THE ABSENCE OF MYTH

The Absence of Myth

The Absence of Myth

ॐ

Sophia Heller

STATE UNIVERSITY OF NEW YORK PRESS

Published by
State University of New York Press, Albany

© 2006 State University of New York

Printed in the United States of America

For information, address State University of New York Press,
194 Washington Avenue, Suite 305, Albany, NY 12210-2384

Production by Kelli Williams
Marketing by Susan Petrie

Library of Congress Cataloging in Publication Data

Heller, Sophia, 1969–
  The absence of myth / Sophia Heller.
    p. cm.
  Includes bibliographical references and index.
  ISBN 0-7914-6589-6 (alk. paper)
  1. Myth. I. Title

BL304.H45 2005
201'.3—dc22

                                              2005002876

10 9 8 7 6 5 4 3 2 1

For Wolfgang Giegerich and David Miller

Contents

Acknowledgments

I would like to thank my colleagues and teachers at Pacifica Graduate Institute for helping to incubate this work, particularly Kristina Berggren, Sue Bozzo, Carrie Clark-Kenny, Christine Downing, David Grady, Gard Jameson, Zena Juhasz, Debra Knowles, Patrick Mahaffey, Dara Marks, Dan Noel, Ginette Paris, Raina Paris, Laura Parrish, Catherine Sanders-Hart, Dennis Slattery, Richard Stromer, Jennifer Taylor, Constance Welch, and Dana White. I would also like to extend my appreciation to Paul Kugler for his thoughtful commentary on an earlier version of this work, and to William Doty, Mark Kelly, and Robert Segal for pointing me toward additional sources.

For easing the transition from San Francisco to Munich, where most of this was written, I thank David Ackerman, Marie Elliot-Gartner, Alois Gartner, Sarah Lenoue, David Mulig, Gabrielle Perrin, Deirdre Reen, Ryan Rhoades, Tracey Rhoades, Leslie Richter, Volker Richter, Monika Steimle, and Kate Wahl.

I am deeply indebted to Wolfgang Giegerich and David Miller, to whom this book is dedicated. Their encouragement and critical readings of each chapter were invaluable. Their own work has greatly inspired mine, and I am grateful for the gift of their participation.

Introduction

The absence of myth is, to a certain extent, a "nonstatement." Echoing what German theologian Dorothee Sölle said about Nietzsche's pronouncement of the death of God—"Those who believed in God were in no way affected by the statement, and those who did not believe in God were also not affected" (see Bierlein 325). Myth means nothing to those who have no use for or interest in it, and to those who hold steadfastly to myth, any assertion of myth's absence or obsolescence will go unheard. However, there is a significant difference between the modern individual who expressly chooses to believe in or look for myth and extant aboriginal cultures still living in myth, because, for one thing, in modernity myth itself has left very little to believe in.

What we have inherited are concepts and imaginings of myth, as opposed to the concrete, living experience of myth. Myth has become a reflection on life without need for the literal reenactment of the reflection or narrative (such as through ceremony and worship). Any so-called living myth today is arbitrary, subject to human rather than divine modification, and lasts for about as long as our interest can hold. One can see how myth's applicability has been whittled down to its romantic appeal and entertainment value; some of the clearest expressions of *myth* are "found" in fantasy fiction and film, such as the recent *The Lord of the Rings, Harry Potter, The Matrix,* and the comic book heroes of *X-Men.* No matter how deeply these creations may engross and inspire us, we still look for the ordinary human being behind the curtain pulling all the strings. No longer content with just the phenomenon itself, the mechanics or science of the creation is what fascinates us.

1

If these popular stories speak of realities, they are abstract, psychological realities. The images in these stories are metaphors for something else, metaphors that need to be analyzed and dissected until what's left is (ideally) a deepened understanding of human nature and the world we live in. But the metaphor itself is discarded in the process. Its role as a placeholder for a psychological truth becomes redundant once we understand the place it was holding, once we get the insight. Hobbits might show us the values of humility and courage, but presumably what we internalize are the values, not the Hobbits themselves. Now, no one without risk of being called delusional would take *Lord of the Rings* as gospel, consider Middle Earth to be real, or think that Tolkien was a god. But what makes myth a myth is, in part, the fact that it is absolutely true because it is real. And what makes it real is the belief that this life, this existence, is how it is, this is how the gods did it; this is what we must now do. When questioned about the reasons for performing a particular ritual or celebrating a particular ceremony, archaic peoples replied: "'Because the [mythical] Ancestors prescribed it'" (Australian Arunta); "'This is how the Nemu [the mythical Ancestors] did it, and we do it the same way'" (Kai of New Guinea); "'Because the Sacred People did it this way for the first time'" (Navajo) (Eliade, "Toward a Definition" 4). Living myth, said Mircea Eliade, means living religiously. Myth is "a reenactment of fabulous, exalting, meaningful events; one is present once again at the creative works of the Supernatural Beings" (5). Living myth is more than telling a good story; it is the reality or truth of lived life, expressed in the form of narratives that are held to be sacred.

In contrast, myths today are studied rather than lived. Since the beginnings of Western philosophy in ancient Greece, myth has been used as a tool for political discourse and, in more recent times, the inception of analytical psychology has enabled the appropriation of myth as an effective means for understanding human nature. The function of myth is critical rather than existential. More often than not, contemporary usages of "myth" tend to be easily interchangeable with the words "theory," "story," and "ideology," defined more by its methodology than by any stable content. Myth is more like a "parasitical form" (Barthes) that feeds on whatever it is applied to (culture, history, literature, psychology, etc.) in order to create a surplus of meaning that can claim for itself a mythic appellation. But as real substance, as the cosmological World Tree centering the individual to the collective and the collective to the gods, living myth has long been outside the ken of modern civilization and, as such, is irrelevant to the necessities of living. Transformed to a metaphorical and conceptual level, myth has lost its former status as an objective reality; it no longer originates in the inviolable domain of Supernatural Beings and instead has become a method to be adopted or discarded at will.

If myth's ontological absence is self-evident, and arguing for the absence of myth subsequently redundant, what exactly is the reason for this study? Why spend time dredging up myth only to refute it, a task that carries the sneaking suspicion that the absence of myth is unacceptable and that there must be a way still to uphold myth as an existential force—even when it functions negatively, through its absence. Such an underlying motivation does, in fact, infuse some of the current myth scholarship cited in this book. On the one hand, a demythologized, scientific world is accepted while on the other hand, this demythologization is subsumed under a larger notion of myth that includes a scientific understanding of reality but is not rendered obsolete because of it (e.g., "the myth of mythlessness"). Yet this is a modern notion of "myth," guided not by divine dictates but swollen instead with humankind's ideas about myth and the need for a comparable substitute, evidenced most conspicuously by the desire for a spiritual meaning in a world or religious tradition that is apparently not providing it.

It is this modern hunger for meaning, whether or not it is explicitly associated with the word *myth* that shows that the "non-statement" of myth's absence has been turned into a statement to protest against. And for those who believe that the remedy for the spiritual void lies specifically within myth, protestations against myth's obsolescence and redundancy are not quiet insofar as pains must assiduously be taken to prove and defend that which is collectively no longer self-evident. Myth then becomes more than an object of historical interest or a psychological tool; it becomes an unwitting pawn in the debate on the meaning of life. As I aim to explicate in this study, myth, in its emptied and malleable status, is thrust forward by scholars and psychologists, seekers alike, as proof that the sacred has not been secularized. And yet theories that have to work especially hard to show how and where myth is still alive

usually point not to myth, but to the desire on the part of the theorist for something that is no more, and furthermore, to the unwillingness to accept what could be a rather ordinary, decidedly
nonmythic life.

Our time is clearly experiencing a dearth of meaning and purpose. One need only look at the self-help, career, New Age, religion, and psychology sections at bookstores to see a deluge of
information, all geared to help the forsaken individual find his or
her sacred purpose, authentic job, soulmate, inner peace, outer
abundance, happiness, God, or the God within. Perhaps this is a
gross generalization, but I do not think it is inaccurate, given that
this book is being written in a time (early twenty-first century) and
in places (Germany and the United States) that have witnessed
such an overload of resources as to how to make one's life more
meaningful that it would be impossible to cite all the cultural
instances supporting this assertion. In any event, my starting point
has little to do with the specifics of how to make life worth living.
Rather, it is to take the observation that this need for a more worthy
life exists and place it within the framework of myth, or, I should
say, myth's absence, for what current civilization has inherited is not
myth, but its absence. And to the extent that the ubiquitous search
for something to fill the void of meaning is directed toward myth or
God, it is worth examining this inheritance of absence more closely,
because the search does not seem to be coming to any closure. On
the contrary, the search for meaning and value has apparently
found its way into a vacuum that must keep recycling infinite variations of the same product ("meaning") in order to calm and piece
together our lonely, fractured selves. If this were not the case, the
popular psychology/spirituality industry would have withered long
ago, rather than exploding into a virtual smorgasbord where seekers can indulge whenever and wherever the urge strikes.

Myths are gone; the gods are dead. This, by the way, is not to
attack one's personal religious beliefs and practices. It is to say that
collectively and objectively, from the perspective of the world and
not pockets of individuals, what was a source of metaphysical and
religious meaning is no more. This godless and mythless state of
the world is nothing new. Wolfgang Giegerich ("The Opposition of
'Individual and Collective'" 12) and David Miller ("'A Myth Is as
Good as a Smile!'" 182) both cite Chaucer's "Wife of Bath's Tale" as

just one piece of evidence that by the fourteenth century myths and mythical figures had already withdrawn.

> When good King Arthur ruled in ancient days
> (A king that every Briton loves to praise)
> This was a land brim-full of fairy folk.
> The Elf-Queen and her courtiers joined and broke
> Their elfin dance on many a green mead,
> Or so was the opinion once, I read,
> Hundred of years ago, in days of yore.
> But no one now sees fairies any more.
> For now the saintly charity and prayer
> Of holy friars seem to have purged the air;
> They search the countryside through field and stream
> As thick as motes that speckle a sun-beam,
> Blessing the halls, the chambers, kitchens, bowers,
> Cities and boroughs, castles, courts and towers,
> Thorpes, barns and stables, outhouses and dairies.
> And that's the reason why there are no fairies.
> Wherever there was wont to walk an elf
> Today there walks the holy friar himself
> As evening falls or when the daylight springs,
> Saying his mattins and his holy things,
> Walking his limit round from town to town.
> Women can now go safely up and down
> By every bush or under every tree;
> Here is no other incubus but he,
> So there is really no one else to hurt you
> And he will do no more than take your virtue.

"What is lost," Giegerich writes, "(and irrevocably lost) is the natural world *as* ensouled, *as* animated, *as* spirited by all sorts of fairies, goblins, and little people" ("Opposition" 13). Though an animated, ensouled nature is just one aspect of living myth, what is relevant is that the "status of nature" is irreversibly changed such that a new mode or logic of being-in-the-world is initiated. In myth, natural phenomena are divinely personified (e.g., in Greek myth, the earth is Gaia, thunder is Zeus, the sun is Helios, the seas are Poseidon, and so forth), but when nature has been emptied of its animating forces, as Chaucer's tale claims, the conditions for myth are also depleted. There is little reason for myth to persist when the repository for divine truth is lifted out of nature and placed into the hands of the holy friar, who is the mere servant of the singular, true (now abstracted into Spirit) God of Christianity. And Christianity, far from being just another "myth," logically and historically represents an intentional overcoming of myth.

Although the absence of myth is, objectively speaking, nothing new, it is a confrontation waiting to happen. As long as there persists a yearning for meaning, the implications of the loss of myth and religion have yet to be comprehended and instead are to be resisted. For religion as well as myth has fallen out of conviction if the question of what makes life meaningful has to be asked. This discussion of the absence of myth, then, is not intended indirectly to reverse myth's obsolescence or rehabilitate the gods/God. It is to delve into the absence, to penetrate and be penetrated by the sense of mythlessness and find out what wants to be known through the loss. My approach is not merely to assume the absence of myth; it is to treat this absence as necessary in its own right, necessary to the very notion of consciousness that is so cherished in the prevalent desire for soulful living. And given that this absence is closer to our reality than myth ever was, it, perhaps even more than myth, requires attention.

℗

This book is divided into four chapters, with each one successively pushing into the ramifications of the absence of myth. Chapter 1 articulates the case for this absence by presenting current myth theory and demonstrating not only that the extensive study of myth is made possible because of myth's absence, but also that the rise of mythology is founded on a profound lack. Whether one deems this a lack of foundation, center, God, or meaning, the point is that, what inspires modern and postmodern myth is the desire for something that is acutely felt to be lost. Although some of the scholarship I review incorporates the loss of myth into an expanded theory of myth, others betray the unwillingness to accept the loss in that the so-called emptiness is shown to be actually quite full—of myth!

Yet whether one subsumes the absence of myth into an overarching theory, or disregards the absence of myth by calling mythlessness just another myth, the modern notion of myth itself must be redefined and translated into contemporary experience to ensure its vitality and applicability. And though I try to place thought *about* myth in contradistinction to examples of archaic or living myth, the redefining of archaic myth into current myth only confuses the seemingly straightforward matter of the absence of myth.

One problem with turning to myth for real sustenance, as indicated earlier, is that original myth is not part of modernity's experience. It exists more in anthropologists' reports and imaginings that can never be entirely objective. Current civilization is very far removed from an oral/aural and ritual-based tradition, and despite the awareness of mythical, cyclical aspects to life (e.g., the seasons, the moon, the calendar), humankind nonetheless lives linearly and progressively, outwardly striving to reach goals and acquire knowledge, determined, in a sense, to master life. Our narratives are not sacred, they are deconstructed; our rituals are public commodities or privately resurrected, belonging more to one's innermost being than to any collective at large.

Living long outside of myth, human thought has emptied the word *myth* of its original value and turned it into a concept that mirrors those who use and study it. Prior to its conceptualization, myth stood for the whole truth; it was the ritualized enactment of the whole of existence itself. But in ancient Greece, where the early philosophers critiqued myths while simultaneously bestowing their value, the distinction between two different periods of myth is absorbed into an already evolving definition of myth that comes to represent both truth and falsehood. And in much of the current, postmodern-influenced scholarship, generated in a time that extols the impossibility of an authoritative truth, myth is perceived as entirely fictitious and ideological. However, the equivocal usage of the same word, *myth*, proves problematic because it conflates the experience of living myth with imaginings about myth and dissolves the cultural specificity from within which myth is realized. This creates a split, or dissociation in psychological terms, between individual and collective, between the myth proponent's personal motivations (such as the desire for meaning) and the outer, objective reality that precludes what is yearned for.

To be sure, not all mythologists insist on the irrefutable presence of myth, nor is there concordance as to the exact manifestations of current myth. But the boundaries between detached myth scholars and passionate myth defenders can be elusive. Modern myth resists precise definition because it has exploded into virtually all aspects of cultural communication. William Doty is one example of a mythologist who embraces an evolving, "polyphasic working definition" of myth, one whose purpose is to "foster a type of [. . .] appreciation that recognizes mythic multidimensionality in both origination and application" (*Mythography* 31, 33). Myth, in part, expresses "the primal, foundational accounts of aspects of the real, experienced world and humankind's roles and relative statuses within it." This, in turn, helps to elucidate "the political and moral values of a culture and provide systems of interpreting individual experience within a universal perspective" (33). Myth as a lens or template highlighting unseen aspects of a particular culture or political ideologies is no doubt a useful tool and, in this regard, much insight can be gained from mythology. But what I repeatedly noticed is that there persists this belief or hope that a thread remains linking archaic myth with modern (notions of) myth, unbroken even in its brokenness. The loophole is that modern myth, while not outwardly purporting to function exactly as its progenitor, is nevertheless presumed to be able to provide the culture and, even more so, the individual, with the same depth of meaning and purpose to life characteristic of archaic myth. Yet to the extent that modern notions of myth easily overlook the distinction between two distinct periods of myth, such a myth will be ineffective in fulfilling the needs of current culture precisely because it is fully grounded neither in antiquity nor in the present time.

Either arguing for the persistence of myth or acknowledging the failure of myth today demands contextualizing any definition of myth within the time that it is functional. This obligation, as well as the dilemma that erupts when historically distinct definitions of myth are muddled, is the subject of the first part of chapter 1. The second part grounds in contemporary myth theory what I have assumed to be a given, the absence of myth. However, my overall intent is to do more than back up the assertion of myth's obsolescence. It is to uncover fallacies inherent in theory that must reconstitute myth to fit modern sensibilities, and to suggest where the theory does the opposite of what the theorist ostensibly intends. This is indicative, for example, of a philosophical and psychological approach to myth, whereby myth becomes conflated with philosophy or psychology and is meant to serve as a means for uncovering truths about human nature and the nature of consciousness, how we see and understand ourselves and the world. This, however, is a kind of truth or insight apprehended through critical thought and analysis as opposed to the acceptance of truth as literal and embodied experience, such as was the condition of myth. One problem with couching current thought and analysis in myth is that myth becomes more of an obstruction and stunts the trajectory of an awareness or consciousness that can only come into its own *after* myth. The irony is that what makes the so-called return to myth possible or even desirable is itself only possible outside of myth. Consequently, any refutation or restructuring of the absence of myth in the name of consciousness becomes unconscious, answering a familiar call to comfort rather than accepting the rigors of reflection in a no longer deified world.

In chapter 2, I take a closer look at one phenomenon resulting directly from the absence of myth: personal myth. Personal myth represents a particular response to the collective loss of myth and religious meaning. Though it may profess otherwise, the personal myth approach does not and cannot seek to remedy this absence because it utterly depends on it. Its philosophy basically says that what the collective has lost, the individual can and should reclaim. And how one reclaims myth and meaning is through knowing and telling one's personal story. However, what separates a personal myth from a mere autobiography, biography, or memoir is the underlying belief or hope that if a personal story is contextualized within myth, it carries an archetypal and numinous significance and, as such, is elevated and geared to replace the metaphysical void created by the departure and death of the gods. This method receives, in part, its inspiration from Jungian depth psychology, specifically, Jung's notion of archetypes as mythological motifs patterning all of life. From this perspective, it seems impossible to be devoid of myth—one need only root out the archetypes to find the myth. The same could be said (and *is* said) for personal myth: one need only identify the archetypes peopling whichever psychological complexes are constellated at any given moment to find the myth pertaining to the individual. But the transposition of myth from collective to individual is ambiguous and incomplete in that myth is simultaneously discredited (for the loss of collective myth is not disputed) and exalted insofar as myth's virtues are now upheld by the individual. Not unlike the redefining of myth to suit modern thought, the shift from collective to personal myth provides a surface solution at best for the prevailing existential concern: how is life to be meaningful.

Chapter 3 confronts the equivocal usages of myth evident in both the first and second chapters. Here I consider the questions, how does the equivocation of myth persist, and does it perhaps serve its own purpose? Expressed another way, how is it that myth lives on amid the general acknowledgment of the lack of a transcendent God? One persuasive answer is found in a postmodern style of thought, a style that opts for imagination and alternating perspectives over literalized and fixated assumptions as to the nature of reality. A postmodern approach to the absence of myth thus welcomes absence or negativity as a general principle because it undermines false or egotistical claims to that which ultimately remains unknowable and is therefore not for the taking. But an absent myth, in this case, does not mean the end of myth; it just adopts a different perspective on myth, meaning, and the divine. God as dead is just one perspective, but it is not to be mistaken for *the* perspective on God's status. Rather, this statement is reversed (e.g., "Nietzsche is dead"—God) and this playful, shifting consciousness creates a space or gap wherein both statements are just as true as they are false. The point is to incite a sense of unknowing, and to dethrone the individual who would claim to know. Ambiguity and equivocation are deemed necessary precisely because they resist a clear, rational approach and compel one to enter the murky "in-between spaces," those liminal spaces between all binary oppositions, such as present-absent, truth-falsehood, inner-outer, and so on. The desirability and necessity of engaging the in-between spaces enable an encounter with the complex, paradoxical nature of life, a truth that can only be apprehended by standing outside of one's habitual mode of understanding.

In chapter 4, I try to give myth and the pursuit of myth the benefit of the doubt. Although I have been contending that one primary motivation for refuting the absence of myth arises from the desire for a meaning that is hard put to materialize, I also think that the persistence and variation of modern and postmodern myth point to another goal repeatedly surfacing in thought and culture: the striving to become conscious. Although the inability completely to relinquish myth can indicate an unwillingness to accept reality on its own, God-less terms, it also carries hints of the desire to reach a level of awareness that does bear a resemblance to mythical cultures insofar as a total consciousness and presence render questions of meaning and purpose irrelevant, the split into dualistic thinking is overcome, and one knows oneself to be held by something much larger and already whole unto itself, whether one terms this God, Being, soul, spirit, or something else. Yet rather than looking at how to redefine myth to meet the evolving demands of consciousness, this final chapter tackles the question—is the idea of pure consciousness itself a myth? Does the process of becoming conscious mean that we will eventually come back full circle and return to myth, not a phenomenal myth as in antiquity but a logical or psychological one? Will a "new myth" emerge, one that maintains the existential equivalency of archaic myth, but without need for concretization through ritual, sacrifice, or worship? In addressing these questions, I continue the progression into the logic of myth as well as its absence, to see if, in fact, the myth somehow contains within itself its own future demise or survival.

CHAPTER 1

The Absence of Myth

The absence of myth is hardly a radical notion. It antecedes the phenomenon called mythology insofar as a loss of myth makes theorizing about myth possible. A culture still living in myth would not need to theorize about that which fashioned the fabric of its existence. The narratives would be self-explanatory and sufficient. The collective that knows without needing to believe (or to write it down) that it is part of a living religion has no need for mythology or for myth, because when *mythos* or *muthos* comes into Greek language as a technical and philosophical term, a separation or rupture from a predominantly prereflective and ritualistic mode of being-in-the-world is already under way. Even the word *myth* itself, then, serves as a placeholder for phenomena that are lost the moment an attempt at capture (or recapture) is made. And any theory of myth posits itself in direct relationship to the loss of mythic and religions phenomena, whether or not such a loss is confronted in the theory.

When I say "the absence of myth," my usage of the term *myth* refers to myth in its most original or archaic sense. It is defined neither as a true nor false story but as the total experience and expression (in narrative form) of life. An example of living myth can be seen in Carl Jung's encounter with Pueblo Indians in New Mexico. The Indian chief told Jung, "[W]e are a people who live on the roof of the world; we are the sons of Father Sun, and with our religion we daily help our father to go across the sky. We do this not only for ourselves, but for the whole world. If we were to cease practicing our religion, in ten years the sun would no longer rise. Then it would be night forever" (*Memories* 252). For the Pueblos, God is

13

self-evident and embodied in nature. There is no distinction between the literal phenomenon of the sun rising and the religious meaning of the phenomenon. God is the sun. And without due worship, the reason for this god, for the sun itself, is changed. As the chief said, it would be night forever. This myth is not a story or hypothesis about God; it is the self-display, in nature, of the truth or reality of this particular culture.

For much of the world, the sun, or just about any other natural phenomenon, is not objectively understood as divine. Our relationship to the sun is scientific when we see a mass of energy, heat, and light. But knowledge of nature is made possible only when the conditions for myth no longer hold. Jung states something similar when recounting this story of the Pueblos: knowledge depends on the sacrifice of myth.[1] And yet—perhaps to say that one is not living in myth because it can be named as *myth*, or because natural events have lost their mystique, is too narrow and stuck in a literal-mindedness that does not consider the modern perspective that one of myth's multiple and evolving functions is to describe the ineffable. If myth is, at bottom, intended to facilitate a discussion and exploration of inexplicable and timeless truths, then, conceivably does it matter which form these truths take, whether ones of cosmologies or natural metaphors or scientific explanations?

Moreover, the assumption that a completely mythic or "primitive" mode of being-in-the-world is undifferentiated and unconscious balks when confronted with the work of Claude Lévi-Strauss, for example, which aims to show that the prehistoric mind is no less capable of intellectual thought than the modern one, albeit to varying degrees. The issue then becomes less one of trying to find a demarcation between myth and mythlessness than of addressing the implications of applying such nebulous terms to today's means for understanding and experiencing life. The need and desire that propel the labeling of current phenomena "myth" demands as much attention as the feasibility of the label itself. For the problem of an absence of myth is not only what one deems to be an indication of myth or not-myth, but that even such a naming is sought. Why would anyone living in what seems to be such a secular world say that there is myth, and what could one point to as evidence?

Adding to the confusion is that myth does not have a fixed meaning. Bruce Lincoln has shown that the prehistory of *mythos* and *logos* in Homer and Hesiod is marked by contradictory representations, where *logos* constitutes falsehood and *mythos* carries the authority of truth (18). This is in contradistinction to the generally assumed, modern definition of these terms, in which *logos* represents truth and *mythos* a fictional story. Thus, for the mind that fastens on contradictory connotations of myth, to say one is not in myth becomes as empty and meaningless as to say one is in myth. The truth or fallacy of such a statement is not only contingent on one's seemingly arbitrary position on or above this continuum encompassing mythology, but is also dependent on a foundation of knowledge that has come to resemble a mirror far more than the solidity of bricks and mortar. And although the emergence of critical interpretation and/or rejection of myth in conjunction with the development of philosophical thought initiated by the pre-Socratics and cemented in Plato is an attempt to clear the smoke obfuscating the mirrors, more often than not this demythologizing paves the way for modern interpreters to *re*mythologize, bringing us back to myth (where some say we have never left, which precludes the need to remythologize in the first place). Properly re-mythologized, we presumably face myth no longer as naïve participants but with a more complex understanding and appreciation of the world, its inhabitants, and the means of reflection.

Lest the fissures implicit in demythologization spread too deep, myth scholarship tends to include demythologization as a subsidiary to the larger concept called myth; even the word *demythologization* itself is contained within another theory of myth. Rudolf Bultmann coined the term and, though far from eliminating myth, its purpose (specifically applied to the New Testament) is to "extricate the true, existential subject matter of the mythology" (Segal, *Theorizing* 24). Demythologization, in this sense, becomes another means to retain myth when the narratives themselves can no longer be accepted literally. It is a way to hang on to the meaning of the same narrative, but the truth of the myth is now transposed from an embodied expression to an abstracted one. However, although an implied thread that remains unbroken even in its brokenness persists in linking human existence under the rubric of myth, there is still this tacit gap or absence. Yes, humankind can be united throughout the ages by the sheer fact of human existential experience, but this unity is made possible by abstracting knowledge from the actual experience, and there is a significant gap between cultures living in myth and cultures living in modernity (to name only two historical periods).

This gap or difference is logical; it can be seen in the changing modes or forms of reflecting on the world. Wolfgang Giegerich points out one example of this in the differences between the dream-time narratives of Australian aborigines and the epics of Homer and Hesiod or the Old Testament. Dream-time narratives have no beginning or end or any distinction from the greater whole; they flow together to make one infinite narrative. "*All* images and narrative events *together* represent a living, ever-changing interconnected whole from which they cannot be separated into individual units" ("The Historicity of Myth" 2). One just dives into the narrative at any given point to pick it up. But when narratives are selectively edited to create a particular order and clearly establish "In the beginning," as in Hesiod's *Theogony* or Genesis, a separation from "the ocean of mythic knowledge" is already under way. Now there is a formal and historical "In the beginning," rather than a mythic beginning that is not really a beginning as such, but a continual renewal and reentering of the whole myth. Consciousness is not immersed as deeply *in* the narrative; rather, consciousness has begun to distance itself *from* the narrative in order to craft and systemize the narrative toward a particular end already in mind.

The absence of myth is not only implicit in the nature of interpretation and analysis that demands a distance so as to obtain a better view of that which seeks to be elucidated (such as in demythologizing), but also in the lack of myth as an organizing and unifying center. This lack of center is by no means revelatory insofar as talk of mythlessness or the death of the gods has been acknowledged by many; no longer is one solely dependent on Nietzsche's famous proclamation or Yeats's loose anarchy or Eliot's hollow men to declare modern Western civilization's secularized and fragmented status.[2] The rise of postmodernism, situated on its lack of credible and mythic "grand narratives" (Lyotard) and virtual reality obviates the need for and resists any unifying center. And

Loyal Rue has even designated the term "amythia" specifically to describe the current mythless condition.

Even so, the Western importing of uprooted customs, watered-down religious practices, and pieces of philosophical systems from every appealing Other (e.g. "Tibetan Buddhism in Hollywood and Krishna Consciousness in airports" [Doniger, "Foreword," Feldman and Richardson xii]) could be seen to betray the desire to alleviate the absence and to be anesthetized from the implications inherent in a void. Much innocence remains to be shattered, for whereas contemporary theories and discussions of myth may give credence to its intrinsic absence, myth in all its positivity remains as a cushion to fall back on. This is seen in the belief that mythlessness is itself just another myth, or that we are in between myths, which is to suggest that when the new myth arrives, the alienation that results from its absence will be eradicated. We will be rescued from our own emptiness. Life again will be meaningful and, if we are to believe Rue, we will stave off our impending annihilation. (Rue fears that in a state of *amythia,* "there is little chance that Western culture will survive very far into the twenty-first century" [3]. Terrorism, crime, the threat of nuclear destruction, deteriorating school and family systems are all indications of a way of life that may not have a future unless we can find a way to come together and reclaim or reestablish a cultural myth.)

To argue for myth's presence (or, rather, myth's *need*) amid its confirmed absence is far from a dialectical debate because in order to establish myth's presence, its absence tends to be refuted. Despite its absence, myth persists. The absence or gap resulting from the shift in how humanity reflects on the world is ignored or covered up rather than allowed to penetrate into today's reality or means of reflecting.

Rue's observations into the state of modern affairs ring true. He knows the church is no longer satisfying or meaningful for many, and he knows that, for a culture to survive, it cannot remain attached to previous forms of life and thought. Things change, they evolve, and the old myths lose their vitality and necessity. "The demands of the present will not be denied, nor will they be well served by efforts to apply to them the solutions of the past" (4). And yet—at the end of his book Rue wants us all to go back to church! He thinks the myth we desperately need is not only possible, but will manifest itself through radically changing the church from within. But he is still attached to the church, to an older vessel of religious consciousness. On the one hand, he accepts the philosophical reality of the death of God (the "impotence of God" [90]); on the other hand, it sounds like he is still looking for a way to have God. I agree that change comes from within, but it seems to me that the change has already happened, especially if the churches are emptying. He does not seem to accept that a true radical changing of the church could result in the death of the church itself, and in the death of the metaphor that he feels is still living and necessary, that of the Covenant. Instead he asks, "What is the Covenant for a world come of age?" (159). Though Rue's focus is on human existence as it is today, and he is primarily concerned with establishing a root metaphor around which the culture can cohere, his choice of and home for the metaphor (the Covenant and the church) betrays the desire for a kind of religious meaning that is no more. Wanting a cultural cohesiveness is not the same thing as it happening, and wanting what we do not have only exacerbates the crisis he sees indicative of our time.

I believe any attempt to revive or recreate that which is no more is a regressive move and can succeed only in one's imagination. Imagination freed from history may work at an artistic or personal level, but when applied to myth, which, for modernity, earned its place and status *in* history, such an application turns against the very phenomenon that is supposed to be respected, honored, and redeemed. And although it may appear that meaning is unearthed in the excavation of myth, more likely what is revealed is not meaning, but rather the desire for meaning. But myth cannot satisfy this desire; moreover, it was never meant to. In living myth, the desire was already answered before it could become aware of itself. The cohesiveness, the center, was already present in the phenomenon. When Jung asked the Pueblo chief if the sun "might be a fiery ball shaped by an invisible god," the chief replied, "'The sun is God. Everyone can see that" (*Memories* 250, 251). There is no need to answer any desire for God or meaning; it is self-evident.

Jung actually expressed the sentiment not so much to save myth but rather to be saved by it: "Our myth has become mute, and gives no answers. [. . .] Today we [. . .] stand empty-handed, bewildered, and perplexed, and cannot even get it into our heads that no myth will come to our aid although we have such urgent need of one" (*Memories* 332–33). And a current Jungian analyst, James Hollis, taking up this lament, writes: "[A] greater intimacy with myth provides a vital linkage with meaning, the absence of which is so often behind the private and collective neuroses of our time" (8). That is, the solution to prevailing psychological problems (feeling lost and alienated) is to be found in myth, specifically personal myth, for that permits one to suffer the death of the gods but still cling to myth. So then, one might ask, why seek to shatter what innocence remains? Why take away myth if myth and a mythic consciousness provide such a reconciliatory and meaningful purpose? Why be a killjoy and criticize the attempt to restore what appears to have only positive benefits for the culture at large?

For one thing, there is an absence that cannot be ignored. Depth psychologists are not the only ones to address this absence, even if the acknowledgment is part of an attempt to find a cure, not realizing that myth itself may be the illness—as opposed to (only) mythlessness. A persistent focus on what is missing will naturally constellate the fervent yearning for whatever is perceived to have created such an absence. In this case, myth. But surely all the talk of mythlessness and death of God must have sprung from some truth, some profound and real experience of change and loss, thus begging the question, could myth even fulfill such a yearning without perpetuating talk of its absence and accompanying unfulfilled need? History prevents a return to an imagined time of myth divorced from mythlessness because mythlessness *is* part of the cultural awareness, regardless of the degree to which one concurs. Moreover, the concomitant search for meaning in the guise of myth unmasks myth's inability to satisfy such a need. But any current desire for myth to serve as an organizing principle around a center long debunked splits myth into two different phenomena, one ancient, the other modern, while purporting to reconcile the two into a continuous unity. Yet any attempted "reconciliation" between ancient and modern myth cannot be a true reconciliation to the extent that it must overlook the real distinctions between differing modes of being-in-the-world. And any so-called reconciliation further muddles the issue so that questions regarding the function or location of myth only serve to create a ceaseless circular reasoning—but not the kind of circle that could provide a center in a center-less time.

Michael Sexson's essay "Myth: The Way We Were or the Way We Are?" can serve as an example of this circular reasoning that ultimately finds in favor of myth. On the one hand, the steady, historical development of humankind's methods for analyzing and understanding the world, whether through philosophy, anthropology, science, psychology, and so forth, presupposes the loss of our illusions about the Gods—an absence of myth. On the other hand, insofar as human beings are "symbolizing animals and myth is a significant form of symbolic activity [. . .] the truth is that we can never be divested of myth" (42). Sexson's argument, which shares Ernst Cassirer's notion of the *animal symbolicum* but not his (Cassirer's) view that the mythical world is flat and shallow (see Baeten 63), seems redolent of this facile way to approach myth. At the core of the argument is a contradiction that can be linked to a prevailing modern definition of *myth* itself: myth is both true and false; we live in a mythless time and we are never without myth. Only, this is a contradiction linked not to any legal inheritance or experience of living myth, but to intellectual thought *about* myth.

It is important to note that not all theorists who study myth do so to demonstrate its incontrovertible presence. One example is Robert Segal, whose extensive scholarship is the result of someone clearly standing outside of myth in order to analyze theories spanning a wide range of mythology.[3] Moreover, one can posit few generalizations about myth today, given the lack of concordance among modern theories as dissimilar disciplines influence how myth is to be represented; for example, a linguistic view of myth (Eric Gould) is entirely different from a history of religions perspective (Wendy Doniger). And both of these views differ from the depth psychological perspective, which either appears reluctant to relinquish myth (C. G. Jung) or aims to see through myth into psychological reality (James Hillman). And, in turn, the mythopoetic approach (Harry Slochower), which shares with depth psychology the inclination toward analyzing mythic patterns, differs in its intent on consciously creating new myths that question and criticize a culture's rigid and potentially oppressive status quo. This does not even address an anthropological, sociological, feminist, or theological approach to myth, which are well beyond the scope of this book.[4]

The point of this all too scant account is to suggest that myth's amenability to extend into and give shape to varying schools of thought is further indication that myth is primarily an empty *concept* and no longer a reality on the level of the literal or the phenomenal. Insofar as outer or literal phenomena do tend to be deemed mythic, more often than not, it is a fictionalized rendering of myth (e.g., calling a particular work of literature a myth) or it entails a conscious dissolution of the phenomena (discovering a hidden layer of meaning that may not be suggested by the phenomena itself). In both instances, myth is abstracted, analyzed, created—a product of mental activity whose contents are entirely interchangeable and reducible. And as a concept bearing the same name of that which once absolutely depended on a stable content *as well as* form (the unity of the narrative and the mythological mode of being-in-the-world, Giegerich would say), it is all too tempting to sustain the idea that myth translates over time and, through this translation, is able to provide a culture with a comparable existential meaning. But transformed to the purely conceptual level, myth can no longer retain any of its former status. Thus, any attempt to find meaning or God at a conceptual level of "myth" must realize that it depends on the sacrifice of myth.

Insofar as underlying all theories of myth, no matter how divergent, is an absence of myth, an exploration of the absence of myth serves as one inroad for understanding contemporary myth theory. My intention for this chapter is thus twofold: to present a brief sampling of modern myth scholarship while addressing how the theories respond to the question of myth's presence or obsolescence. Some of the theorists reviewed are less well known and have not published as prolifically as others, but I chose them, not only as representative of modern thinking about myth, but because their arguments serve as good examples of what I perceive to be essential issues that either refute, permit, or redefine the absence of myth. However, to the degree that any recognition of absence is influenced by one's definition of myth, it is useful to look first from a general overview at the problem of defining myth.

WHICH MYTH?

Although Bruce Lincoln's exposition of the shift in meanings of *mythos* and *logos* may serve as a necessary disarming of any assumed claims on truth for today's sensibility, one does not want to over-look that prior to theoretical and philosophical thought, myth was the truth. Lincoln expects the modern reader to be surprised on finding the "traditional" values of the terms *mythos* and *logos* reversed in ancient Greek texts, but this only reveals how far removed the modern conception of myth is from itself. Although Homer and Hesiod were already outside of myth insofar as they attempted to systemize mythology through crafted narratives and genealogies that presuppose some degree of critical thought and reflection, myth as truth still lingered. Lincoln notes that in their work, "*mythos* often denotes [. . .] a blunt act of candor. Nowhere [. . .] does it mean 'false story,' 'symbolic story,' 'sacred story,' or anything of the sort" (17–18). Moreover, Mircea Eliade would not even look to Greek poets and thinkers for an authentic definition of myth since "it was only in Greek culture that myth was subjected to prolonged and penetrating analysis, from which it emerged radi-cally 'demythologized.' If the word 'myth,' in all European lan-guages, denotes 'fiction,' it is because the Greeks declared it to be so twenty-five centuries ago." But living myth, "far from portraying *fiction*, expresses the *supreme truth*, since it speaks only of realities" ("Toward a Definition" 3).

Yet even taking pains to affirm the truthfulness of myth obscures the reality that original myth exists prior to any distinction between truth and falsehood, prior to the word *myth* itself. There is only the unmediated experience of one's life and world, which is truthful in that it is necessary and real. "Mythology is not simply a mode of expression in whose stead another simpler and more read-ily understandable form might have been chosen," wrote Karl Kerényi (Jung and Kerényi 3). A culture living in myth has no choice other than to live its myth, bound to serve its God and exempt from the alternative to live and worship anything else. The French sociological school (Marcel Mauss, Georges Dumézil) found that "[m]yth is above all *obligatory* in nature; it does not exist unless there is a sort of necessity to reach agreement on the themes that are its raw material and on the way these themes are patterned. But the constraint comes solely from the group itself, which tells the myth because it finds its own total expression in it" (see Deti-enne, "Interpretation" 7). And from Bronislaw Malinowski: "Myth [. . .] is not an explanation in satisfaction of a scientific interest, but a narrative resurrection of a primeval reality, told in satisfaction of deep religious wants, moral cravings, social submissions, assertions, even practical requirements. [. . .] These stories . . . are to the natives a statement of a primeval, greater, and more relevant reality" (qtd. in Eliade, *Myth and Reality*: 20).

With the distinguishing of true versus false gods in Hebrew scripture[5] and the differentiation between true and false speech beginning with the pre-Socratics, the door to myth shows itself to be closing, paving the way for the phenomenon called mythology. However, as a phenomenon, mythology is notably modern. Burton Feldman and Robert Richardson's critical anthology of the historical development of modern mythology suggests that prior to around 1700 mythology was "rarely studied for itself and not considered important in its own right" (xxi). With the Enlightenment and the Renaissance, particularly Giambattista Vico (1668–1744), myth's importance rises and assumes its place as a central object of interest and study, anticipating the primary modern approaches to myth that would follow. But why would myth come to the surface at this time, especially if it had been pretty much relegated to the background for well over two thousand years? Marcel Detienne argues that the new science of mythology emerges when a religious consciousness no longer holds, thus enabling someone like Jesuit missionary Joseph-François Lafitau, who found connections between North American savages and the ancient Greeks, to discover in the early eighteenth century a religion beyond Christianity. Mythology "appears when dogmas disintegrate and Religion is overshadowed. It appears with change" (*Creation* 4). Although Detienne argues that for Lafitau and other early mythologists like Bernard Fontenelle myths are seen as beastly, scandalous, or silly, a "result of ignorance," it is "of an inquisitive ignorance trying to account for phenomena and for the world itself" (5).

Yet the loss that would compel one to seek truth and understanding begins much earlier, in ancient Greece, where the early Hellenic philosophers seek a "critical distance from such sinful plots" as well (43). Detienne quotes Thucydides: "Truth inherent in acts is so powerful that it has no 'need of a Homer to glorify it nor of anyone whose tone of voice may charm momentarily but whose interpretations must suffer in the light of true facts'" (60). If the first mythologists, whether those of classical Greece or eighteenth-century Europe, deem myth as scandalous, illusory, the "carrier of the irrational which leads to the decline of true religious feeling" (Wilhelm Schmidt qtd. in Detienne, *Creation* 17) and as threatening to truth (Pindar qtd. in Detienne 47), then myth as representing the living truth of a collective is no more. It would follow that the study of myth surfaces precisely when myths, and later Christianity, no longer provide this source of religious and existential meaning. One consequence is that humankind is left to its own devices and the mythologists are free to "discover" a new myth, even if disguised as an old one.

One responsibility toward a discussion of myth is to clarify what is meant—the time of living myth or the time after it. For once myth is no longer the presupposed truth, its role begins to expand and mimic those who examine its remnants. Even the distinction between two different periods of myth is absorbed into myth itself insofar as myth comes to represent both truth and falsehood. Beginning with Plato who used myth to mean both,[6] or considering Claude Lévi-Strauss's approach, in which the meaning of the myth is secondary to a structure that contains and orders binary oppositions,[7] myth as holding the opposites comes to serve as an effective tool in public discourse and an analysis of culture. But the logic that apprehends myth continues to change. Myth begins to dissolve and deconstruct in the work of someone like Detienne, who interprets myth as empty, "consciously delimited fiction, deliberately exclusive [. . .], fragmented and empty; [. . .] a dead rumor" (128). With the progression of myth from truth to falsehood, while covering everything in between, it is little wonder that the definition of myth proves increasingly more complex and elusive.

Insofar as myth, in a prevailing modern interpretation, holds on to the truth while being widely understood to be fictitious, it, perhaps more clearly than any other form of expression, contains its own negativity and thus resists any stable definition or attachment. Jean-Pierre Vernant observes that, beginning with classical Greece, from whom modern Western civilization has inherited its concept of myth, "In one way or another myth, as such, is always exorcised. [. . .] Myth is either defined negatively in terms of what it lacks or fails to offer, as non-sense, non-reason, non-truth, non-reality or—if it is granted any positive mode of being—it is explained away as being something other than itself" (223). Yet in Greece this negativity coexists with the belief in myth as providing an important cultural, social, and spiritual framework. If, as Vernant says, "It is as if [myth's] existence depended upon it being transposed or translated into some other language or type of thought," this simultaneously questions any existence of myth in its own right besides asserting its vitality in everyday life. Amid this paradox, however, the dialectic of myth stagnates—not necessarily within myth or within a particular story, but of myth itself. The exorcism of defining myth then resembles more a chipping away at a concept of myth where the shards land someplace else, only to grow and either subsume themselves under or consume in their own name what was trying to be differentiated.

Bruce Lincoln and Wendy Doniger are two mythologists who resist defining myth and prefer instead to demonstrate what a myth does.[8] This supports Robert Segal's assertion that "theories of myth are always theories of something broader that is applied to the case of myth" (*Theorizing* 1), which echoes Vernant's remarks that even the Greeks needed to translate myth into "something other than itself." In this regard, myth's amenability to extend into other fields can increase ad infinitum. "Myth is now so encyclopedic a term that it means everything or nothing. We can find in it whatever we want to say is essential about the way humans try to interpret their place on earth" (Gould 5). In its equivocal usage, *myth* lends itself to a superficial conformity that attaches itself to any referent or phenomena, whereby on interpretation, a new order of meaning emerges. However, any mythology now tends to expose a mythologist's ideology rather than settling on an objective definition of myth and satisfying the problem of meaning. In order to extricate a more precise definition of myth, each of these referents would need to be defined and ideologies unmasked. But the boundaries of myth blur in the process and put into question the existence of such a boundary or limit, meanwhile forgetting that any need or ability to choose or settle on what myth is precludes an intact collective still living in myth. The fact that contemporary mythologists draw on current events or narratives to prove the existence of myth indicates not only that the absence of myth has been given little more than lip service, but also corroborates the "fabricated real,"[9] that the reality that is sought is easily found or created—made all the more viable in an abundance of phenomena from which to choose. And today, with the technological erasing of cultural barriers, if only at a virtual level, one has an endless influx of cultural forms of expression to appropriate, including as well the capacity to borrow from historical or invented periods of time.

As previously indicated, part of the problem in defining myth is that what is deemed to be a phenomenon of myth is contingent on how one wields the word, often resulting in a conflation of two entirely different denotations of myth. The word *myth* or, more precisely, the experience of myth, is specific to one's own time and culture—this seems obvious given that a culture's myth is composed of its own particular, living narratives. And yet in much of contemporary usage, the concept *myth* remains attached to an *idea* of a phenomenon rooted someplace else and in the past, or outside of time—while simultaneously being transferred to modern phenomena. We examine ancient narratives to understand what a myth means or how it is structured, but then the mythic pattern is abstracted and applied to a newly created narrative that we then can call our myth or use as evidence that myth is still alive and well (e.g., interpreting the success of films like *Star Wars* as proof of the vitality of myth). To label modern phenomena mythic more often than not results in a new and even more comprehensive definition of *myth* that of course will be entirely relevant to today, given that today's events and cultural forms are what are being looked at. Although theories of myth may be recognized as a lens applied to something broader, often the reverse application is not performed: the phenomena that are being looked at (specifically those that are considered to "prove" the existence of myth) are not analyzed on their own terms and by means of their own forms—outside of myth. The problem is not so much that the word *myth* is ascribed to modern phenomena. Rather, it is the intentionality that infuses the word, the desire for what is identified as myth to provide a source of meaning and fulfill a comparable function as if science did not already render it obsolete.

Giegerich addresses this discrepancy in Jung: At the phenomenological or semantic level, Jung concedes the absence of myth, but at the formal or syntactical level, Jung's theory indicates otherwise, for when confronted with the implications of the loss of myth as a social phenomenon, Jung turns inward to seek his own personal myth. "Now you possess a key to mythology and are free to unlock all the gates of the unconscious psyche." But then Jung asks himself, "Why open all gates?" Jung knows there is no more living myth, that psychology requires the analytic dissolution of myth. And yet Jung does not unlock the gates; instead he asks himself, "[W]hat is your myth—the myth in which you do live?" (*Memories* 171). This, Giegerich says, reveals the "modern experience of the present. One moment, one now unfolds as the double movement of radical negation of the past and a longing for, indeed an insisting on, a new future." Inasmuch as this envisioned future—complete with a new myth—"includes a debunking of myth in the first sense" (myth as the "religious tradition that precedes one's personal existence") then dissociation ensues, not only from one's origins if a new beginning is mandated, but from the ability to experience the actual *now* as it is (Giegerich, "The Flight into the Unconscious").[10]

Approaches to the Absence of Myth

Although it may be assumed that the world is no longer animated to the degree that it is for cultures still living in myth (notwithstanding those who advocate the protection of "Mother Earth"[11]), the absence of myth, seemingly straightforward, provokes disparate responses. Four approaches to be discussed are briefly summarized as follows:

- **The refutation of absence**. The intentional confounding of form and substance is evident in thinking that strives to meld philosophy and myth. The boundary that marks the emergence of philosophy *from* nontheoretical myth is erased in an attempt to show that myth has always been present and, furthermore, remains the truth even at a conceptual level. Two contemporary theorists, Elizabeth Baeten and Milton Scarborough, draw on philosophy to resuscitate myth from ill-intended and false reports of its absence, redefining myth in the process and applying myth to one of modernity's phenomena that resulted precisely from the end of myth: the split between subject and object.

- **The incorporation of absence.** The "myth of myth" can best describe the approach that assumes the loss of myth but subsumes it under a larger interpretation of myth that "sees through" itself to reveal its ideology. Two theorists, Bruce Lincoln and Robert Ellwood, allow myth to abide in its negative, fictitious status while uncovering the political ideologies shaping myth theory. Similarly, two representatives from the depth psychological perspective, Christine Downing and Adolf Guggenbühl-Craig, assume the infiltration of ideology into myth and one's personal role in directing myth, but ultimately maintain the liveliness of the symbolic realm.

- **The necessity of absence.** The postmodern awareness of absence and the impossibility to settle on a solid meaning is projected onto an ahistorical reading of myth in the work of Eric Gould, which unwittingly removes myth from the grounding it *did* have and perpetuates its absence. The modern experience of a lack of grounding and meaning are unavoidable but necessary for creating myth, which must strive to find meaning anyway. Absence is the center, perhaps the only center. Exemplified in writings by David Miller and Joseph Campbell, emphasis is placed on a purposeful lack of meaning, for any posited meaning obscures direct experience as well as the larger context containing and unconsciously influencing any assured proclamations of meaning or truth.

- **The simultaneous acknowledgment and discrediting of absence.** Wendy Doniger's approach to myth presupposes its absence insofar as myth is essentially a tool in the hands of humankind. At the same time, myth is redefined such that its fragments, whether to be found in popular culture or Eastern religion, point to an undeniable reality of myth. Not only a reality, but a necessity because myth, one's stories, are all there really is in a demythologized (but actually remythologized) world to provide life with depth and meaning. While a comparative mythology is certainly instrumental in enabling one to view his or her culture from the lens of another one, living by other people's myths carries the potential of overlooking the consequences of an absence of myth in one's own land.

As this is far from an exhaustive survey of contemporary myth theory, it bears restating that the reasoning behind these selections is such that I consider these theorists to be illustrative of primary approaches to an absence of myth, covering the range from denial to acceptance to even a celebration of sorts. To be sure, these theories overlap into other sections as I have outlined them and obviously address additional issues in regard to myth. But for the purposes of this discussion, I trust they will assist in magnifying the topic at hand.

THE REFUTATION OF ABSENCE

Elizabeth Baeten: Myth as Mirroring Thought

In *The Magic Mirror: Myth's Abiding Power*, Baeten writes, "Human history, the processes of culture, and the advance of our understanding of the workings of the world are seen, in large part, as progressively divesting human life of myth" (6). But through the examination of four very different theorists, Ernst Cassirer, Roland Barthes, Mircea Eliade, and James Hillman, Baeten aims to show how "theories *about* myth have come to play the roles of myth," thus precluding any real divesting of myth (19). She sees the same "dangerous myth" coursing through these divergent theories; namely, that the "*telos* of human existence is absolute and unbounded creative freedom." Yet rather than addressing existential issues of freedom and the boundary between what is human and what is not at the philosophical level at which they are raised, she wants consciously to guide philosophy's head back into myth. In her words, she intends to "remedy this relative dearth of serious philosophical investigation into the nature of myth" (19, 7). This then becomes an *idea* (and not a phenomenon) of myth that has to fuel the requirements of both structure and phenomena. The distinction between structure and phenomena or form and substance is purposely effaced. This may make it easier to perceive how modern theories of myth function the same as myth itself, but this is an unspecific, unlimited view of myth. Not only does it already contradict her theory of myth of something that is distinctive, this view of myth ignores the fact that living myth (as opposed to the theory) requires a unity of—not an effacement—of form and substance. The myth is the narrative and the embodiment of the narrative, the mythic mode of being-in-the-world. But ideas of myth cannot stand in for both.

Baeten is a theorist who criticizes the lack of a concrete definition of myth in most scholarship. "To refuse to give definitions or set limits" prevents humankind from fulfilling its purpose of self-creation, an act that she believes is played on the stage of myth (212). This innate need for creation can only function amid constraints and boundaries; every telling of a myth, then, or a theory about myth is an act of "creating the boundary of human being" (39). Myth itself is the ultimate boundary. It is the demarcation between what is human and what is Other; what is not human but the "world for human being" (165). In this respect, opposing theories of myth can all be joined under serving this same function of defining and delimiting what it means to be human. Insofar as myths have performed this function since time immemorial, then not only can we never be without myth, but any theory of myth adds another outer ring to this circular thinking, with the circle broadening itself to allow for a conjoining among differing historical (and now thoroughly abstracted) usages of the word *myth*. Despite Baeten's acknowledgment that mythlessness is part of our cultural inheritance, the continuity of myth must prevail; the bubble cannot be burst. Although the idea that we can never be without myth reveals its other, hidden face: that we, or Baeten, at least, does not *want* to live without myth. This underlying motivation allows a clinging to the hope that any connection between archaic myth and an analysis of myths exists somewhere else besides human intellect.

For Baeten, unbounded freedom will be seen as dangerous because it does not allow for one to be free from myth and to see that it is precisely such a release that could structurally fulfill a comparable purpose as to what is imagined or sought for in myth. Her argument overlooks that in living myth, having fewer options may presuppose a lack of freedom, but it also renders the issue of freedom irrelevant. Joseph Campbell wrote, "[F]ormerly, for generations, life so held to established norms that the lifetime of a deity could be reckoned in millenniums" (*Masks of God* 677). The known gods and myths endured and with that endurance came the commitment to serve one's god and myth. But in a time where "there is nothing now that endures," where the "known myths [and] the known God cannot endure" (ibid.), where the established norms do not last for very long and are subject to human rather than divine intervention, it is impossible to return to a time when one had no need to speak of freedom because life was contained in the gods.

Furthermore, in myth there would not be any reason for humankind to fulfill any purpose of self-creation, for one believed this task fell to the gods. (Two examples from Egyptian cosmogony: at Heliopolis, the first couple and subsequently the world were born from the masturbation of the god Atum. In Memphis, the artisan god Ptah thought and felt the world before speaking the world and making it real [Derchain 91].) Baeten's own creative and philosophical reading of myth bespeaks a higher degree of intellectual freedom unlikely to be experienced (or needed) by archaic societies. Yet the trajectory of her own method, an idea of unbounded freedom, must be thwarted. Her idea must be removed from its course and wrapped in myth, not just to absolve the need to answer for mythology as primarily a modern phenomenon, but also to support her theory that any theory of myth plays the same role of myth. She and the theorists she discusses are specifically mythmakers and not just regular storytellers, thus laying claim to myth's "abiding power." But myths were not theories, and if one is a theorist, one cannot be a mythmaker. Theories demand arguing, proof, and further define themselves through falsification. Myths, on the other hand, do not require proof; they simply *are*. To conflate theory with myth may be one way of trying to come to terms with philosophical issues for today, but this conflation unwittingly adds another boundary or layer of resistance and occludes the understanding that was presumably sought.

Baeten's analysis also unwittingly reinforces the boundary between myth and mythlessness. "The mythical is a kind of gateway, hinge, turnstile or threshold [. . .] for myth to maintain its status as myth it must continue in its function as the boundary between incommensurables" (166). But despite her saying that myth functions as a permeable boundary, myth acts more as a barrier to be consciously erected, a one-way turnstile going in reverse, toward some time protected from both myth and present-day reality. The split between the opposites is strengthened, because the "other" that is not-myth, the "other" that historically turned against myth and initiated great cultural and religious transformation, is not fully allowed into awareness. Whatever is not-myth must remain outside.

Baeten does argue against pluralistic thinking being reduced into dualistic thinking, given that underlying each examined myth theory is an ontological reduction that favors one category over another (e.g., Barthes's history opposed to nature; Eliade's sacred and the profane). Baeten herself is a proponent of the philosophical school of naturalism, which does not view "nature" as a category to be opposed to any other (194). And yet in positing myth as a boundary between what is human and what is other, although what is deemed other is flexible in its range, her entire argument rests on a dualism that she would strive to work against. Through myth, human beings are placed in direct opposition to what is other, but there is no room to allow that what is other (such as living without myth) might also be part of a larger domain that does not insist on a drawing of "a line between what is ours and what must remain outside" (193).

Without assuming responsibility for what Baeten has left outside awareness (mythlessness), then not only meaning but knowledge as well must safely reside in myth and, no, humankind will not be free. The need for a consciousness of absence to make itself known through humans will be repeatedly frustrated. The reflection in myth's "magic mirror" shows the other as something that must remain on the other side of the boundary in order to define the one who is looking in the mirror. Although what is other is "therefore what belongs" (perhaps because it defines those of us looking at the other), what is other is not to be invited *fully* in, into human awareness.

Furthermore, what exactly is this receptacle called "myth" in which knowledge is safely to reside? Beaten agrees that there is "no stable content to the concept of myth" and that the "meaning of 'myth' can only be determined by the work it performs" (176).

With a lack of stable content, the emphasis by default is placed on the form of myth, but here myth as a form cannot be considered entirely on its own terms, nor can it be allowed to transform into something else, such as a new form of consciousness. In this case, myth remains an old form in search of new content. It must continually be applied to something else, like contemporary psychological or philosophical theory, to bolster its so-called irrefutable existence. Myth as a form that has lost its own distinct boundary in its multitudinous definitions is attached without restraint to phenomena that intend to display "the work it performs" in the hopes of recovering meaning. But the meaning conveyed through present forms and phenomena that already dominate in an already established mythless time is obscured by such an attachment. Additionally, overlaying modern conceptions of myth onto an imagined immortal myth obscures the fact that living myth does not have a boundary to be lost or found. (Recall the dream-time narratives of the Australian aborigines: "Like an unending band they flow along, merge into each other, intertwine and disentangle again, break up abruptly, only to reappear, like a subterranean watercourse, at another place" [Uber qtd. in Giegerich, "The Historicity of Myth": 2].) Baeten's utilization of myth as a boundary mirrors the progress and expansion of *thought*, not myth. She might concur, given her philosophical approach to myth, although her agreement would differ in that myth would have to be swept up and carried along with intellectual development, rather than being left alone as just one, earlier form of reflection in the life of the mind.

Setting aside the question of freedom, it is important to note that the level of form or thought is the *only* level on which such different theories could be argued together. In abstracting a common pattern or function to these theories, Baeten has not only purposely removed this discussion from the level of substance, but in doing so has removed the theories themselves from the same level, notwithstanding her careful summaries of each theory. This follows the same pattern as her argument, namely, a mirroring of the ideas embedded in each theory with the theory itself. This is not to say that her insights into these individual thinkers are not worthy of consideration (although for the purposes of this discussion they are not relevant) or that she has failed in discerning philosophical issues in myth *theory*. But the distinction that needs to be made is that not only does such a blurring between form and substance hinder or prevent one from seeing what wants to be known through absence, but that myth itself may not even be the ideal (let alone a possible) platform on which to discuss the existential questions posed. Is it not fair to suggest that other forms of expression or reflection besides myth, such as music, science, and art, could also define what it is to be human? When Baeten subsumes the modern need to define what it is to be human under myth, she not only suppresses the range of human reflection, but she also suppresses it under an inflated and generic usage of myth. And because a generic usage of myth loses all cultural specificity, it is less likely to define humanity adequately.

If, as Baeten argues, "the subject of myth is a mirror reflecting our intellectual concerns, our intellectual concerns mirror myth as well," then questions about the *telos* of human existence will never get out of the confines which would give rise to such a question (163). The question will be thrust back onto the questioner. Even if questions of existence are ultimately unanswerable, this becomes a conversation that could best be served outside of myth, given that myth is so easily identified and conflated with conflicting means of understanding and apprehending not only the world, but human faculties as well. Baeten's mirror metaphor is unspecific and, in one sense, does a disservice to myth. We know myth by what is not-myth; such a distinction is necessary to distinguish myth from intellectual concerns. Furthermore, as long as modern ideas of myth continue to look backward while purporting to look ahead, what could potentially provide a response to today's intellectual concerns is hidden from view—philosophy's dependence on a differentiation from myth denied. This is not to criticize or deny the wellspring of meaning available in studying myth as a historical text. The question is whether such a study is intended for its own sake or is an attempt, among many things, to show that the meaning couched in logically differing usages of the word *myth* is essentially the same.

Toward the end of her book, Baeten recounts a creation myth from the Snohomish Tribe in Washington State, in which scattered peoples came together and, raising poles made from fir trees, lifted the sky (which the Creator had made too low). For her, this myth resonates today insofar as "we have carved out a niche where we can live 'without bumping our heads.' We work, in concert and in resistance, with other natural products and processes, to shape what we find in nature into a human abode. But the sky is now closed to us; this is the price we pay" (193). The price is the loss of the belief that by lifting a pole made from a fir tree, heaven and earth are literally separated, and equally the price is the loss of the living religion that accepts this as the truth. We cannot go back to a time when such a ritual would be common knowledge or practice. Although Baeten would not literally have us go back to such a time, she would keep the pole so firmly planted that it and her thinking are still utterly bound to an experience we now call myth (the ritual of the Snohomish creation), and, moreover, bound to a notion of myth that is collectively regarded as fictitious. By defining myth as a necessary boundary, she is bound to the idea that heaven and earth are irrevocably separated, never to be united in their separation and thus keeping the need for myth in its reconciliatory role burning. Baeten may be applying the logic of the creation myth to today's methods of understanding our world, but she only goes halfway.

The creation myth ritualizes in narrative form the simultaneous separation *and union* of heaven and earth. The divine progenitors of the world are joined in their sacred marriage and separated for the sake of creating life and consciousness. In Greek myth, Gaea (Earth) gives birth to Ouranos (Sky) who then covers her, and so begins the creation of the cosmos. With the loss of myth and ritual, the same dialectical movement between union and separation or same and other is still required for consciousness to come into existence. We have not stopped reflecting; we are still in the process of creating consciousness. Only now this movement is no longer enacted externally and concretely, as was formerly appropriate for cultures living in myth. Now this separation and union must be realized internally. For it is not that the sky is closed to us, as Baeten says. On the contrary, the sky has fallen—into moonwalks and space travel and reflected at the other end of the astronomer's telescope. Not a literal fall, obviously, but an internal and formal fall, the loss of the sky's mystery and divine inhabitants. The act of union and separation must be commensurate with this new, inverted, and negative status, with the form of reflection appropriate to *now*. This act must correspond to the same structure—only it is now centered in the mind and cemented in the progression of thought.

Even if fragments or traces of myth linger in our imagination, they cannot perform this role. Insofar as Baeten's efforts to continue the process of a differentiating awareness are tied to myth, the differentiating is caged in. The greater price modernity thus pays is not the loss of myth, but rather the loss of the now internalized dialectical movement between union and separation. With a philosophical myth, we get stuck in the space between union and separation. We get mired in the gap between heaven and earth, immune from both, and prevented from creating new life (consciousness).

Milton Scarborough: Myth as Overcoming Dualism

For Milton Scarborough, another contemporary theorist, the boundary between inner and outer does not need to be steadfastly maintained *by* myth, but is "devastating" *for* myth, because myths or modern theories of myth are either about subjective experience or the outer world, not both. "Myth must be about one or the other." No longer can myths tell the whole story of the universe (12). Yet rather than accepting this as a necessity or truth of myth—really of modern experience, given that theories of myth materialize out of such experience—Scarborough intends to "overcome the inner-outer dichotomy and set forth a definition of *myth* which does not depend upon that dualism or the features of modernity that spring from it" (73). But if the split between inner and outer is our inheritance, then seeking to overcome it is a disguised rejection (although perhaps not so disguised in this case, given his apparent disdain for the state that myth is in) of the tradition we live in. This sets in motion another dichotomy between an idea of wholeness that cannot allow for the split and a worldview that has incorporated the split into consciousness.

The act of reflection, epitomized in the mirror that Baeten sees as a powerful reflection of myth, is for Scarborough an instrument of corruption. Or, rather, limiting myth to just one kind of reflection is what defeats myth. His book opens with a recounting of the disintegration that befell a small Stone Age tribe in New Guinea upon receipt of mirrors and photographs of themselves by the anthropologist Edmund Carpenter, in 1969. When the anthropologist returned to New Guinea six months later, the sanctity of the tribe's ceremonies was no more. Their sacred mysteries were now open to full disclosure, male initiation rites were no longer mandatory, and the most scared ritual objects were put up for sale. Carpenter cited poet Matthew Arnold in his report: once a cohesive collective, the tribe now consisted of individuals who "wandered 'between two worlds, one dead, the other powerless to be born'" (qtd. in Scarborough: 2). However, for Scarborough this implies less a loss of myth than the "embodiment of some larger cultural force" still at work behind the scenes (3). The problem, as he construes it, is not looking in the mirror. The problem is in identifying the images on the "visualist blackboard" with ourselves and succumbing to the misguided belief that self-consciousness and living myth are mutually exclusive. For behind the outer reflection is the always present "prereflective world" of myth. This is more than the true nature of myth, it is undying myth that is waiting to be restored to its rightful status (125).

Thus, in New Guinea, the fact that the "traditional myth [. . .] has not been replaced by a new one" indicates to Scarborough that "myth is not so much dead as it is broken, enervated, numbed" (6). Precisely because no new initiation rites were established and no new mysteries were discovered, because nothing came in to replace what was lost, he sees this as evidence that even when secularism presides over the sacred, myth persists. And not just any myth, but in essence the same myth that infused the life of this tribe, even if now in a fragmented or numbed state. If this particular myth were really dead, it would have easily given way to another myth, to another chapter of gods and rituals. Ignoring the possibility that perhaps nothing could come in to amend this rupture (meaning a real death) or that such a rupture not only necessitates modernity but is the only way an abstract, content-less myth can be imagined to perform the same unifying function of archaic (and decidedly concrete) myth, Scarborough tries modernity as the killer of myth. But he has a trap door, for myth has not really been killed. Modernity merely pushes it underground with what turns out to be just another myth. "Far from suffering from the absence of myth, the West has been and is now under the spell of a particular and somewhat peculiar myth—namely, the myth of origin in Plato's *Timaeus*" (48). Again, here is the intentional equivocation of the word *myth*. An absence of archaic myth, such as the loss of cult and ritual life experienced by the tribe in New Guinea, is essentially disregarded and conflated with a philosophical discussion framed in an *idea* of myth, Plato's *Timaeus,* itself a product of demythologization. Although if one wants to believe, as Scarborough does, that any notion of an absence of myth is really a "retreat before the advance of myth," the equivocation is needed in order to maintain an allegiance to myth (33).

Following the school of phenomenology, Scarborough argues for the "world [as] the ultimate context for all human activities, including thinking." And myth "is the primordial and comprehensive grasp of this life-world and, therefore, is always present in the tacit dimension to orient and guide all reflective analysis" (94). Moreover, tacit knowing is rooted in the body, related to Maurice Merleau-Ponty's "body-subject," that exists prior to the abstraction of subject and object. This "primordial [and non-dualistic] being-in-the-world" is not only still accessible, it is also what can overcome the dichotomy between inner and outer (qtd. in Scarborough: 80). The larger cultural force running behind the Stone Age village in New Guinea is the "true" and persistent myth that intends to recover a primordial and prehistorical mode of being-in-the-world. This is despite a definition of myth rooted thoroughly in modernity, and in a theory that exposes its ignorance about the real experience of living in myth, all attempts to exhibit otherwise notwithstanding.

Scarborough's definition of myth is severed from the gods and narrative details, no longer symbolic and seemingly no longer attached to any phenomena, whether historical or current. His is an idea of myth as a wholeness enveloping all, although another dichotomy is set in place in that the body, supposedly an instrument of unity but posited against other sources of knowing or subsuming other loci of consciousness under itself, for example, "mind is bodily," ends up as only part of the whole (81). As long as one regards myth as ahistorical and eternal, then one will undoubtedly find myth everywhere. Yet Scarborough's need to fight so hard at establishing the illegitimacy of an absence of myth betrays a larger cultural force that is not "true myth," but precisely the opposite.

His intention is explicitly for a postmodern notion of myth: "My aim is not [. . .] to attempt a comprehensive treatment of myth but to concentrate upon the ways in which my view of myth goes beyond those of modernity" (84). In asserting a view that is not only to be unique to modernity but also a reflection of his own uniqueness, his theory smacks more of a personal agenda than a thorough grasping of any world. If the story of the New Guinea tribe can be isolated from the very real details that marked an irreversible change in their own apprehension of life and relation to the gods in order to demonstrate that myth either exists or can be recovered (despite the "hostility" of mirrors and photographs to myth), then it follows that any experience can be removed from its reality as well. An anachronistic sequestering carried out whereby reality—not myth—is pushed underground to mend a split that "is the defining mark of modernity" (13). Only it is a mending that in turn will have little bearing on reality and subsequently little hope for overcoming the dichotomy that is real.

Any understanding of myth requires a reflective process and thereby creates a split between subject and object, a loss of myth in order to see myth. Like the proverbial fish in water, we cannot know what we were once immersed in until we get out of the water. Yet for Scarborough, the loss of myth must be remedied by what has just been realized as being lost—myth. But it is far from the homeopathic method where like cures like, for his definition of myth is so far removed from itself that, like Baeten, his argument does the opposite of what he is seeking to accomplish. By virtue of ignoring or obscuring differences between conflicting usages of myth and contrasting ways of grasping the world (for one thing, numerous scientific and philosophical theories are reduced into either manifestations of the *Timaeus* or Genesis myth), the split itself is addressed only superficially. Therefore, how could it be successfully overcome?

The intentional equivocation of two logically distinct periods of myth functions like blinders that must be steadfastly held on to as long as one wants to maintain a current and vital presence of myth. Myth only needs to be updated; yet substituting myth's old clothes for new ones effects a surface change at best. A new myth that seeks to replace and redefine the old one can never provide meaning for humankind at the level that needs it most. Otherwise, a successfully altered myth would render questions of meaning and meaninglessness irrelevant. Given the excessive and at times despairing quest for meaning and purpose running rampant in the twenty-first century, I think it is safe to presume that myth, whether a new or re-dressed old one, is not fulfilling the function it once naturally upheld. And insofar as modern treatments of myth attempt to recover its status as truth, specifically via philosophic discourse, as a result neither myth nor philosophy is able to apprehend the truth. For the merging of the two disciplines endeavors to bring together two modes of expression that in order to be true to themselves, cannot coexist.[12] Whereas myth was previously the outward expression of self-evident truths, philosophy took on that role, now interiorized, once religion no longer carried the collective. Both are bound by a lack of choice—those in myth are bound to their gods and the philosophers are compelled to express the truth of their age. Yet what was unreflected only in the sense that it was assumed and accepted for the culture still in myth is, for the philosophers, contingent on critical questioning, reflection, and choice.

THE INCORPORATION OF ABSENCE

The awareness of one's subjectivity influencing one's theory of myth further removes the filter from myth's authority because any mirroring of myth and its theory is traced to the peculiarities of the theorist as opposed to proving the irrefutable existence of myth. Recognizing the power to affect myth rather than be unconsciously affected by it must presuppose a granting of the absence of myth, because the question is no longer, "what are the myths of a mythless time?"[13] but "which ideology is calling such-and-such a myth?" Yet even perceiving ideology in the place where myth once stood runs the risk of being overshadowed by a larger umbrella of myth, where myth must be inflated to see through itself—but still have something left over that can be called myth. The issue of myth's truth or falsehood becomes secondary to the consciousness of one's role in determining myth; a myth is "true" insofar as someone believes in it (what is important is to examine those beliefs) and a myth is "false" in that it is sustained by ideology rather than the gods.

Christine Downing and Adolf Guggenbühl-Craig: Myth as Psychological Method

Christine Downing is one theorist who argues that a given theory of myth reveals the methodology of the theorist. She writes, "In the study of myth the method of approach obviously largely determines what we find and is itself shaped by our deepest assumptions about what it means to be human" (3). Similar to Elizabeth Baeten, Downing advocates a closer look at the "underlying assumptional patterns" within each method in order fully to comprehend a theory of myth. Yet whereas Baeten seeks to unearth evidence that theoretical discussions of myth serve the same purpose as telling stories around a fire, Downing's analysis remains contained within the particulars of the theorists and their theories (4). In a work analyzing Freud, Jung, and Lévi-Strauss, specifically in relation to the Oedipus myth, the method does not play the same role as myth—the method *is* the myth. There is a distinction between these two approaches: while Baeten's approach can be likened to a perpetuating or rippling of concentric circles that define and emanate from myth, Downing enters a more personalized interior to show that an analysis of myths is "*never* disinterested, objective [. . .]. The analysis of myths, of primitive thought, is always in part self-analysis" (4).

For example, Downing views Claude Lévi-Strauss's structuralist approach against his personal failure in the search for "the primitive and archaic, for his progenitors" (60). His search for the primordial literally took him to South America, where he soon realized that what he desired most, authentic contact with the "other," was removed from his reach by the very means employed to achieve it. Of the natives in the Brazilian jungle Lévi-Strauss wrote, "They were as close to me as a reflection in a mirror. I could touch them, but I could not understand them. I had been given at one and the same time, my reward and punishment. [. . .] I had only to succeed in guessing what they were like for them to be deprived of their strangeness" (*Tropiques*, qtd. in Downing: 62). Either it was impossible to connect with the other or their similarities proved that the otherness did not exist. Subsequently, Lévi-Strauss's impetus to search *personally* for the other was no longer. But his loss and alienation deliberately became part of his method. Lévi-Strauss returned to Paris to study other peoples and their myths from "a point of view sufficiently lofty and remote to allow [the anthropologist] to disregard the particular circumstances of a given society or civilization" (*Tropiques*, qtd. in Downing: 64). Lévi-Strauss still sought to forge connections with others. Only he looked beyond the myth's narrative, beyond the mythmaker's personal or emotional intent, beyond aesthetic dimensions, and entered the structure of the myth itself to find connections based on universal patterns of thought. So, for him, the myth of Oedipus was to be understood by breaking it down into binary oppositions and analyzing all of the myth's variants. The "meaning" of the myth is to be found in the order and the pattern that emerges, a meaning that has little to do with one's personal life or one's feelings about identity. It is not an existential meaning but a logical one, and is, moreover, subject to change whenever the pattern changes.

Despite the realization that one's beliefs determines one's approach to and corresponding definition of myth, to name the method as myth, as Downing does, is to enliven a mythic consciousness in which myth itself is not entirely stripped of its power or necessity. The power of being lived by a myth is celebrated alongside the conscious usage of myth as analytical tool, as a lens for seeing through to something else. But—does it work to live in a half-baked form of myth, to subject myth to modification while simultaneously asserting that we are the subjects of myth? Here, the equivocal usage of the word *myth* comes into play again. A confluence between different approaches to myth is now found in a symbolic realm, where, Downing notes, even Oedipus himself was being lived by a myth, lived by the archetype with which his story would come to represent. "The bloody deaths, the incest, the calamities/You speak so glibly of: I suffered them,/By fate, against my will!" (81). To be sure, Downing's assertion that "avoiding the myth is what got [Oedipus] into trouble" while connecting this with the need to live one's myth consciously is not a naïve presumption that this has anything to do with archaic myth. Nor is it a call to live in a time other than this one. But using the same word and choosing the symbolic realm as the meeting place reveals the hope for a bonding between differing phenomena of myth, that a "mythic consciousness" is not an oxymoron as if modern consciousness did not depend on an absence of myth.

This particular equivocation of myth is indicative of a depth psychological approach in which psychology is equated with mythology. Jungian analyst Adolf Guggenbühl-Craig says a psychology with soul "necessitates the connection of the objective to the subjective" (*Old Fool* 39). The joining of the opposites is performed by myth and symbol; insofar as such a connection requires the discernment of unconscious or invisible motivations behind individual or collective behavior, "everything becomes mythology, because it is only through stories, narratives, and images that it is possible to come closer to psychological phenomena" (39). We need myth to know and see the workings of soul. Mythologizing and demythologizing are therefore struck together, one implying the necessity of the other. Our "ideologies, idols, models, policies, visions, demands, slogans, psychological theories" must be detected for the myths that they are, while at the same time the myths must continually be created, for they are the stuff that life is made up of (42). Even when the myths are recognized as fantasy, ideology (our own creation emerging out of the social climate and personal complexes), they, according to Guggenbühl-Craig, must continue to be created. "Nothing comes nearer to soul than myths and symbols" and soul is the depth psychologist's container for modernity (41). But, I would contend, how can a choice of slogans or policies or models substitute for the kind of containment found in archaic myth? This kind of myth feels more akin to a game, a Ouija board in which the players want to hold all the pieces, but hope that something else is providing mysterious guidance.

A problem I find with this approach is that steadfastly keeping the symbolic realm as recourse dilutes and dulls the process of dissolving the phenomena so as to see what calls it into existence, supposedly the role of a psychology as mythology. Georges Bataille wrote, "because a myth is dead or dying, we see through it more easily than if it were alive" (*Absence* 48). But the death is aborted. Guggenbühl-Craig's acknowledged mistrust and caution against the dangers of one-sided myths are important to consider in any discussion of myth, yet he also says, "we could avoid much trouble if we did not constantly transform our myths into ideologies" (77). This statement echoes the sentiment that, at bottom, we still have myth and ritual, no matter how diffused into modern society and no matter how secularized.[14] Despite the allowance for opposition and the need for demythologizing, if *everything* is a myth, then everything sooner or later falls under this protective blanket that prefers to wrap the experiences of a meaningless or mythless time in symbols that belie the meaninglessness. And, in the meantime, the separation that allowed consciousness to begin to become aware of itself is smothered.

As Downing sees it, the question raised in the myth of Oedipus, as well as reflected in Freud, Jung, and Lévi-Strauss's approaches to myth, is that of genesis or origin, not merely the lineage from which one descends, but "the desire to be self-begotten [. . .] to overcome, misread, rewrite [our] predecessors" (2). Moreover, the question of origin "can never be recovered literally, only metaphorically, only mythically" (5). Again, there is no denying a richness afforded by a mythical perspective and the imaginal realm. But the call to speculate on one's origins, the need and ability to create oneself not only split the Now, as Wolfgang Giegerich sees as the state of modern consciousness, but also presuppose a lack—a lack of taking for granted or assuming that there is one story to contain it all, one way to live. How can this be construed as anything less than a necessary movement in human consciousness, given that this lack cracks open to reveal difference and multidimensionality? The expression of being alive is no longer limited to a collective dreaming for itself as a whole, but is reflected in endless refractions—unique, but shining from a fragmented mirror. For Downing, the analysis of myths is not only in part self-analysis, but "self-analysis is always also self-creation" (4). It is an act of creative living that must be wary of identifying with only one myth, of reducing one's life to a monomyth. The task, rather, is to know that one lives many mythic roles (85). However, this self-creation is standing on emptiness and loss. To have the option to create oneself carries within it a loss of knowing how to live and supplants it with a perpetual curiosity and urge to know.

A further dilemma with this depth psychological approach lies in the unresolved contradiction of wielding myth as an analytical tool or as a lens with which to read individual or collective phenomena—while insisting on an all-encompassing power of myth. This not only splits the present status of consciousness, like Jung's semantic concession of the absence of myth ("Evidently we no longer have any myth") but syntactic denial of the absence when he turns inwards to find his personal myth ("But then what is your myth—the myth in which you live?"). This double, contradictory usage of myth as psychological tool and immutable force also defends against the split that did occur in consciousness.

Recall the Stone Age New Guinea tribe that fell apart six months after the introduction of photographs and mirrors. In living myth, one's reality and existence are tied up in the collective, in the narratives, rites, and rituals of the myth. There is no "subject" as modernity understands the concept, because one's subjective thoughts, feelings, and so forth are integrated within the larger, objective life of the collective and practice of the myth ("We do what our sacred Ancestors did"). Yet the mirrors and photographs introduce a new self-consciousness and initiate the split between subject and object. In the process, the "new" subjects are expelled from the containment of the myth. "Suddenly the cohesive village had become a collection of separate, private individuals" (Carpenter, qtd. in Scarborough: 2). The tribe was no longer identified with their mysteries, initiation rites, and sacred objects (all objective loci of existence) because the mysteries were disclosed to outsiders, the initiation rites ended, and the objects were sold. The tribe was now made up of individual subjects, and though they may have appeared "detached, [. . .], lonely, frustrated, alienated" to the anthropologist observing them (3), their existence was nonetheless bound now to their subjectivity.

This splitting in consciousness is irrevocable. To keep the opposites held together in *living* myth (which is more an imagining of what living myth would be like) obscures the split from awareness. Accepting the split would require fully realizing the irrevocable loss of myth, or, to be more exact, the rupture that allowed myth and mythology to come into knowledge. Instead, the fragments of myth are pieced together into ideas about myth and reality. Yet an absence of myth ultimately prevents any new myth from cohering for any myth is now subject to revision, analysis, interpretation, criticism, above all subject to the choice of determining its mythic status. What Downing or Guggenbühl-Craig calls a myth, I could call something else. And with the inability for a new myth to adhere, the way is paved for ideology to fill in the gaps.

Bruce Lincoln and Robert Ellwood: Myth as Ideology

Bruce Lincoln's treatment of myth is dryer than a depth psychological approach. His analysis is removed from a mythical or symbolic consciousness as he methodically reviews theorists who are also essentially removed, for his aim is to expose myth as "ideology in narrative form" (147). Narratives justify themselves, telling stories within their own stories "as a means to define, defend, reflect upon, romanticize, analyze, legitimate, exaggerate, mystify, modify, and advance its own position, not to mention that of its practitioners" (21). So that in the *Odyssey*, for example, praise for poetry and the poets presented in the form of a poem legitimizes and claims for itself the very powers extolled in and by poetry. Not just the poem that is the *Odyssey*, but reminders of poetry's virtues are peppered throughout the story as well, such as when Odysseus praises the poet Demodocus: "Truly it is a good thing to have heard a poet/Such as this, resembling the gods in voice" (21). Beyond moving Odysseus to tears and compelling him finally to reveal himself, Demodocus's song of the end of the Trojan war also serves to fill in the gap between the end of the *Iliad* and the beginning of the *Odyssey*, "a void so well-known as to need no narration but also too dreadful to permit any speech" (19).

Through this reconciliatory act, "poetry shows itself capable of filling in the inevitable gaps that mar any narrative, ideology or line of discourse," but again, this is only a story about poetry (22). "Although poetry has only limited capacity to effect such reconciliation in lives outside fiction, its real genius may lie in persuading audiences that this sort of healing is possible, all evidence to the contrary notwithstanding" (22). The tension between the opposites, whether male and female or victor and vanquished, may be resolved through the pathos of a poem, but, Lincoln shows, this healing remains essentially a fiction, taking place in a fictitious domain, and presumably lasting only for the duration of the poem or story. Homer and Odysseus's poetic ideology may be more subtle and pleasing to the ear, but there are still politics at work that aim to convince the listener of the power of poetry.

The burying of fictions within fictions is by no means limited to Homer. Lincoln traces an ideological thread through myth scholarship leading up to modernity. His purpose is to demonstrate that a myth or theory of myth is basically a story told about another story, tightly wound with the historical, social, political framework that influences and intertwines both story and theory. In a similar exposition, Robert Ellwood examines how the mythologies of C. G. Jung, Mircea Eliade, and Joseph Campbell originate "not from the perspective of eternity, but [are] as much a product of its times as any intellectual endeavor, and [are] interwoven with the subject's own life and political context" (xii). So that, for example, Eliade's experiences as a young political activist fighting for Romania's identity, his association with the anti-Semitic and fascist-leaning Legion of the Archangel Michael, subsequent imprisonment, and later exile from his native land are linked to his theory of myth that, in seeking to return to the magical and primordial world, *in illo tempore*, strives to be free from the "terror of history" (Eliade, qtd. in Ellwood, *Politics* 99). Moreover, Ellwood also suggests that Eliade's pluralizing and universalizing of the sacred is a result of totalitarianism, where "he could well have been led to perceive totalitarianism's opposite and exile's opportunity" (97).

For Lincoln and Ellwood, myth in its mirroring function clearly provides a useful reflection of the ideals that impress on culture and theory. The work is to see them for the ideals that they are and within the context that they emerge, not as a natural given or isolated and objective truth. Accordingly, they call myth a myth. But, in this context, to regard myth as a myth is to turn myth in on itself, as if myth is now only known in its negative, fictitious sense. Ellwood comments, "Myth is really a meaning category on the part of the hearers, not intrinsic in any story in its own right" (175). And yet even if myth is granted some vitality in its negative or fictitious status, to imbue this kind of myth with meaning, as Ellwood does, contradicts the terms by which myth is now endorsed. At bottom, it reveals the hearers' and tellers' *need* for meaning, along with the desire for an experience that could fill such a need.

If, following Lincoln and Ellwood's lead, myth itself is a myth, then there is no end to the metanarratives that can pile up on top of each other in the attempt to offer new perspectives on myth or glean something of value. Inasmuch as this is an attempt to experience a corresponding truth of today's collective and individual life, corresponding to the function of myth as informing both the surface and depth of life rather than as a source of information to be picked through at will, then there are only more layers to dig through—not to find a new interpretation, but to find a comparable meaning for today's "myths." Ellwood holds no claims that we can be "saved by myth," but he is willing to shroud the myth of myth in its now seen-through and tattered cloak. "In a semi-secularized and rampantly pluralized world in which the hold of objective religious truth is increasingly problematic, but in which religious questions and yearnings are certainly real, mythology is a viable and not ignoble alternative to a stark choice between dogmatic religion and sheer secularism" (177–78). Myth, by Ellwood's standards, permits us to retain our status as both inside and outside of myth, perhaps caught between two worlds but unable to enter the next one as long as the implications of being caught in a gap are not accepted without keeping myth as an ace up one's sleeve.

To the extent that myth is seen as a means for containing and transmitting ideological assumptions, then, yes, I would agree that we are never without "myth" (meaning ideology), given that one's very act of living is itself a narrative infused with ideas of what it means to live. And to the extent that any text or scholarship carries the author's proclivities in the choices made as to what to disclose or exclude, then anything can be construed as a myth, however repackaged. But in the case of myth, it is crucial to look inside the packaging. Both Ellwood and Lincoln are essentially saying we are in a story, even though this is what they call myth. Or, conversely, what has been generally and historically regarded as myth is really just a regular story, even if at various times weighing more politically and culturally. The continued use of the word *myth* amid discussions of ideology would therefore be an attempt to course-correct modern and romanticized ideas of myth. Although Ellwood still clings to some mythical dimension ("we need to make the world safe for myth and dream" [178][15]), Lincoln prefers to tease out concurrent narratives, to bring the stories down from their mythic status and see them against the backdrop of human history and in light of any given story's relationship to those who tell and receive it. Little is attributed to a transcendent power or archetypes. Matters of one's personal soul are not relevant. What is relevant is the responsibility attributed to storytellers and hearers, not necessarily to impart the stories with meaning but rather to gain enough critical distance from any meaning that might cloud the capacity to excavate the ideological and other assumptions forming the stories.

Even as a modern construct, even seen through to its ideology, myth cannot and perhaps should not articulate the truth of lived life, for life has become too complex and nuanced to be articulated in one grand narrative. Narratives may offer engagement or escape, but they can no longer satisfy the soul to the degree that they once did in living myth. Neither can religious dogmas. Collectively and predominantly, we want comprehension, proof, and explanations.[16] Moreover, any narrative that would purport to be large enough to speak for it all today, however unlikely, would be seen as functioning repressively and accused of gross generalizing that minimizes and obscures differences in race, gender, culture, politics, and so forth. Similarly with myth theory: "The hope for an elegant master theory has atrophied. Those twentieth-century thinkers who have attempted such a theory—Frazer, Jung, Freud, Lévi-Strauss, Eliade, among others—have kept the customary authority of intellectual ancestors, but their powers of persuasion have lessened. [. . .] [T]he process of change is well under way" (Patton and Doniger 2–3). Nonetheless, our intellectual development and creative prowess come at a price. Just as Demodocus's song fills in a gap both created and relieved by Homer, our words and texts also seek to fill and erase the gap created by the loss of myth with myth. But it is a fictitious endeavor for us as well.

THE NECESSITY OF ABSENCE

In other theories of myth, absence is not only presupposed but is relegated to a more central status when the apprehension of absence or nothingness points to an essential reality underlying the basic means of encountering life. However, the experience of absence is not exclusive to the modern situation that becomes aware of it. Rather, absence is assumed to be an inevitable and integral part of human existence, and is projected backward onto premodern modes of experiencing life, namely, myth. From this perspective, absence *precedes* myth—not the other way around.

Eric Gould: Myth as Language

"I do not believe that we must differentiate sharply between some pristine, original, and sacred myth of origins which has somehow receded from our grasp, and which we can only pessimistically hope to recover and, on the other hand, myth as a semiotic fact" (10–11). So writes Eric Gould, who does not pretend that true myth can exist in modernity but believes that "mythicity" or the nature of the mythic exists as long as language is used to understand the world. Although this potentially reads like a casual dismissal of the problems inherent in myth's equivocal usage, it assumes that whatever loss did occur was so long ago that it merits little cause for concern or argument. It is as if the need to differentiate between religious and linguistic myth is a lingering in a world already exposed as fictitious. However, the level of Gould's discourse is at a place at which a loss of myth is ostensibly irrelevant because language is given precedence over myth. Inasmuch as myth is determined by language "and not the reverse, [. . .] mythicity is no less modern than it is ancient" (12). The mythic link between antiquity and modernity has little to do with the actual experience of the gods enacted in ritual, although by no means does Gould discount myth's role in attending to the numinous. The link that is emphasized is language. Myth exists through the ages by way of using language as a metaphorical means of finding truth and the attempt to recover the sacred—regardless if the attempt is actualized.[17]

The absence of myth is not the issue for Gould. Absence in relation to myth is, for at "the heart of myth" itself lies a gap that can never be completely filled. But this gap finds an approximate expression in myth as metaphorical language because language "describes what is *not* present." Language is inherently gappy, it is "the *lack* presupposed by our speaking anything at all, rather than a direct presence" (Gould 7; Doty, *Mythography* 203). In semiotic terms, it is a gap that results from "the perpetual tension we find in any sign, between the signifier (in all its arbitrary indifference) and the signified (which depends on our intention to locate meaning in language)" (Gould 7).

I have been suggesting that theories of myth are connected to the extent that they can be seen as resulting from the loss of myth. For Gould, myth is a result of the loss itself, of the inevitable gap that surrounds meaning. Myth is not merely a result of but a direct response to absence or nothingness, for myth "reminds us strongly today that without a sense of Nothing, there is no selfhood or freedom" (10). Following Heidegger, Gould believes that myth is "the history of our inability to authenticate our knowledge of Being, and yet it is at the same time a history of our attempts to understand that inability" (10). The loss that gives rise to myth may be temporarily appeased by myth (language), but the absence cannot be overcome by myth. If myth is identified with language and, furthermore, language cannot escape the semiotic gap and is built around "an absent center" that "cannot contain its own origin," then this is an absence that cannot and should not be mistaken for any kind of presence, least of all myth (138).

Though Gould assumes the absence of myth, his argument still depends on myth's equivocation. He sees myth as materializing from a lack of grounding and not-knowing, but this is a reading of myth that overlooks the embeddedness and grounding in nature and the world that *was* the reality of myth. Kerényi writes that the one who lives in myth, the *Begründer* (founder) "dives down to his own foundation, founds his world. He builds it up for himself where everything is an outflowing, a sprouting and springing up— 'original' in the fullest sense of the word, and consequently divine" (9). The point of myth was precisely an act of grounding. It represented the solidity that comes with knowing one's place in the world, and knowing that one's being is inaugurated from a common divine origin. It is the questioning of this knowledge, questioning the answers that are already presented simply by virtue of existing, that slowly loosens the foundation. Gould's abstraction of myth (to his term "mythicity") permits him to posit a certain vitality and continuity to myth, but then myth *as* grounding is made to bear the brunt of modern experiences of nothingness while simultaneously being usurped of the role it once served. Despite an "absent center," myth is cloaked in a definition that forces it to find a foothold in a world whose ground has been receding.

Gould argues that in the attempt to make events known and thereby meaningful, myth strives to do the impossible: close the "ontological gap between event and meaning" (6). However, the gap can never be closed, only repeatedly interpreted and reinterpreted through which myth makes the "imaginative leap over the gap" (134). Without the gap, the impetus to interpret any symbolic language would cease and without interpretation, the meaning would remain hidden, an attempt at knowledge and truth thwarted before even having a chance to realize its limits. The gap is necessary—and unavoidable. The distance between event and meaning can never be completely overcome, yet myth as language and interpretation reaches into the absence to bring forth a meaning no less relevant to ancient than to modern mythmakers and myth-receivers. But the ensuing meaning is essentially a fiction compensating for an implicit and undeniable absence. Myth as language that aspires to make sense of the world is fictitious, an inversion of reality. "By definition, all fiction, however much it looks like reality, is a refusal to accept that the real world is ever quite enough. We need it in more vicarious, even abstracted forms, for it to be fully alive" (138). The perceived insufficiency of reality (perhaps resulting from a loss of living myth despite Gould's statement that one need not distinguish between original and semiotic myth, especially if language precludes the possibility of directly participating in and being held by myth) thus compels one to find meaning in fiction, and for Gould it is specifically in modern literature that the mythic intention is preserved.

The narrative of life once contained in nature is now contained in the narrative of modern literature. It is an abstracted and fragmented myth that exposes how the mythic nature is merely "dissipated" rather than "weakened" in the modern (134). The author and potential mythmaker (Gould focuses primarily on James Joyce, T. S. Eliot, and D. H. Lawrence) occupies "the borderline place," becoming more mythic when he "realizes the impossibility of closing the gap" while the reader, through interpretation, attempts to shorten the gap (254, 44). Although the gap is never fully closed, the attempt to close it anyway serves to provide meaning and some relief to the ontological question, even if any meaning or answer is essentially couched in fiction.

If, as Gould suggests, humanity is linked by the need to interpret the world around it, whether through spoken language in prehistoric (or "without writing" as Lévi-Strauss prefers [*Myth and Meaning*, 15]) cultures or with the written word of modernity, the gap between event and meaning will remain a permanent fixture. To that extent, a severing from an undifferentiated world would not have taken place because such a world would never have existed for humanity. The whole concept of myth would have been founded on an imagined loss of itself. Myth, then, or more precisely the modern inheritance of myth, would serve to differentiate not its own existence, as Elizabeth Baeten would argue, but to measure everything else against its absence. "'Myth' is born illusion. Not one of those fictions unconsciously made up by the earliest speakers, one of those shadows that primordial speech casts on thought, but consciously delimited fiction, deliberately exclusive" (Detienne, *Creation* 128). Moreover, if we were truly in myth, how would we know to answer in the affirmative or the negative until the *idea* of myth had already come into consciousness? But once myth produces itself as an idea or concept, it has replaced the experience that perhaps it can never fully speak for.

Gould would agree that myth today could never speak for the entirety of experience, given that the language of myth is only an approximation. But a problem I have with his approach is that he seems to overlook the fact that the experience of living myth would have been prior to any concerted efforts to find meaning. In archaic myth, humanity did not need to interpret the world; humanity lived and celebrated the world's already given "interpretation" (its myth). Once myth is no longer self-evident and reduced to semiotic terminology, it shows itself as dissipated *and* weakened, contrary to Gould's belief. His argument is confusing because on the one hand, he says we do not need to distinguish between "some pristine, original" myth and modern myth. And yet his argument depends on this precise distinguishing.

As long as it is *myth* that is meant to suffice for a reality that is not enough, the gap that myth tries to bridge can only widen and the need for meaning intensify. Furthermore, myth's attempt to close the ontological gap between event and meaning unwittingly sets up another gap, one between meaning and the gap itself. Despite Gould's argument for an a priori nothingness and the impossibility of ever closing the gap, absence is deprived of its own truth as long as the fictional attempts to eradicate it are what is meant to provide the meaning. He speaks of gaps and nothingness, but that is not enough—a layer of meaning must be added. To say that mythicity "is preserved in the gap which has always occasioned it" implies the inextricability of myth and absence (12). Only in this case, myth and absence are staring at each other across another gap, a gap occasioned by the need to try and fill the first one in order to have meaning. We need myth to mollify the real, negative implications of absence.

The consequence of this kind of reasoning is that the cycle of meaning and meaninglessness will continue unabated. As long as it is *meaning* that is perceived to be absent (rather than myth), then the need for meaning remains activated but never entirely satisfied, just as Gould says the ontological gap can never be closed. A meaningless reality is not only insufficient, but insofar as there is "a risk of becoming obsessed with this ontological gap as the fatal condition of myth, [it] can pessimistically force us to acknowledge our incompleteness and drive us to apocalyptic theories" (7). Apocalypse and its implications are to be avoided in favor of attempts to "preserve a sense of the numinous today"—however, *not* through today's phenomena (some of which are decidedly apocalyptic), but through "a renewed awareness of ancient mythology" (7–8). Gould would perhaps agree that today's phenomena are not being considered as vehicles for the numinous, given his assertion that we need reality in more vicarious and abstracted forms for it to be sufficient. But whether the numinous is to be recovered in fiction or in something past (itself a problematic endeavor), the same issue remains: whether the means for recovery is called myth or language, the very process of such a recovery is trying to reclaim something that is no more, now through means determined as fictitious—and therefore unlikely to succeed at such a reclamation. Furthermore, the absence that would compel one to search for the numinous in fictitious phenomena is neither fully comprehended nor accepted. The impossibility of directly experiencing meaning today (which would require an *entering* of the gap itself as opposed to an entering that really tries to close it) keeps the need for meaning alive but never quenched.

David Miller and Joseph Campbell: Myth as Mythoclastic

Myth's movement *into* absence is exemplified in David Miller's discussion of myth as "mythoclastic," where it is the purpose of myth *not* to settle on any meaning or to try and fill any gaps. Identification and coherence are to give way to difference and disidentification. "Serious dogmatism in religion, the ideology in culture, and the literalism in historiography are smashed by myth, which, through dealing with powerful ideas and meanings, is after all merely myth. It is fiction, story, and hypothesis misread as biography, science, and history" ("Fire" 89). Myth as mythoclastic serves to smash any fixated meaning and reveal it for the myth (fiction) that it is, a meaning that taken too seriously or literally runs the risk of functioning repressively and oppressively—a different connotation of mythoclastic that smashes people rather than ideologies. This is a damaging function of myth that, Miller argues, has been exposed in much of contemporary myth scholarship (86).

Myth as mythoclastic (in the first sense) is, for Miller, illustrated in the work of Joseph Campbell, particularly in his 1957 Eranos lecture, "The Symbol without Meaning," in which Campbell argues that in a progressively demythologized and scientific world, religious meaning can no longer be found attached to any symbols. Symbols that engage or attach are a trap, trapping the "energy-evoking and directing agent" of the symbol itself (178) and trapping those who would cling to such symbols for an idea or truth of something (such as God). Ultimately, Campbell says, this kind of attachment obstructs any direct experience of meaning. But it is in a symbol that *dis*engages, purposely withdrawing meaning from itself, and like a bow, propels itself repeatedly into the unknown that "meaning" is to reside. The point is to evoke a state of being and a reality beyond meaning. "What is the meaning of a flower?" Campbell asks. "And having no meaning, should the flower, then, not be?" (188). We may have lost our mythic centers, but this opens us up to the depths and horizons of existence, of the soul. "The circle has been broken—the mandala of truth. The circle is open, and we are sailing on a sea more vast than Columbus." Today's circle is one "whose circumference is nowhere and whose center is everywhere; [. . .] our meaning is now the meaning that is no meaning; for no fixed reference can be drawn" (189–90).

However, the problem of a symbol without meaning is that despite the intention for a withdrawal and disengagement of meaning, any discussion of "no meaning" carries its opposite, the desire for and a positing of meaning. Campbell is still concerned with meaning; he is just defining it negatively. Moreover, any symbol perceived to be living (even if it has no meaning) presupposes if not a living myth, then at least the wish for one. Talk of no meaning is not really *no* meaning, because this is another way of providing meaning. Now the attachment is to silence and space, to a lack of meaning that, if we could just learn to live with, it might make life once again meaningful. Although to be fair, Campbell would argue against attachment in favor of the unknowable, and against meaning in favor of experience: "People say that what we're all seeking is a meaning for life. I don't think that's what we're really seeking. I think that what we're seeking is an experience of being alive, so that our life experiences on the purely physical plane will have resonances within our innermost being and reality, so that we actually feel the rapture of being alive" (Campbell and Moyers, *Power* 3). And Miller points out that Campbell's work "implies a hermeneutic beyond meaning and meaninglessness" insofar as he (Campbell), as a "prepostmodern," holds no false pretensions that myth or religion can hold of its own accord without being propped up by ideology or being dissolved by intellectual thought, thus presupposing the futility of satisfying questions of meaning ("Comparativism" 175).

"Myth is mythoclastic, when it is functioning truly as myth" (Miller, "Fire" 89). Absence is to be sought, rather than bridged. "True" myth is to look for the holes and find the myth in and of any proclaimed certainty. Whereas fragments of myth might be perceived as surviving despite an absence of myth, in the mythoclastic view, it is fragments of *mythlessness* that remain. As mythoclastic, myth in its negative, fictitious sense persists. It is like shards of itself hardening around an empty middle, unable to see through itself with the same force that it sees through ideologies. The circle may be broken, but new ones keep being created in the attempt to know what is recognized as unknown and to talk about what is out of the reach of language. And in the process we reveal ourselves first and foremost. This is not unnoticed by Campbell and Miller in their awareness that "all statements about myth and religion betray the provincialism and ideology of their authors [. . .] that includes this statement, too" (Miller, "Comparativism" 172).

Yet if myth is to be regarded as fictitious, then by implication one is really talking about mythlessness—even if using the word *myth*. One is just speaking of myth negatively. The mythoclastic function of myth can only apply to modern experience and modern ideas about myth, for living myth as "absolutely true" would predate any notion of fixated ideologies and dogma. *We* are the ones who see the dangers of dogmatic thinking. The rupture received by myth is thus exposed. No longer capable of standing for the truth of a collective (or interested, for that matter), the mythoclastic myth is now used to deconstruct any rigid claims on truth. But if one truly means to talk about mythlessness, then myth needs to be dropped from the discussion. Otherwise, the hook is still held out to myth, even if the hook is thrust into the void. Looking to myth in its negative form for a negative meaning betrays a hope that myth will provide *some* meaning, even amid ostensible notions of meaning pointing otherwise (or nowhere). Although a postmodern definition of myth attempts to have some consciousness about the theories (fictions) living us, thus making it impossible ever to be divested of "myth" (meaning: theory), it is precisely because of myth's easy identification with "theory" and "story" and "ideology" that it is all the more necessary to see through *that*. In the final analysis, an understanding of the absence of myth must leave mythlessness behind as well, before it, too, becomes solidified and codified into yet another myth or ideology.

THE SIMULTANEOUS ACKNOWLEDGMENT
AND DISCREDITING OF ABSENCE

Wendy Doniger: Myth as a Tool

For Wendy Doniger, a loss of archaic myth and ritual may be part of our inheritance, but rather than something to be mourned or rectified, it is, in a sense, to be taken advantage of and celebrated. Now we are free to look at and enjoy *other* culture's myths, which are not only enriching in and of themselves, but can in turn shed light on our own surviving myths. Defined partially as "a story that is sacred to and shared by a group of people who find their most important meanings in it," myths for Doniger are seen everywhere, alive and kicking even in a demythologized world—"reports of the death of mythology have been greatly exaggerated" (*Implied* 2 [Doniger O'Flaherty] *Other* 135). Myths are found in popular fiction as well as classic literature and religious texts. Even if thinned out into mythological "kitsch," the traces thrive in theater and films and television; they are in the details and messiness of everyday experience and cultural expression, in and of itself meaningful and truthful. Even if any given myth cannot bind a collective or guide an individual, if the myths are received in fragments, if there is no ritual to accompany the myth, as long as stories are told to frame human experience and meaning, the myth is real. Universal experience binds humanity, not necessarily a particular myth or god. Experiences such as pain or joy, that while invisible and irretrievable once the experience is over, repeatedly "generates [...] the stuff that myths are made on" (*Implied* 61).

Myth may be the reality, but it is not an immutable or biological reality. Myth may speak to religious questions, but it is not a divine reality. "Myth is not an active force in itself but a tool in the hands of human beings" (2). It is the transparency of such a tool that may mistake itself for an unquestionable reality and a meaning in its own right, but, as Doniger stresses, the transparency and meaning come from the human experience behind the myth. Myth has merely proven to be a highly effective and multifocal lens with which to view and interpret the experience (80). The fact that Doniger believes that human experience gives meaning to the myth rather than the other way around—that human experience is meaningful *because* of the myth behind it—could be taken as further proof that we are living within an absence of myth. No doubt, this facilitates the appropriation of myth as a tool. Although Doniger defines myth as a tool, I think she would be less likely to contextualize this within an irrevocable absence of myth, for one can always pick up or set aside a tool. Two metaphors Doniger employs to describe this mythic tool are the microscope and telescope: one lens shows the particular and personal while the other pulls back to look at the universal and abstract. Both perspectives are contained in myth, which, in simultaneously engaging both ends of the continuum spanned by binary oppositions, uniquely supports this double vision.

As a tool in our hands, Doniger implores us to be aware of which perspective we exercise or exclude as we use this tool. She wants us to be wary of the fact we "are always in danger of drawing our own eye" when we think we are drawing the world, and to "apply the methods without the ideologies" (11, 151). How is this possible? Through a comparative mythology that in its own unceasing rigorousness acts as a sort of dissolution, made possible by the freedom from myth while simultaneously taking its own liberties with myth in an eclectic gathering of material with which to work. As exemplified in the Indian myth of the hunter and the sage whose lives become intertwined and physically altered on entering the heads and dreams of each other,[18] Doniger would have us enter a dizzying display of myths until we forget the level of consciousness to which we have become stultifyingly habituated (but without forgetting ourselves). She would have us give up our illusions of control and certainty and find ourselves completely in the myth, in someone else's story that also contains our own and, if all goes well, in the heart as well as the head of the story. The "hunting sage" is how she would envision the historian of religions or mythologist, to have in one's study as much objective awareness and understanding as possible without denying the emotional and experiential, all-too-human component (*Other* 12).

To bestow our myths with the appellation *myth* is, for Doniger, ironic, given that the word comes down to us from ancient Greece, "one of the very few cultures in the world from which we have almost no example of real, live myths, of myths as part of a vital tradition" (*Other* 25–26). And as far as she is concerned, any imagined golden age in which the classics were alive and shared by the community was not all that golden, so why look backward? Moreover, by her own personal account, Doniger's inherited religious tradition, Judaism, was unable to provide her with the depth of meaning that Hindu mythology came to serve. All of this bespeaks a loss of myth and meaning. But although she would look for meaning in other people's myths, the search (for her) is not futile for she finds remnants of it in the presence of nearly any story, it seems, so that any loss or rupture is tacitly accepted but by no means a deterrence or a barrier for leading a myth-full (meaningful) life.

One old story Doniger tells in favor of comparative mythology is of the Sufi Nasrudin searching for his lost keys, not in the place where he lost them, but outside, where it was lighter.[19] "An eclectic who searches outside of his own house has many lights with which to search, and finds many keys (not only his own) to many enigmas" (*Other* 146). But does he find his own keys? Does this overlook the obvious, the need to look in the darkness, where the loss occurred and therefore the best place to find the "key" to the loss? Doniger recognizes that in her own culture, the "symbols [. . .] have become degraded," that "the rejection of the religious community into which they were born, their given ritual community, has left the majority of secularized, demythologized Americans with myths that have been stripped of their power to shock" (133, 131). And while it is not possible casually to borrow rituals from other cultures to go with the empty shells of our lost or degraded myths, "we still can be shocked by the myths of other people" (135).

Only to have to go to other cultures to be shocked into recognition—shocked into life—one role Doniger attributes to traditional myth and ritual, assuages having to really experience and take in the emptiness that would inspire such a crossing over to other cultures in the first place. Is it possible to be shocked into recognition by our losses or have we become immune? This seemingly carefree approach to myth, though held in all seriousness and necessity by Doniger, suggests an imperviousness to the reality and meaning of *this* culture, to deny events (some of which are extremely shocking, e.g., school shootings enacted by progressively younger gun-toters[20]) of their own intrinsic value and what they call into recognition—without having to be a symbol or myth.

Doniger does not deny her inherited religious tradition. She references a well-known Hasidic tale, the story about the rabbi who repeatedly dreams of a hidden treasure in another country. After staking out the area where he was to dig, the rabbi tells an officer guarding the area the reason for his arrival, and after hearing the rabbi's dream and decision to act on it, the officer laughs in his face and reveals that he, too, has had a dream, that of a treasure buried in a rabbi's house. This, of course, turns out to be the very same rabbi, so he returns home to retrieve his treasure.[21] The "treasure" is our myths *and* other people's myths. Why deprive oneself of such a veritable resource, especially given not only the capacity to access but also the increased and unavoidable intermingling of other cultures? Taking other people's myths seriously is no light endeavor, and Doniger more than meets her own rigorous standards for a comparative mythologist, which includes mastering the language of the culture whose myths one intends to study (enter). And whether she is finding an abundance of meaning or intensely looking everywhere *for* that meaning, her process of doing so nonetheless shows how, as a tool, myth is highly effective in shedding light on culture.

By Doniger's methods, comparative mythology keeps one from becoming complacent or lazy with myth or asking myth to perform a role that it no longer can, because no myth is given preference. No single myth is responsible for solving any lack of meaning or answering a religious question. No myth is removed from its contextual layers and no myth stands entirely on its own for too long before it is faced with another different but similar manifestation of itself, fragments giving way to other fragments as one falsifies the other, or brings into focus what the other one cannot see. "Comparison is our way of making sense of difference. [. . .] Silence too is a statement, but one that we can only hear when we compare it with other sounds" (*Implied* 28, 40). Even when a collective can no longer function as a collective (at least in the traditional sense), comparative mythology maintains a dynamic relationship, a call perhaps to balance the scales between oneself and other, same and different, a relationship that Doniger would liken to the very act of living. And in today's world, rather than quibbling over an absence of myth, it would do better to receive the myths as they are, where they are.

> The historians have demonstrated that there is no such thing as an even theoretically impartial observer, and the anthropologists have cynically undermined our hopes of getting inside the heads of other cultures, relativistically or otherwise. The linguists and philosophers have, finally, hopelessly defamed the character of language as a possible vehicle for mutual understanding. So we are stripped down to our naked myths, the bare bones of human experience. They may be our last hope for a nonlanguage that can free us from these cognitive snares, a means of flying so low that we can scuttle underneath the devastating radar of the physical and social sciences and skim close to the ground of the human heart. (*Other* 166)

At heart may lie human experience, and that experience may be inherently narrative—but, I would point out, that does not diminish the fact that when the film ends, curtain falls, book shelved, most ordinary people who are not so facile at using other people's myths are still left with the loss of their own. Maybe Doniger is different; she even says about herself that she has "come to be more interested in the imagination than in what other people call 'real life'" (*The Bedtrick* xxii). The problem is, real life cannot be denied, no matter how active an imagination, and the existential malaise enveloping many still seeps through. No longer assured by the community and no longer sustained by myth and ritual, nations like the United States are composed mostly of individuals, a large percentage of whom are looking more and more to a plethora of self-help books and workshops, to gurus in the form of television celebrities and talk show moderators for direction and guidance on how to live, how to find their personal "path." But, Doniger asks, how "can an *individual* have a myth at all? How can an adopted myth remain a myth when it is no longer the property of the group that validated its status as a myth?" (*Other* 142). A critical question, no doubt, but one that disappears into the gaps as long as individuals try to squeeze myth into current social phenomena without sacrificing their prized individuality.

In a twist on Socrates's dictum that the unexamined life is not worth living, Doniger says, "it is also true that the life that is not lived is not worth examining" (24).[22] But we are now in a culture that is obsessed with self-examination as if that could either make a life worth living or show that life was worthy enough to merit examination. Doniger's emphasis on the *experience* of living resonates with Joseph Campbell, but what is essential to note is that having to talk about or remind others about the basic experience of living shows a lack of knowing how to live and is a further removal from experiencing *this* life, as it is, whatever it is. The emphasis on experience over meaning is a further abstraction—now it is not enough to know that one is simply alive. One needs special experiences to authenticate life, to prove that one is really living, as if a common and even mythless existence were somehow less than.

To the extent that Doniger is concerned primarily with human experience and all the myriad imaginings of experience, then her approach to myth—or rather, storytelling—is certainly valid. Her emphasis on myth as a tool rather than a transcendent force curbs the myth from grandiose claims of truth and meaning, which, I have been arguing, is no longer possible. Doniger clearly loves and values a good story, in all the forms stories come in. Of course one can learn from and be tremendously enriched by stories. But are they myths? That would depend on the definition. Yet it is clear that one consistency among differing and equivocal usages of myth is the concern for meaning, whether to posit the presence of meaning or to deconstruct any certified meaning. The ability to decide on meaning indicates, if nothing else, that we are no longer in the phenomena that once answered to this. If we were immersed in myth and meaning, there would be little need to look for or talk about it. (Do people go to therapy if everything is working well?) If with the loss of myth comes the loss of knowing how to live, perhaps the question to live by should not be, what or where are the living myths now, but, rather, can an absence of myth teach me how to live?

On the other hand, holding resolutely to an absence of myth can become the next trap, when myth is not really accepted as absent but continues to provide fodder for debates on whether or not the absence is real or to what degree it permeates existence. Then the more appropriate question would be, can we forget about myth so that we may learn about life through our own phenomena? Myth may be transparent, but it is still an overlay, as is mythlessness. The moment one places it over something else, the experience that called for such a placement is covered before it can be apprehended. A relatively small moment, perhaps, and therefore easily overlooked, but nonetheless it is what we are standing on.

This simultaneous acknowledgment and discrediting of an absence of myth that I find within Doniger's approach (she herself says, "Where 'either/or/ was, let there 'both/and' be" [*Implied* 154–55]) underlines the focus of the next two chapters. Equivocal usages of myth form the belief in personal myth, a notion of myth that depends on an absence of collective myth but insists that a personal myth can carry the same degree of vitality and purpose. This is the subject of the following chapter, and a postmodern approach that similarly requires and rewrites the absence of myth is explored in greater detail in chapter 3.

CHAPTER 2

The Personalization of Myth

Delving deeper into the absence of myth and into the fragmentation that results from a lack of collective center, one confronts the individual crux of the matter: namely, what is the lone individual to do when there are no collective myths to orient him or her? If one is committed to salvaging meaning where one can, one option is to seek out the sacred stories in other people's myths, as Wendy Doniger does, and find inspiration in the realization that a distant culture's story can hit closer to home. Or one can take up the sword of meaning for oneself. This effort, the determination to find or create a piece of personal grounding for oneself, forms the basis for the movement called "personal myth."

Essentially, personal myth is the absence of myth taken personally. The absence of myth is refuted not so much by scholarship that modifies the definition of myth to fit modern sensibilities, but by the conscious intention to fashion one's individual myth out of the void. To ask the question, "What is my myth?" supposes that any so-called absence of myth can be redeemed, simply, so it would seem, by refusing to believe it. Myth may no longer guide and unify the collective, but its absence affords the opportunity to discover *my* story, *my* myth, to satisfy if only for myself the need for a meaningful life in a meaningful world, irrespective of a world reality that may indicate otherwise. And it is precisely the attempt to fill this vacancy through myth that reveals one motivation for the study of myth, displayed even more prominently in the phenomenon of personal myth.

Personal myth is situated in the gap rendered inevitable through the loss of myth. It plays inside the space between inner and outer, subject and object, self and other, in efforts to demonstrate that what was formally declared empty is actually quite full. Assembling one's personal myth requires connecting the dots between imagination, inner experience, and outer events to discover the hidden depths beneath the surface of ordinary life. Personal myth involves abstracting the narrative structure from the old stories and transposing them onto today's. So that, for example, one's life experiences and obstacles or one's depression is located within a larger, impersonal context, nestled in a timeless and ubiquitous pattern that infuses every "hero's journey" and "descent to the underworld," two motifs themselves considered emblematic of human experience (and that will be explored further in this chapter). For the moderns who choose to follow the map of personal mythmaking, they are as solitary explorers in their own (but also not their own) world, learning to read the signs and dreams along the way; once lost but now told by a growing number of personal myth coaches that if they can put themselves into a myth, they will be found again.[1]

Stanley Krippner traces the development of personal myth as a concept, beginning in 1926 when the term "private mythology" was employed to describe artist Paul Klee's worldview, and continuing through a range of psychological writing.[2] One of the earlier introductions of personal myth into psychotherapeutic literature was linked to Ernst Kris in 1956 "to describe certain elusive dimensions of the human personality" (139). Without wishing to minimize the differing denotations of personal myth that have evolved among varying schools of psychological and social thought, it is my intention to focus on the concept of personal myth within the framework of depth psychology. While C. G. Jung, and even more so, his followers,[3] are not the only ones to question the individual role in creating or sustaining a myth, depth psychology's vocal love of myth provides a strong foray into examining the ramifications of personal myth. And to the degree that personal myth retains its viability, regardless of what one looks to for supporting theories, it is reasonable to assert that one underlying consistency is the issue of personal meaning. Even Krippner's delineation of the variations on personal myth is grouped under an all-encompassing purpose. "Personal mythologies [. . .] perform the functions of explaining, confirming, guiding, and sacralizing experience for the individual in a manner analogous to the way cultural myths once served those functions to an entire society" (138–39). Similarly, William Doty writes, "Each of us develops a personal set of *mythostories*, a means of relating our own existence to the larger cultural and universal meanings that have been treasured in the past" (*Mythography* 44).

As noted in chapter 1, when Jung was confronted with the loss of religious and social myth and recognized that he did not live by what was presumably the predominant myth (religion) of his time, Christianity, he turned the question of myth inward. "Evidently we no longer have any myth. But then what is your myth—the myth in which you do live?" he asked himself (*Memories* 171). In posing such a question, the absence of myth is deflected while the significance of the individual continues its ascent, now carrying myth along for the ride instead of the impossibility of being carried by myth. Although the collective may be devoid of meaning and thereby justifies the shift to the individual as the locus of meaning, the collective's own story and history is essentially lowered in status to achieve this. Rather than accept a secular and meaningless world, favor must further be bestowed on the individual, hoping that if the individual can support enough of the weight and responsibility, meaning will be restored to the world. Thus, the pronouncements of myth's absence are proved erroneous, for myth has simply moved from one house to another. Resuscitated through the individual, myth merely requires subjective eyes to search it out and call it by its rightful name.

Jung prefaces his memoir, *Memories, Dreams, Reflections*, with, "Thus it is that I have undertaken, in my eighty-third year, to tell my personal myth" (3). And yet this work does not purport to be a "personal myth" in that it does not lay claim to a higher, archetypal truth. Jung proceeds to write, "I can only make direct statements, only 'tell stories.' Whether or not the stories are 'true' is not the problem. The only question is whether what I tell is *my* fable, *my* truth" (3). Jung is essentially saying that he has nothing else to draw on except his own subjective recollections and interpretations, his own inner and outer experiences that may or may not have anything to do with an objective, worldly truth. Perhaps the use of the phrase "personal myth" provides one clue as to how the personal myth movement finds a certain authority in Jung's work, and yet, in the original German, this phrase does not exist. Jung writes, "den Mythus meines Lebens zu erzählen," "to tell the myth of my life" (*Erinnerungen* 10). Here, myth is not personal. "Myth" is used critically; it is a mode of reflection that, in recounting the story of one's life, understands the line between truth and fable to be indeterminate and entirely subjective. Jung's usage of the term *myth* corresponds more to the definition of myth as fictitious. It is as if it is the scientific equivalent appropriate to the complexities of this particular "science," namely, the act of recounting one's story by means of inner thoughts, visions, and dreams. As, according to Jung, myth (story) expresses one's individual life more precisely than science can, myth is thus the best approximate appellation for an undoubtedly personal project.

To be sure, the line is subtle. Proponents of personal myth would say that Jung's example demonstrates exactly what a personal myth is—it is my story, my subjective viewpoint, my critical self-reflection, which has to come from me if it is to come at all, because no one or nothing outside of myself, least of all the collective, can supply this "truth" or shed light into my personal reality. Little fault could be found with this belief, for who can tell and make sense of one's story better than oneself? But the problem, and the critical focus of this chapter, lies in the reading of personal mythology that *would* seek a higher, archetypal, more authoritative truth or meaning to one's life. The dilemma arises in the assurance that this higher meaning unequivocally exists and is available for the taking, or rather, reclaiming. Semantically, one may profess to simply tell one's story, but, syntactically or structurally, one's simple story is deemed insufficient because now it must be endowed with a specialness. And before too long, a movement develops around the inflated individual, all the more insidious because the movement is believed to move of its own accord, sanctioned by the Gods while kneeling before the individual altar.

Two contemporary advocates of personal myth, both practicing psychotherapists, allude to the fact that myth was not always personal. D. Stephenson Bond, a Jungian analyst-in-training at the time of this publication, writes, "I appreciate that the phrase *personal myth* is a contradiction in terms" (29). And Stephen Larsen, the official biographer of Joseph Campbell, similarly writes, "The term *personal mythology* contains an inner contradiction. Myths are by nature transpersonal—beyond individuals [. . .]. How then can they be 'personal'?" (3). Yet beyond such cursory acknowledgments, the basis of both of these authors' arguments is to show that myth can be equally personal as transpersonal, thus justifying the movement from myth as a cultural phenomenon to an individual one. For even if a cultural myth deteriorates, each individual's ability to "restore the cultural imagination" through the inherent need to frame life in images and meaning suffuses the empty shell of a dead myth with life-restoring energy (Bond 29). Precisely due to the decay of cultural myth, personal myth is enabled to step forward and adopt its place, not necessarily to salvage the remains, but because it alone can navigate the absence running rampant in modernity and still manage to deliver the same degree of meaning.

Larsen concedes potential difficulties with personal mythmaking, such as bestowing myth with more meaning than it warrants and succumbing to "mythic fundamentalism." But then he proceeds to ask, "Don't these problems arise precisely because in modern times myth is so 'fallen,' dismembered, and dispersed?" (17). If myth had not "fallen," the inclination for personal myth would be nonexistent. Personal myth is born out of humankind's unwillingness to endorse the loss of myth, not because of any problems with myth. To contend that the dangers involved in personally appropriating myth are a result of a loss of myth makes little sense. It is a pretense, a simultaneous admission and disavowal of the absence. Moreover, if "fallen" myth means that myth is now set loose on the world for individuals to mold conceivably and fallaciously in their own image, then this would argue against ushering in personal myth. Perhaps it is better to bury the vestiges rather than fuel the fires of fundamentalism and overzealous foraging for meaning. Nevertheless, once again myth suffers the hunger of those who cannot let it go. Whereas in the scholarship reviewed in the preceding chapter, myth was frequently split into two different phenomena, archaic and modern, now it is further divided between collective and individual, each with its own notion of myth desperately trying to find some middle ground. And in the meantime, myth is stretched to cover both, forced to check any negative impulses from either side so as to ensure that talk of dismemberment is treated as rumor.

There is little presumption that collectives in Western civilizations are still living in an intact myth, and yet the crossover to personal myth carries a certain entitlement, resonant in the expectation that what was good for the collective is good for the individual. "If individual cultures have always developed a unique integrity through myth, why not the individual person, who also seeks to give coherence to his or her internal parts?" asks Larsen (15). And Bond stresses the point that a culture living in myth is composed of individuals, each of whom sustains the myth through living it. "Where do the sustaining myths of culture come but from what were once personal myths in individual lives?" (29). The idea that myths come from individuals is a misconception—myths are always cultural. "Myth is always a happening in which the magnitude and importance of the individual agents or victims are swallowed up" (Otto 34). The notion of a private life, an individual self comes later, notably in Christianity. Thus, for personal myth to prevail, the modern notion of the individual with a legitimate claim to a personally fulfilling existence is projected backward so that even the individual in antiquity is assigned more importance than he or she rightfully had. Moreover, if it falls to a culture and its individual members to uphold the myth, then it is fair to assert that any major disruption received by the culture will determine the condition and future existence of the myth. But to imply that myth is waiting in the darkness, ready to illuminate and be illuminated, is to undermine the culture's role in killing and seeing through its own myth. Humankind is thus able to recall myth while its deleterious actions are dismissed. Such logic is one-sided. It betrays the unwillingness to tolerate the waning of myth's influence and a lack of responsibility toward knowing one's participation in shaping one's reality. And if myth were this amenable to regeneration, it would have less need for humankind's remembering.

While purporting to speak directly to the heart of the individual, and through that person, to the heart of the culture, personal myth is actually based on a further abstraction of myth. In its own heart, it is removed from the concrete individual it is designated to serve. For myth to be personal, it must be thrust into the existential void, forced to balance the nebulous concepts of subjectivity and objectivity, so that neither one takes precedence, both maintaining an equal partnership. For Bond, this is what makes personal myth unique. "[T]he possibility of a personal mythology lies precisely in that middle ground between the subjective and the collective" (29). But living myth existed prior to the subjective distinction between subject and object. Personal myth as a modern construct embodies yet one more reiteration of the split in awareness, in that it is both contingent on and a response to the split. Personal myth is made increasingly possible because of the increased awareness of the separation of the subject from the object (the world); the subject is now free to look for and create a myth. And personal myth is a response to the split because it consciously tries to bridge it, to find that "middle ground." Despite its reliance on the split, personal myth simultaneously tries to mend it with as little a seam showing as possible in order to appeal to individuals and cultural ghosts alike. And yet if the absence of myth empowers personal myth, any expressed concern on the part of the personal mythologist over this absence is hypocritical. It is a contrived condolence that barely conceals the need for a meaning to find its way deep into the individual.

Contrary to all appearances, the narrative details, the stuff of which personal myths are made of, ultimately prove secondary to the need to establish a connection between inner experience and outer events. The details are replaceable and recyclable, subject to choice and modification depending on how one feels, or where one is in one's own developmental process. But reflecting on what mythic themes mean, whether death and rebirth, loss and reward, solitude and community, and so forth, and particularly what they signify to the individual, filters the direct experience and diminishes the presence of that which was supposed to "prove" itself as myth. The reflected narrative is no longer understood as containing the immutable truth. No longer is the narrative the full expression of the myth; it is whatever layer we put onto or read into the narrative that dictates the so-called myth. The narrative itself, however, is now as formulaic as it is responsive to revision. And despite its efforts to provide a balanced whole, personal myth inevitably betrays an inflated importance of the individual, further contributing to the relative arbitrariness of the narrative. When personal myth becomes programmatic, a prescribed path to follow so that one may emerge from life's ordeals transformed, it remains under the supervision of the individual ego. The narrative now serves the ego, rather than the ego serving the narrative. What was once in living myth free from interference ("we do what our sacred Ancestors did"), although, to be sure, not directed specifically toward the individual, is now to be sculpted and monitored as each individual consciously carves out his or her niche of meaning. The awareness that life is more than one's subjectivity falls on deaf ears as long as a personal myth remains something to be consciously sought, rendering any transformation, at best, incomplete.

Personal mythology is far more concerned with the personal than it is with myth. Bond writes, "The personal myth is [. . .] the vehicle through which a person becomes an individual. The myth opens up a way of life through which the potential can be lived" (72). Its appeal lies in promises of living more soulfully and authentically. One can redeem one's regrets for all the 'I never's' of an unlived life and one can rewrite challenging circumstances, not by minimizing the affect, but by putting one's story into a much larger context and looking at it through alternative lenses. This certainly has validity; there is always another perspective to any given situation. But why must such a perspective or story be glorified as myth? This is not to disparage self-awareness or being true to oneself. But self-alignment and self-discovery do not presuppose endowing one's stories with myth-like and godlike qualities.

To be sure, one can find recurring patterns in myths and modern stories; such is the commonality of shared human experience. The problem arises when one likens one's story to that of the immortals, imagining that, even if they no longer exist for the culture, they are inside the individual, potential resources just waiting to be tapped. One need only access one's inner Aphrodite or Artemis to find love or know one's wild independence, for example, to know that "there are many 'goddesses' in an individual woman" (Bolen 2).[4] Even quotation marks around 'goddess,' perhaps intending to shield the reader from literalism and inflation, do not stave off the message that the goddesses and gods are active *inside* us, "the more complicated the woman, the more likely that many are active within her" (2). This almost reads like an endorsement for collecting archetypes, an invitation to make things more complicated so that one can be sure not to miss out on any goddesses before one's life is over. "How swollen we must be to contain all these invisibles," says James Hillman. "What pretension, what anthropocentrism, what imperialism!" ("Look Out" 161).[5] By no means does this deny being inspired, driven, moved, or consumed by something seemingly outside of oneself. The problem arises when people ascribe to such experiences a higher significance than they warrant; when, for example, motherhood must take on the sacred qualities associated with earth and mother goddesses and cannot just be plain motherhood. Never mind that any appropriation of the goddess is only partial and abstract, unable to incorporate the full range and power of what she represented when actively, obediently, reverently, communally, and fearfully, if need be, worshipped.

Not all writers on personal mythology regard it in terms of storytelling. Thomas Moore argues against piecing together fragments of one's story into a coherent mythology. For him, "[t]he personal myth is not a story at all, though we might try to reach and express that myth by telling stories" (22). Moore's definition of myth corresponds to the postmodern view of myth as fictitious ("Myth is not true. I would say that myth doesn't even convey truth" [20]), but he still believes that mythology and by extension personal mythology is extraordinarily useful as a tool for imagining, whether one's own life or the life of the culture. Personal myth is a myth; one's story is another fiction out of many other possibilities. History and truth-seeking only interfere with the richness and value afforded by unleashing one's imagination. Thus, what sustains the myth is the telling and retelling of one's stories, fantasies and dreams, without worry for exact beginnings, middles, or endings. Insofar as myth is a fiction to be kept alive, and a purposeful fiction at that, this speaks to the sensibility behind myth that seeks meaning and depth—the poetry of life—above anything else. But the loophole that repeatedly surfaces is that, despite the freedom and willingness to work within modern conceptions of myth, the desire for a fictitious *myth* to satisfy the quest for meaning and restore soul to the world betrays the belief or secret hope that whatever lingers of myth today has some correspondence with archaic myth, where, it bears restating, meaning and soul were never perceived as missing.

To the degree that myth and meaning are synonymous as they are eternal, any search for meaning by default will lead one to myth. "What is myth but the meanings that structure our lives? What is myth but the story that takes each individual moment of a life and places it in a context, a plot, a cohesive movement? [. . .] That's what 'meaning' is. Meaning is mythological. Myth is meaning"

(Bond 57). However, to insist on our stories as *myths* not only belies their imagined inadequacy but also reveals one prime clue indicating that this is a psychological and not a mythological matter, and that is *need*. Bond states it succinctly: "The need for myth is the need for meaning" (25). No doubt, he would agree that such a need points to a psychological lack and suffering. But a persistent need that must be fulfilled by something commonly understood to be gone speaks only to the irrevocableness of the loss and the subsequent failure of looking to myth for meaning. Equating mythology with psychology cannot appease the loss, and only sends one on an endless chase after elusive symbols that are far more familiar as commercial products and marketing techniques than as something that can generate real mythic, religious, metaphysical meaning.[6]

Bond's work explicitly draws on Jung's, yet he does not reference the Jung who "knew full well that psychology presupposes the obsolescence of mythology" (Giegerich, "Patriarchal Neglect" 29). Jung wrote, "It seems to me that it would be far better stoutly to avow our spiritual poverty, our symbol-lessness, instead of feigning a legacy to which we are not the legitimate heirs at all. [. . .] Only an unparalleled impoverishment of symbolism could enable us to rediscover the gods as psychic factors" ("Archetypes," *CW* 9.i, sec. 28). Understanding the gods as psychic factors (which personal myth unequivocally needs to relate the archetypes to one's individual psychological process) can only come once the symbol is dead and we are, so to speak, no longer under its spell. Although Jung did not follow his own insight, because for him the gods did not become mere psychic factors, they became diseases ("Commentary," *CW* 13, sec. 54). But naming the god in the symptom or "reverting the pathology to the God" does not release it back into the world, as Hillman might prefer (*Re-Visioning* 104). All too often, the god, diseased and emptied of its religious vitality, moves no further than behind the "I." To declare, "I am (whichever archetype one wants to invoke)" no longer carries the same weight of discovery that it did for Freud, whose insight "I am Oedipus" is well known for its role in shaping his theories. Now the phrase "Oedipus complex" has found its way as easily into colloquial speech as it has into the analyst's office, becoming something of a restriction or joke, a costume rather than a liberation.

I do not want to dispute the personal examples presented by Bond and other therapists who find mythology to be a veritable resource in helping individuals. Nor do I want to deny the feasibility that individuals can transcend their subjectivity and authentically experience something larger than themselves. But such experiences need to be carefully distinguished from myth. Any personal numinous experiences are exactly that—personal and private. In modern, Western civilization, religion and spirituality are predominantly relegated to the sidelines, extracurricular activities that require a special commitment and a concerted effort to incorporate into daily life. Personal myth intends to allay the individual need for religious meaning, and, through the individual, the culture. Yet how is a private affair to sway the movement of a cultural and historical reality moving in the opposite direction, compounded by the advance of postmodernism that questions the tenability of the subject?

Furthermore, to be completely immersed in the phenomenon obviates the need to cull any meaning from it. One simply lives the experience and has no inclination to render it meaningful. Most satisfactory meaning today comes from the psychological process of reflection and integration of phenomena. But this "meaning" is more like an explanation or internalized, noetic understanding *of* an event, which presupposes already being outside the phenomena. It is not the external mythic or religious meaning experienced by immersion *in* an event that is meaningful just by virtue of its existence. Were the phenomena used for current psychological reflection to retain their mythic status (such as narratives), whether experienced in waking or dreaming life, they would remain essentially untouchable in their mysteriousness, immune from noninquiring minds. Not only is this not possible today given the capacity and thirst for awareness, but it is unacceptable, especially for the person who wants to actualize his or her full potential.

Realizing one's potential precludes the outer, positive reality of myth or any phenomena that ignites a personal spark or hint of recognition. It requires a process of interiorizing that not only enables any recognition of "I am," but also must move through it. The object of recognition is dissolved so that what was initially perceived in its latent form, as potential, actually becomes available to be integrated into individual consciousness. To use Jean Shinoda Bolen as an example, who insists that there are goddesses in every woman; what I am sure she intends to convey is the fact that women and men have the potential to access different forces or patterns of behavior and responses to life, which she, like many Jungians, personifies in the gods and goddesses of ancient myth. So that a woman who has known herself predominantly in a mothering, caregiving capacity and to the exclusion of all the other facets of what it means to be a woman, can reclaim or discover her independence, her intellect, or her own need to be nurtured. What I am saying is that the recognition and integration of a new or suppressed part of one's self necessitates the dissolution of the personified archetype. It is not the literal goddess (or the myth) one needs to reawaken; it is the psychic qualities formerly represented by the image of the goddess, but now understood and available *as* psychic factors (as the qualities of independence, intellect, nurturing, etc.)—precisely because the goddess as a living, numinous symbol is dead.

To label the process of realizing one's potential as "finding one's myth" and with this endeavor, aim to bring back cultural myth, is like putting a stopper in the whole reflective process. The alleged psychological benefits to be gained from personal myth are turned against themselves, and personal myth is itself deceived, as long as an inflated notion of myth is granted an authority beyond what it holds in the imagination of modern humanity. The sky has fallen and the gods have come down to earth, the reality they once stood for available to human awareness. *Mythos* gave way to *logos*; the mythic became psychic. However, those who insist on a personal program of meaning (in the religious or metaphysical sense) are not here to witness the fall or subsequently partake of the spoils. They have fled the earth in search of the gods, either without realizing or expressly intending that the only gods they'll find are heightened versions of themselves.

Personal myth may be implemented to assuage the loss of myth and meaning, but there still persists the loss, wanting its voice to be heard and its own significance grasped without the need to be fixed or smothered. Clearly, the loss is acutely felt at an individual level, given the prevalent urge to find oneself and the appeal of a personal mythology. And personal myth might even imagine itself as incorporating the loss into its program, such as by seeking its archetypal value and mythical referent as a means of allowing the presence of loss in one's life. Nonetheless, two particular psychological phenomena, each feeding and fed by personal myth, reveal a grandiose relationship to this loss rather than an honest incorporation of it. The result is that the individual ends up filling the gap with himself, which neither mitigates the absence nor transforms it into the kind of meaning that endures. For once one embarks on the quest to find a personal myth, it becomes like a merry-go-round that never ends, the need for meaning not permitted to subside. As long as one must seek or create the requisite symbols to accompany every stage in life, one dare not stop, lest the threat of meaninglessness creep back in.

In brief, these psychological phenomena are:

- The sense that without something larger to contain me, without meaning in my life, I am nothing. My life is nothing. The personal lack is either exaggerated, in that one holds on to his or her inadequacy at all costs, or medicated, whether through the pharmaceutical industry or a personal psychology that dresses it in mythical garments. Consequently, neither serves what is a decidedly real absence and provokes the question, how do we suffer our losses without suffering over our suffering?
- The other side of the same experience, the inflated sense that in order for my life to have meaning, I must be a special somebody. Personal myth proffers the template of the hero's journey, teaching individuals how to recognize the extraordinariness of their own drama. However, one aspect of the hero's journey complicates the translation into modern personal growth, namely, the bringing back of the boon, the elixir that is specifically meant to restore the collective.

It is my intention for the remainder of this chapter to step further into the gap and explore these two phenomena, along with the phenomenon of self-writing, which serves as one concrete means of affirming oneself, whether negatively or positively. Furthermore, personal myth grants the authority of self-validation to the individual, even while asserting that the validation comes from something outside oneself, the archetypes. But when one's validation is not matched in the collective, the split between the individual and the collective widens, leaving the individual trying to navigate the world trapped between personal and impersonal notions of truth and meaning, or lack thereof. It is with this in mind that I will also consider the issue previously alluded to—the added dilemma of personal myth in a postmodern and deconstructed world, where the death of the subject has superseded the death of God.

THE BURDEN OF MEANING

Absence is detected through the penetration of its invisible edges into thought and experience. Inherently empty, its form is shaped through responses to its perceived presence, each response groping in the darkness for something that, despite being "nothing," wields so much power such that whole philosophies develop to mold or make sense of it. Nothingness extends itself without cessation or reservation into all modes of apprehending life; ever since the fundamental gap opened to allow for the faculties of thought, choice, and questioning, nothingness has proved itself a faithful companion to humanity. Despite its lack of concreteness, absence is easily found. It arrives in the moment of something else's departure and stays to persuade any subsequent questioning or searching, for the nature of a search, whether for meaning or understanding, presupposes a lack seeking to be filled. But any search will ultimately disappoint as long as life is perceived to pivot on uncertainty and absence. The resources employed to carry out one's search or quest will in the final analysis be construed as insufficient, leaving the individual who has inherited the absence of myth simultaneously the designated source of his or her own power and impotent.

There is a particular brand of nothingness currently afflicting modern experience. It stops short of the freedom to create or the responsibility to choose, for it feels abandoned of all possibility and choice. This is a nothingness that is taken so personally that it sees nothing outside itself. Such an absence is slower and duller, brightening only with a heightened sense of unworthiness and the promise of death. It is absence absorbed with itself, with loss, and yet cushioned by this absorption it is unable fully to comprehend or relinquish the loss. The steadfast belief in and commitment to deprivation obscures the hollowness so that one's nothingness becomes something to worship rather than remain as nothing. It is the abyss of the depressed, the despair of those who cannot tolerate a lack of meaning and purpose to their life. It is the self-fulfilling anguish of those who know they do not matter and consequently cannot believe in their own matter, in any real substance to their being. Julia Kristeva writes of Bellerophon, "the first Greek melancholy hero, [. . .] self-devouring because forsaken by the gods, exiled by divine decree, this desperate man was condemned not to mania but to banishment, absence, void" (7). A life shadowed by nothingness is endured in its insufferableness, a tabula rasa condemned to be wiped clean every night, save for lingering traces of accumulated hatred and rage.

The World Health Organization predicts that by 2020, depression will be the world's second most debilitating disease.[7] The sense that something is missing predominates, that authenticity and meaning have been replaced by persistent banality. We are caught in an endless routine of balancing too much work and the minutiae of life, finding relief primarily through a combination of entertainment, shopping, and antidepressants, to name a few popular outlets for escape. Given the world axis spinning around consumption and profit (even simplicity and relaxation require the right magazines, accessories, classes/workshops, and location to achieve maximum benefits), it is little surprise that depression floats, buoyed by its genuineness amid a sea of manufactured meaning. "When your only prophet is the supermarket, is it any wonder that spiritual satisfaction is hard to come by?" (Lasn and Grierson 37) And when escape into consumerism can no longer provide a good enough escape, when aimlessness overwhelms and those desperate for meaning seek to peer below the surface of superficial relationships and a personality or User ID that has usurped character, an escape disguised as its opposite is sought. It is the turn toward finding one's self, an escape into personal programs of meaning that can hopefully deliver some purpose. This disguised escape differs from a depression that accepts absence or nothingness as its purpose, for the search for meaning has not yet been resigned or deemed futile.

But in a massive media culture, this escape into one's self all too often entails turning to others for the answer, picking from an "endless banquet table of philosophies" to be directed on "what to do, think, read, and feel next" (33). Like chickens running without their heads, the search for meaning takes on a frenzied and blind look, discarding one packaged meaning as soon as a newer and more appealing one beckons.

One danger (and the American way) lies in assuming happiness to be a "default setting" (37), an inalienable right taken as God's word even if God is presumed dead. Medication, pharmaceutical or otherwise, thus serves as an expensive means to claim one's right to be happy, to "pull us back to 'normal'" and drown out the "malignant sadness" in favor of a fulfilling life, perhaps glimpsed somewhere else but never completely tasted for oneself (37). The solution, recommended by the authors of the article cited earlier, lies in creativity. "The most promising way to happiness is [. . .] through literally creating a fulfilling life for yourself by identifying some unique talent or passion and devoting a good part of your energy to it, forever" (38). This may be true, but, paradoxically, asserting it as such further compounds the problem and clearly does not diminish depression as a collective phenomenon and stable industry.[8]

Instilling in individuals the notion that they are left to their own devices in forging a unique identity is problematic when it becomes the next task to be added to the list, the next special effort to be mustered and squeezed into the schedule. Feelings of dissatisfaction and meaninglessness are to be acknowledged but then surpassed on the way to create resolutely that which will fulfill. Go straight to the happy ending and adjust the kinks in the road along the way. To be sure, criticizing the quick-fix mentality of the "pharmacologizing of America" is justified (Smallwood 42), and it is refreshing to be reminded that happiness as a default setting is a modern construction and preference as opposed to an incontrovertible right.[9] However, to claim that all one can really do is try to create a unique and meaningful life for oneself somehow belies the observation that happiness is one more entitlement expected by an entitled nation. The depression may not be medicated but now it is invalidated, sidestepped in order to seek fulfillment. But if this endeavor fails, what then? Depression confidently takes the lead again, whispering sweet nothings into one's ears and confirming one's uselessness. Because the solitary individual failed at the kind of lasting creativity that could shut the lid on the question of meaning, because whatever answer to authenticity was found could not escape the banality pouring out of the airwaves, nothingness announces its presence, its seat warmed by the underlying suspicion that nothing is ever enough as it is.

The incessant talk of and need for personal meaning indicates that few want to live a meaningless life, though apparently many do. Regardless of whether one focuses on meaning or meaninglessness, the two define and perpetuate each other. Meaninglessness implies an expectation of meaning—why would anyone be concerned with meaninglessness otherwise, were it not for the belief that meaninglessness could and should be transformed into its opposite, meaning? The expectation of meaning today acts as if "meaning" is a given in its own right and therefore could easily be culled from any event or experience, if only one knew how. But this neglects or detracts from the individual onus to engage with one's life as it already is, which in practice requires forgetting about meaning. This kind of presence and immersion in life, freed from the endless chatter of what is meaningful or not, is presumably what is perceived as missing and consequently desired by those who are obsessed with meaning, those who would likely be attracted to personal myth. But anticipating the rescue of meaning and a meaning-laden rescue from today's banality act as a barrier to such an immersion or engagement with life. The individual is trapped, caught between the demand for meaning and the dread of meaninglessness. The very search for meaning is its opposite. By default it requires that one *already be* identified with meaninglessness—this is what propels the search. But in the process of the search, the individual is distanced from the only experience that could conceivably stop this exhausting cycle—the experience of living life without any expectations that it be more than it already is.

Furthermore, seeking to transform banality into specialness is as problematic as a life perceived to be meaningless is. It is a denial of the reality that incubates such experiences. Real suffering or apprehension of a real loss is magnified such that the loss itself is eclipsed by an inflated outrage over the loss. Suffering itself becomes something to protest against. Although just as the idea of meaninglessness carries the assumption that there must be meaning, the idea that a loss (such as the end of myth) needs to be suffered carries the belief that there should be *something* else—to blame, reclaim, mourn. We need something that not only "proves" the indisputable presence of loss, but also justifies the attempt to make amends, such as turning to personal myth to rectify the loss of cultural myth. When such a loss is judged in contradistinction to other times or cultures, the fantasy of entitlement is furthered. This is particularly apparent with personal myth because it looks backward to give its existence credibility: others had myth and meaning and though it may have been lost or buried, it can and must be found again. Yet just as an insistence on the presence of myth can overshadow and deny the absence of myth, a protracted emphasis on the notions of absence and loss themselves can equally be a denial of a present-day reality that appears to manage well enough (notwithstanding complaints of meaninglessness). The task is to live life under the conditions in which it is given—which is always *now*. But when the drive for meaning unwittingly or intentionally screens life, the problems that instigated the drive are only exacerbated and the price for human fulfillment becomes even more exacting, forced to pay for individual identities that can rectify a cultural loss.

One psychologist, Roy Baumeister, argues that as a culture emphasizes each person's autonomy and uniqueness, the burden of such a creation overwhelms people along with the increased desire to escape it, contributing, among other things, to drug and alcohol abuse, compulsive spending, eating disorders, and higher suicide rates. To the degree that "our notions of ourselves are imposed on us, to a great extent, by our culture and society [. . .] the human being can't necessarily tolerate being aware of itself—*being* itself—all the time. [. . .] The weight of self-knowledge can be crushing [. . .] and the duty to self can become onerous when the self becomes tyrannical in its demands" (210, 213). Baumeister's opinion that creating a self can imprison one stems from an empirical psychology, wherein ideas of self are determined and identified by one's outer role within the culture. This takes on a rather comic (or desperate) dimension when one considers that the culture determining identity is presumably composed of individuals similarly struggling with concepts of selfhood. The pull toward personal meaning then becomes nothing more than the reflection of a myopic perspective unable to find solid ground. Within a culture both demanding and unable to meet its demands for personal meaning, even a manufactured meaning cannot find its home, unable to lodge itself within the individual who launched its quest in the first place.

What if the call to uniqueness is not only burdensome, as Baumeister argues, but impossible to achieve? What if against the dictate of "finding oneself" one cannot find anything extraordinary? What if one's unique ability is to be just as banal as the next person? Uniqueness *is* trivial. Everything that exists is unique, snowflakes and insects no less than human beings. The inflation girding personal myth thus extends even into the word *unique*, required to stand for greatness before it can stand alongside another person. One is no longer sufficiently unique just by virtue of being alive; one's value must be exquisitely mined and discovered before one can rightly be called a self. The intention for uniqueness may seem like a thrusting of the individual outward and upward out of the careless throngs of mass man, armed with the determination to make a stand and let one's self be counted. But then one hides behind the desire and the grandiosity. One is excused from having to live one's possibly quite mundane life to the fullest.

The *desire*—whether for meaning or uniqueness—may stem from sincere intentions or from real pain, but it is a desire that ultimately defers the thing that is desired. If one is caught by or enamored of the yearning, then one must remain in the position of the "not-have's"—so that one has something to yearn for. This creates an additional distance between oneself and the desired object or experience. (It is like when the yearning for romantic love becomes more appealing than going on a series of ordinary and possibly boring dates in order to get closer to finding that love.) And yet one must be wary of surrendering one's desire out of the hope or hidden intention that such a surrender will bring the object of desire to one's life. Not only is this still wedded to the ego, and is therefore only a partial and conditional surrender, but also the reality of these mythless times is such that meaning itself leaves much to be desired. How can meaning even be possible when its search has become a commodity, propelled by those who would negotiate the findings into acceptable, self-determined terms? If the loss of myth tempts one to redeem this loss through an overpersonalization of myth, the same could be said of meaning: the loss of (mythic, religious) meaning tempts one to redeem it through an over-identification with meaning, only this "meaning" does not envelop us but rather has been abstracted and commoditized by us.

"Why have we so conflated the two quite separate notions—a) self and b) worth?" asks another psychologist (47).[10] In a culture concerned with self-esteem, one's self will always be highly valued, even if the individual is plagued with low self-esteem. For as long as self and worth are tightly bound, there will be no shortage of justifiable excuses to orient meaning around oneself, prodding one on the path toward self-fulfillment. Low self-esteem claims for itself, no less than high self-esteem, the right to self-worth. In fact, low self-esteem surpasses high self-esteem in self-importance, for one's afflictions, particularly depression and melancholy, uniquely afford the opportunity to feel special when all outward attempts prove inadequate. Abandoned in the throes of nothingness, convinced that no one else has suffered this life in such inevitability and such truth, chosen to wave death's flag among the oblivious and shallow living, the depressed person finds an intensity of meaning in its perceived lack. Romanian philosopher E. M. Cioran embodies this negative self-aggrandizement well: "I am: therefore the world is meaningless. What meaning is there in the tragic suffering of a man for whom everything is ultimately nothing and whose only law in this world is agony? If the world tolerates somebody like me, this can only mean that the blots on the so-called sun of life are so large that in time they will obscure its light" (14).

Depression at least slows the tendency to look outside of oneself for answers or the right recipe for how to become a unique individual. For there is nowhere to look save into the darkness, and at bottom rests the belief that there are no answers. As exemplified in the work of James Hillman, depression is one vital way to be reminded of the tragic, to touch the depths of soul found in the depths of life. The challenge is to live one's depression without identifying with it, to accept its role in life rather than using it as a means to deny life. Depression brings "refuge, limitation, focus, gravity, weight, and humble powerlessness. [. . .] The true revolution begins in the individual who can be true to his or her depression. Neither jerking oneself out of it, caught in cycles of hope and despair, nor suffering it through till it turns, nor theologizing it—but discovering the consciousness and depths it wants" (*Re-Visioning* 98–99).

Similarly, David Miller asks, "Could it be that the malaise so many feel really wants not to be gotten rid of, not healed, but deepened and [citing Jung] 'accepted as our truest and most precious possession'? It is our worst enemy only because it turns deep nothing into something" ("Nothing" 17). Speaking primarily to concepts of self and no-self in depth psychology and religion, Miller argues that treating a self who experiences itself as nothing, whether through antidepressants, New Age spiritual transcendence, or even psychological labeling, is not only futile to the degree that the symptoms of nothingness persist, but also denies any purpose nothingness may hold. Moreover, methods seeking to treat nothingness barely hint at the dilemma. It is the "fantasy of the 'self' as some-thing, worth something, full of itself, attached to itself" that compels the individual to run from absence and more importantly, hinders the nothingness from working on the individual or the collective (17).

An egoic or self-centered perspective that demands something of itself, such as uniqueness, will undoubtedly feel betrayed when nothing answers the call. Consequently, the nothingness is suffered loudly and with much fanfare, molded in the image of the individual simultaneously creating and trying to eradicate it. In the process, the individual does not realize that what was nothing is a now a something *imagined* to be nothing, for any real nothingness has long slipped out of reach. To be sure, depression is vividly real to the person living it—although this proves itself to be far from nothing. Yet to prostrate oneself as a victim at the mercy of depression, or to situate oneself above the depression in seeking to transform it, obscures the view into whatever lies beneath. Realizing what might want to be known through depression is thus thwarted in favor of securing for oneself a piece of meaning more suited to individual temperament and ideology. It is as if even depression and absence in and of themselves cannot be counted on to comprehend the loss of meaning. Instead, these realities require human intervention and magnification to compensate for a loss that is still waiting to be understood for what it is.

Personal myth also risks preventing the consciousness desired by depression from being fully apprehended, although at first glance it may appear otherwise. Under personal myth's gaze, depression is validated but restrained from taking center stage as it is placed in a larger, archetypal context. The "descent to the underworld" is one mythological motif used to amplify depression and the transformation that can occur through plunging into and facing the depths and darkness of experience. The Sumerian goddess Inanna-Ishtar descends to the underworld to see her "dark sister" Ereshkigal, whose husband his died; the Greek goddess Persephone is abducted by Hades one day when she is gathering flowers. But in withstanding the ordeals of the underworld (Inanna must bear witness to the rage and suffering of Ereshkigal, who also kills Inanna and hangs her rotting corpse on a peg), the one descending is initiated (Persephone is no longer an innocent maiden [the Kore]; she becomes Queen of the Underworld who divides her time between the realms of both the living and the dead).

One's suffering may feel painfully isolating and personal, but when looked at in the context of myth, the suffering belongs to all humanity, for the myths still depict the truth of what it means to be human. One can, in a sense, find permission for depression when one sees it as a precursor and initiation to a new phase in life; the old must die and be grieved before the new can come in. And yet the modern individual does not confront his suffering through and by means of the collective and a *living* myth. The individual is essentially alone, even with the aid of a therapist, as he is encouraged to travel further inward and attend to dreams, fantasies, feelings, personal history, and so forth, in the hopes of acquiring a deeper understanding of the particular role depression plays in his life. This aloneness is not only the reality for many; it has unto itself its own necessity, its own ability to bring consciousness. Jung wrote, "The patient must be alone if he is to find out what it is that supports him when he can no longer support himself" ("Introduction to the Religious," *CW* 12, sec. 32). Campbell said, "The call is to leave a certain social situation, move into your own loneliness and find [. . .] the center that's impossible to find when you're socially engaged" (*Reflections on the Art of Living* 77). Personal myth does ostensibly seek to promote consciousness while aiding the individual in discovering his or her individuality. The mythical map once serving the culture is now placed within the individual's possession, with the hope that it can still teach one how to live, even in the darkness and the depression. Nonetheless, personal myth functions more like an intellectual drug or escape into fantasy, enveloping one in unconsciousness rather than meeting the demands of consciousness.

It goes without saying that depression is also an illness that is quite debilitating to those who endure it. The challenge, then, is neither to invalidate it through repression nor to romanticize it through over-extolling its virtues; yet both invalidation and romance befall depression in the hands of personal myth. Seeking to contextualize one's personal depression through personal myth can function as repressively as antidepressants or a New Age/popular psychology mentality. Mythical motifs such as the descent or abduction into the underworld may feel true to form, but by holding to the myth as a model, one is actually caught in mid-descent. The real descent is not permitted to complete as long as it remains supported by mythical personages whose psychological value is contingent on the dissolution of the myth and, moreover, is conceivably guided by the individual with ideas and imaginings of depression already in mind. The descent cannot descend while it is held up with scrutiny and explanation, or while the persistent hope or belief that the gods have not truly departed breaks the fall. The real descent happens when one realizes it is *not* a descent to the underworld or to any other haven in the mythic universe. If there is nowhere to go, no secret hope or expectation of transformation, then one is truly "down."

"We are drawn to the abyss when we no longer experience the presence of the Divine in the world. At the abyss, in the depths of grief and suffering, we meet the gods who have taken flight from the world," writes Robert Romanyshyn (197). He feels that we "need to be called to the abyss because we have lost our capacity to grieve," and because we have "forgotten how to feel and be touched by the world's suffering" (195). This perspective insists that one suffers the abyss only to meet and bring back the merely departed but not deceased gods, but it is clinging to a proxy erroneously believed to be the real thing. The hope that the loss of myth and meaning is only temporary, remedied by a good cry, insults the depression and belies the pervasive and insidious sense of loss. If one were to let go completely, realizing that loss is loss, then one might face the abyss, whose nothingness would be less amenable to being filled with any-thing, least of all with oneself. Otherwise, depression, like personal meaning, remains in limbo—stale, recycled air with nowhere to go except where it has already been.

What if today's depression does not want to fit the old map? Looking to myth not only defends against new, possibly less attrac-tive forms, but also removes the responsibility of suffering what one must suffer *without* a map. Even if one were committed to using myth as a guide into the underworld, one at least needs to remain faithful to that myth; otherwise the use of myth for one's psycholog-ical process becomes just an arbitrary selection of metaphors that have no real substance. When Inanna descends into the under-world, she must pass through seven gates, where she is repeatedly stripped of all her outer garments and trappings. This is a myth that is saying, don't use the myth! When going under, the myth will not help because it is just an accoutrement that will be removed. As previously mentioned, Innana is finally "turned into a corpse, / A piece of rotting meat, / And was hung from a hook on the wall" (Wolkstein and Kramer 60). Maps (and personal myths) do not make a difference when one is truly "in the underworld."

One's suffering may be alleviated somewhat through psycholog-ical maps, but then it has not been fully heard. This is by no means a heartless summons to endure suffering without cause, although it is clear that many suffer already without any command to do so. Rather, the issue is how much humankind's endeavor to relieve suf-fering unwittingly ends up exacerbating it. Insofar as personal myth or the search for personal meaning directs the relief efforts, the individual remains trapped, unable to yield the desire for oneself and unable to escape the self that desperately misses meaning. So long as one is determined to find meaning inside oneself, one's ordinary suffering will turn inward as well. Yet confined to the space drawn by the individual, it intensifies in its enclosure, alongside the invisible swell of the absence inspiring this whole search.

The Indiscriminate Hero

The yearning to make an impression and not merely be impressed on, the wish to be the real thing and not a shaky imitation, the desire to excavate the true self inside who would not get lost in the translation from conception to expression, the rumbling urge to be a *somebody*—all are desperate cravings that surface when one subscribes to personal nothingness. And all these cravings find hope of alleviation and transformation by way of personal myth. To discern the reason for one's existence, to know that buried inside one's psychological wounds lies a precious gift waiting to be opened; to see one's life as a journey where each episode and obstacle is not only a necessary lesson to be learned, but one stride closer to the mastery of one's inner and outer kingdom—such is the promise of the mythic hero's journey or, more precisely, the hero's journey lending itself as a psychological pattern directing the life of the individual.

Joseph Campbell's *The Hero with a Thousand Faces*, a comprehensive study of the hero myth, is perhaps considered his most popular and accessible book. His identification and illustration of each stage of the hero's journey, excerpted from mythologies all over the world, give credence to the monomyth, the one myth of individual transformation and reclamation of the mystery between hero and god. Yet despite being primarily confined to ancient myths, Campbell's analysis easily paves the way for the absorption of the hero template into the modern task of finding meaning. Each stage, such as the call to adventure, crossing the threshold, facing unknown trials, receiving unexpected aid, and returning home with the life-restoring elixir, is mined for its psychological value to demonstrate that the hero of myth is not only fundamentally the hero within, but also the hero of *today*. And to the extent that the hero's journey is a symbolic story perpetually held to link timeless patterns of existence with individual experience, the continuity and relevance of the journey are assured.

The modern appropriation of this motif, the "how-to" of embarking on a personalized yet archetypal quest for this inner hero, is deceptively alluring as it seduces the individual into believing that the hero's journey is neither elitist nor self-indulgent, but available to anyone who wishes to take up the task. One such advocate, Carol Pearson, writes, "This call is not about becoming bigger or better or more important than anyone else. We *all* matter. Every one of us has an essential contribution to make, and we can do so only by taking the risk of being uniquely our own selves" (xv).

Insisting that no single person dominates in the realm of importance may level the playing field, but the field is nonetheless elevated as long as the individual is compelled to address overtly his or her importance by means of the hero's journey. The moment one's individual responsibility, whether to oneself or others, becomes the overly conscious subject of a path to search out and follow, it becomes objectified. One now serves the object or the idea of what it means to live authentically or "heroically," rather than just being one's subjective self. The explicit intention to serve one's self obscures the actual service and is exposed as inflated self-importance. The hero's journey then becomes one more justification to maintain an ego stance, but it is an insidious ego stance when it is disguised as personal myth's intent to bind the individual to a greater, archetypal truth.

In myth, heroes were summoned not by the need to find meaning or personal satisfaction. Heroes were called to face a certain predicament within the society, on whose outcome the society or kingdom's livelihood usually depended. Whatever meaning and satisfaction that resulted from their journeying were secondary to the tasks before them, more like a side effect rather than a consciously sought objective. It might be easy to look at the myths and say, well, since dragons or multiheaded monsters did not really exist, this is one more indication that myths are psychological, that one must confront one's *inner* dragons, a task available to anyone who chooses to look inward. Yet especially when reading mythology as psychology, the structure of the myth cannot be ignored or changed in order to suit the individual. And the structure of hero myths, such as Moses leading the Jews out of Egypt and procuring the Ten Commandments, or Aeneas's finding the city of Rome, is such that one is called to find a concrete solution to a concrete situation within the collective—*not* to discover his or her uniqueness or inner selves. Pearson's statement that "we *all* matter" may comfort or inspire those besieged by low self-esteem, but, the truth is, most people do not matter a whole lot, except to maybe a small group of friends and family. And there are even those without that circle, those who when they die are little more than a statistic, easily forgotten, and perhaps having made no "essential contribution" other than to reduce the population.

"Not everyone has a destiny," Campbell notes (*Hero* 228). Not everyone can tap into some underlying current of creativity and emerge with powerful and influential life-renewing possibilities, writes Adolf Guggenbühl-Craig, for creativity has little to do with the individual's personal psyche (*Wrong Side* 5). Anyone assuming the general accessibility of the hero's journey is bound to suffer a severe setback or remain adrift in a comfortable illusion when his or her life fails to follow the formula. But the success of personal myth unequivocally depends on its lack of discrimination and open door policy. No single individual seeking meaning must be turned away. Rather, it would do better to herald them as heroes, those courageous souls willing to reclaim myth, personally and internally, in a world that has allegedly forgotten it. "In the current time," says Stephen Larsen, "more than ever, when our grand mythological projections have been so withdrawn—from the theater of outer events to the inner life—do we need to become aware of [the] psychological dimension of the hero quest. [. . .] Everyone is to take the hero adventure within and there seek the Grail" (105).

Lest the fragments of myth completely disintegrate, the modern hero—who is not a hero by destiny but by choice—must strive harder to keep the flame of myth alive, self-alight with the special task of restoring meaning to life. Yet, to use Larsen's image, the structure of the search for the Holy Grail is precisely such that few were permitted to behold it. The reasoning that translates the Grail story into an allegory for any individual's psychological development runs counter to the truth of the myth. Moreover, it naively presupposes that everyone has the same depth of inner landscape and possibilities in life. The symbol of the Grail is abstracted such that it can be obtained by anyone, notwithstanding the long and harrowing journey to find it. But in the process, the power and worth of the Grail, that which was sought in earnest and hope, are weakened. The object one seeks and ostensibly recovers is not the Grail, not the God substance, but the hollowed and Hollywoodized gods of modernity, closer to the Grail of Monty Python.

Campbell apparently held little misconceptions about the viability of the hero myth in modernity. The final chapter of *Hero with a Thousand Faces*, entitled "The Hero Today," acknowledges that the "timeless universe of symbols has collapsed" and "the dream-web of myth fell away" (387). Further on, "the problem is [. . .] nothing if not that of making it possible for men and women to come to full human maturity through the conditions of contemporary life. Indeed, these conditions themselves are what have rendered the ancient formulae ineffective, misleading, and even pernicious" (388). And yet despite his astute observations on the conditions of a mythless world, where the "social unit is not a carrier of religious content, but an economic-political organization" (387), Campbell seeks a compromise that diffuses the repercussions of such a world. For at the very end of this chapter he writes:

> The modern hero, the modern individual who dares to heed the call and seek the mansion of that presence with whom it is our whole destiny to be atoned, cannot, indeed must not, wait for his community to cast off its slough of pride, fear, rationalized avarice, and sanctified misunderstanding. [. . .] It is not society that is to guide and save the creative hero, but precisely the reverse. And so every one of us shares the supreme ordeal—carries the cross of the redeemer—not in the bright moments of his tribe's great victories, but in the silences of his personal despair. (391)

These concluding remarks betray a dissociation between the recognition of the state of modern society and the concomitant reaction to this reality. Without myth and symbol, the world is depraved, materialistic, secular, and a whole slew of other evils. Even so, it is possible to rediscover and redeem meaning—now through the individual as vehicle. To assert that the individual is responsible for saving society, that it is "precisely the reverse" from the old heroic pattern, is no less attached to the gods and living myth. It is just moving in the opposite direction. But in order to propel this movement, the individual must be pumped up with excess significance, riding on the belief and hope that the internal journey can match in equivalence what was formerly enacted in public. Campbell does not outwardly suggest that the hero's mythic journey function as an active formula in modernity; nevertheless, he leaves the door open for others to annex this template with determination, faith, and gusto.

Examples abound of the proliferation of modern hero pre-scriptions. Maureen Murdock in *The Heroine's Journey* maps the woman's inner quest, which, in her opinion, received short shrift under Campbell's model. Christopher Vogler's *The Writer's Journey* has transplanted the formula into a successful screenwriting manual, ensuring that the same movies will be churned out for years to come. Jean Houston, one of Campbell's associates, in *A Mythic Life*, aims to show how her personal experience is a living example of the veracity of the journey, an invitation and inspiration to others to take up the mantle of their greater story. And Carol Pearson, one of the authors cited earlier, followed up on her original book on the hero within, which only contained six archetypes to live by, with a sequel doubling in value: *Awakening the Heroes Within: Twelve Archetypes to Help Us Find Ourselves and Transform Our World.* While all these authors have different stories to tell, one message is repeatedly the same: the journey of the hero (or heroine), previously narrated in myth, works. It is a psychological truth, a depiction of an individual's successful transformation or individuation. In fact, it is more relevant to today than the time of myth in light of the possibilities for now understanding and integrating the myth's meaning.

Setting aside the issue of willfully assigning the task of one's transformation to the empirical personality, it remains to be asked, how well does the hero's journey translate in a psychological rather than mythological age? One fundamental aspect of the hero's journey is to bring back the boon, the fire or the gold, the "runes of wisdom, the Golden Fleece, or [the] sleeping princess, back into the kingdom of humanity, where the boon may redound to the renewing of the community, the nation, the planet, or the ten thousand worlds" (Campbell, *Hero* 193). In the myth, the boon or the elixir restores and rejuvenates the spiritual life of the collective, not simply the individual, for it is as "ego-shattering" as it is "life-redeeming" (216). The hero has undertaken the journey to serve something outside of personal proclivities—not out of the inclination to know himself better. Given that the contemporary status of the collective is understood to be fragmented, imper-sonal, secular, composed of individuals each going about their solitary business, how is the gift of the boon to be made manifest? If one were to remove this stage of the journey, sweep it under the carpet as irrelevant to today's self-centered world, then it is no longer the same journey, all the trials and ordeals ultimately for naught and the much sought after benefits reduced to mere trifles. But this part of the journey need only be rewritten to find its place along the personal path of mythmaking. For the boon of modernity is tailored directly to the soul-searching individual in a community-deprived culture. It is "the boon of increased self-awareness," the idea that if one heals the self, one heals the world (Jung, qtd. in Jaffé 140).

When self-consciousness is cradled in a popularized rendition of the hero's journey, it is not the same thing as bringing or restoring consciousness to the world. It is too much awareness focused on one's life, rather like taking extensive notes instead of just living. Insofar as the boon is to be deliberately placed in the hands of the individual, the boon is discharged of its boon-ness, sheltered with the individual from the world he means to save. It remains safely ensconced in a mirrored box that reflects exactly what was hoped for—one's self. The need for a unique purpose to one's life receives a respite from any accusations of self-centeredness in the notion that "every time we [. . .] move deeper into the ongoing discovery of who we are [. . .] we bring new life to ourselves and to our culture. We change the world" (Pearson 1). The real impact of this kind of myth-seeking or mythmaking is to further an abstract and inflated fantasy of meaning, rather than provide the world with any substantial changes. No doubt one's immediate circle of family, friends, and colleagues are affected (which is different from being changed themselves) when one consciously endeavors to live more truthfully—but the world? It would be impossible to get an accurate reading of the ripple effect one's actions may have, but the problem occurs when the desire or belief in such an effect *precedes* or even accompanies one's actions. Then, the hero's journey provides yet another excuse for feeling good about oneself, this time inflating one's importance under the guise of benefiting humankind. One's honest choices in life have little to do with the self-importance infusing personal myth, yet the honesty is overshadowed by the grandiosity that seeks to identify an archetypal equivalent. But the impetus to label parts of one's process as Warrior or Magician or Wanderer, to name three examples discussed by Pearson, does not come from within those archetypes themselves. It is the ego revealing itself as the ever-present center.

The boon or elixir brought back by the hero was gold as the substance of God, the "mineral light," the symbol of "supreme spirituality and glorification," divine illumination and intelligence (Cirlot 119–20). The gold of today represents otherwise. Devoid of its metaphysical value, it is little more than an analog for the one universal God remaining, the Economy or Money (Hillman, "Once More into the Fray" 17; Giegerich, "Once More the Reality"). And yet it may appear as if the hero's journey survives in its original form after all. For the boon of gold, even if stripped of its spiritual properties, clearly dominates the life of the collective. Money, just like a God, is "observed faithfully in thought and action, joining all human kind in daily acts of devotion" (Hillman, "Once More" 16). However, if this is used to corroborate the subsistence of the Gods and myth, it must be recognized for the inversion and perhaps perversion of what they once represented. A modern boon of gold is a parody of itself, abstract and emptied of any real value. It is bonded more to fluctuating and fleeting bottom lines and stock portfolios than to the life-blood of a community. Far from funding divine illumination and "supreme spirituality," gold or money mostly subjugates one to perpetual cycles of earning and spending and investing, so much so that the life of the collective is dictated by it above all else.

It is, for one thing, the excessive wealth marking modern civilization that provides the backdrop for the endemic emptiness and quest for meaning. Our unprecedented wealth is balanced by our spiritual poverty. In lesser developed countries, there is little time to be bored and to ponder how to live a more fulfilling life. The whole point of life is to survive, to make do with the resources one has, often which are nowhere near enough to achieve a minimum standard of health. The feelings of nothingness that persist even when one has everything reflect the other, less abundant side of living in wealth. And as seems to be the pattern when confronted with uncomfortable or difficult psychological phenomena, official pathologies are now circulating around the economic surplus, quickly gaining momentum as the next problem to be combated. These new diseases have recently been identified as "Affluenza" and

"Sudden Wealth Syndrome." Intent on showing how the American Dream has become the American Nightmare, symptoms include loss of motivation, low self-esteem, depression, loss of self-confidence, preoccupation with surface things, compulsive consumerism, guilt and shame, feeling disconnected, increased anxiety and stress, identity confusion, fear of losing control, sleep disorders. It seems as if the whole gamut of neuroses can now be attributed to living in excess.

Personal meaning is clearly a by-product of this environment, a symptom in its own right of the sense of alienation and exile. Yet personal meaning is also what people turn to when the environment fails or is seen as lacking. Perhaps the goal is now a *simpler* personal meaning, unfettered from monetary shackles (save for the cost of therapy and other self-help measures). But to the degree that personal meaning remains ipso facto the nucleus to which all seek to return, the other, negative side of the search for meaning—the void that does not seem to get filled, no matter how hard one tries—still remains shadowed, content in its own dim illusions of grandeur and redemption. The agenda for the Money, Meaning and Choices Institute, the people responsible for coining "Sudden Wealth Syndrome," is specifically to facilitate people in "finding a higher meaning for their lives" (see mmcinstitute.com). Similarly, the Affluenza Project aims to help "people of all economic classes build a new American dream" (see affluenza.com). Given that these very ideals contributed toward the predicament that the culture now finds itself in, who is to say that the proposed treatment will not breed a different, but similar beast, one that eventually falls victim to the fallout from expectations of higher meaning and purpose? Even so, from here it is a very short step to personal myth.

Personal myth is primed by the modern condition. The vigilant attention to the economy fosters and encourages the flourishing of a movement that claims for itself the antidote to such compulsive materialism and soullessness. Expressly intending to speak to and from the soul, personal myth proffers the kind of individualized care and attention sorely lacking in the coldness of a demystified and impersonal world. It plants itself in the middle of the frenzy and the emptiness and beckons the individual to come closer, slow down, look behind the outer trappings of life and beyond one's inner imprisonments to find vestiges of God's grace and the truth of myth. But to maintain its credibility and ensure its continuity, personal myth needs evidence to give the individual the incentive and the means for living authentically, uniquely, soulfully. Inasmuch as the hero's journey manages to prove the invincibleness of myth as well as the originality of the individual, it is an ideal template in which personal myth can trust and on which individuals can depend. Even if the template must be restructured to suit modern sensibilities, such as the relocation and redefinition of the boon from a gift directed outward to a rightful inheritance based inward, personal myth need only fold any structural changes into itself, nestled against the determination to milk meaning out of anything.

Personal myth intends to serve the individual before the collective, for it is the individual who will see to the restoration of the collective. Yet if the collective cares little for individual meaning and frankly has no inclination of being restored, any missionary efforts on the part of personal myth, however indirect, will only reinforce a barrier between the reality of the collective and the desire of the individual. It would be easier to argue for the success of the hero's journey if it is conceded as a negative one, only this is unacceptable to those who would insist on reading contemporary phenomena through the lens of myth. Peering out from behind the comfort of myth and the promises of personal myth, one might have to realize that in today's technological world, "the economy is no longer there for the well-being of humans, but humans are there for the well-being of the production process and count only to the extent that they are needed for the advancement of production." In a world revolving around globalization and profit maximization, the "human being is dethroned [. . .] and made redundant" (Giegerich, "Opposition" 16–17). Similarly expressed, "In corporatism [legitimacy] lies with the group, not the citizen. The human is thus reduced to a measurable value, like a machine or piece of property" (Saul 33).

If personal myth considers itself an antidote to the dis-ease of the collective, and yet is ostensibly about serving the collective, it has no alternative other than to split itself off from the very reality it feeds on. Amid the pervasive belief that individuals are solely responsible for what they make of their lives, the proposed remedy of personal myth far surpasses this belief in its own conviction that what is good for the individual must be true for the collective. But insofar as the collective regards its members as replaceable, personal myth will repeatedly come up against a wall that it will be unable to transcend. No matter if it is a losing battle, personal myth intends to stake its claim anyway, steadfastly holding to individual prospects against the threat of individual obscurity. Moreover, any honest relationship between individual and collective is precluded as long as the individual is held in direct opposition to the collective, whether posited as its savior or presumed to be independent of it. John Ralston Saul writes, "It is as if our obsession with our individual unconscious has alleviated and even replaced the need for public consciousness. The promise—real or illusory—of personal self-fulfillment seems to leave no room for the individual as a responsible and conscious citizen" (54). The promise of self-fulfillment can never be completely kept as long as it subsists at the expense of the larger whole (the collective), and one's self can never by fully filled as long as it depends on one-sided promises to see it through.

To be sure, there are times when the collective comes together somewhat, such as through sporting events or when a woman gives birth to surviving septuplets or a dog abandoned at sea is rescued, but these times are marked by emotion and intensity, and presumably last as long as the feeling or the event. Even when tragedy and crisis connect people and bring out the communal spirit, after a time the bonds remain mostly with those in one's private circle. Although written in 1970, Michael Novak's contention that the center of consciousness in the United States is based on the simple affirmation, "I feel," still rings true today. "We are not metaphysical but sentimental," he writes (10). Contrary to Descartes's maxim, "I think, therefore I am," in the United States, "[n]o 'therefore' is available, or needed. The eye of consciousness yields to affect, percept, kaleidoscope. [. . .] [T]he primary sense of reality is shaped [. . .] mostly by cinema, television, and records" (5). One need only substitute CDs and MP3s for records, and add the Internet and video games to have an updated list of stimuli. But intense experiences and emotions function more like a drug and less a representation of a community that shares communal values and responsibilities. Either better, faster, flashier stimuli must be produced to keep the collective going, or otherwise one might be forced to recognize that society accepts itself as a show. Whatever truth is held by the collective is only truthful or valuable insofar as it makes for good entertainment, good ratings, and good business. But when the phoniness and the fraudulence dawns, the experience of nothingness sneaks its way to the forefront of one's consciousness again, leaving one at that pivotal point of what do next.

However, what is perceived as nothing need not be equated with emptiness, but, rather, a transparency allowing for a comprehensive vision that holds presence and absence together without succumbing to either one. In her book *Mona Lisa's Moustache,* Mary Settegast traces the slow dissolution of cultural forms, indicating that reality itself has become a collapsed notion. There is no longer any one pattern that could meaningfully make sense of today's postmodern world. "Breakdowns of structure are everywhere to be observed: in social and moral codes, in gender distinctions, in literature, music, architecture and painting, in politics, economics, and personal relationships. There is no longer an absolute, a 'proper' form, anywhere. If we're not yet at a place where *anything* goes, we seem to be very close" (8). Opportunities for experimentation and exploration abound in an Aquarian era, leaving one confined to little save for ideas and the infinite possibility of something new. And even though notions of subjectivity are dissolving as well, the ideals of individuality and freedom remain firm, as if all one can hold onto in a rapidly changing environment is one's self, however tenuous that relationship may be. Settegast draws on an Eastern philosophical perspective, where the challenge is simultaneously to recognize that one can in reality cling to nothing, as well as use the dissolution of forms as an opportunity for self-realization. To live in the present moment, to be free from constricting ideologies, and "to meet the next situation clean"—this is the way to meet life meaningfully, to "authentically make a difference, in our own lives and in the life of the world" (137).

Learning to be present is undoubtedly one of many useful teachings coming from the Zen tradition, but importing Eastern philosophy cannot be as effective as long as it is situated on top of a Western philosophy that no matter how much it has shifted, still grounds and inspires the belief that every individual deserves to lead a special and meaningful life. The dilemma lies in the idea that even when confronted with dissolving forms, the individual not only tastes freedom, but must also use this freedom to find the truth of one's own individuality and create a meaningful life. Conflict is bound to arise as long as "meaning" remains part of the equation. A clash will ensue between the deconstructive and "anything goes" mentality, for the individual will take any and all measures to find something to hold onto, even amid the growing recognition that there may be nothing.

SELF AND PRESERVATION

The phenomenon of autobiography and memoir, or self-writing, well reflects the attempt to claim one's individuality, for it provides the seeker something tangible to control and cling to in the search for meaning and identity. Self-writing actively supports and is supported by questions of selfhood, for it is as much about self-creation as it is about history and recollection. The distinction between what is fact and what is imagined is blurred, with truth and history secondary to the desire to know one's self or prove that something is worth knowing. The act of setting this knowledge in writing further cements the undisputed centrality of the self, as if the imprinted text could ensure an imprinted self. Visibly admitting that it is both subject and object, the autobiographical self boldly assumes its self-sufficiency, if not its completeness, ever faithful to the task assigned to the individual set loose in an enlightened and fragmented world. And as ideas of selfhood evolve or dissolve, the form of self-writing changes in reciprocation. Even the doubt and impossibility of fully knowing or positing the self is incorporated into a content that nonetheless insists on positing something.

Self-writing could be construed as a lighter form of personal myth, insofar as it does not necessarily have any pretense of archetypal significance. However, to the extent that one equates myth and story, one's memoir or autobiography will be seen as another means to find one's personal myth. Maureen Murdock argues for this perspective, contending that memoir, no less than myth, serves to orient the individual to his or her surroundings and to become aware of the unconscious processes influencing the individual life. "Myth provides the pattern; memoir provides the details. In telling our story we realize the deeper pattern of our lives; we can't go home until we tell our story, where we have been" (133).

With self-writing it is no longer sufficient to cultivate self-awareness or simply to speak one's story; one must memorialize oneself. And yet, as Peter Shabad argues, the inclination to memorialize may be appropriate. If we have suffered a traumatic loss, it needs to be witnessed and mourned (memorialized) so that we can be freed from the confines of the loss. We need "to elaborate our experience into the memorable status of something real and objective" (199). "Without another person to validate the 'event' of our suffering, we are forced into the awkward, involuted position of bearing witness to our own experience" (200). Suffering is too much for one individual to bear alone, not just because of the inherent psychological difficulty, but also because suffering something alone makes it easier to doubt the veracity of the event that caused the suffering. Without a witness it becomes easier to question, did this really happen? And without outside validation, one's symptoms to the traumatic event (whether rage, depression, apathy, and so on) then assume the role of memorializing, thus ensuring an undue faithfulness to the symptoms and the suffering. But a memorial built on objective validation and not one's symptoms helps one to heal and move on.

Of course the validation of suffering is an important part of counseling and psychotherapy. But if one takes Shabad's argument to a cultural and collective level, one could suggest that the phenomenon of self-writing is an attempt to combat the forces of insignificance and meaninglessness. Whether one's personal approach to this reality is defiance (my life is not meaningless, and here is my personal myth to prove it), or sensitivity (I am just a speck of dust on the end of a single hair), the act of self-writing enables one to objectify one's existence and show that we and our experiences, our joys as well as our traumas, are very real, regardless if there is an official living myth or not. Our self-memorializing is one way of releasing our symptoms back into the world, so that we do not have to bear their weight alone or defer to our symptoms beyond what is due. However, in a whole other sense, the stories we write about ourselves are stories perpetually waiting to be written, more like an unfinished monument. Writing captures a living process, freezing one moment in favor of another yet to be told or overlooked. Self-writing may acknowledge its partiality or futility in establishing a meaningful self and may in fact remain caught in the *attempt* for meaning rather than its imagined fulfillment. But inasmuch as the aim is to attain some coherence to one's life and prove that our suffering has not been for nothing, self-writing and personal myth both share the burden of the individual need for some sort of attention and affirmation.

The conversion from public to private history corresponds to what George Gusdorf calls an "*in*volution of consciousness" rather than an evolution. "The truth is that one is wonderstruck by everything else much sooner than the self. One wonders at what one sees, but one does not see oneself [. . .]. The subject who seizes on himself for object inverts the natural direction of attention" (32). But it is this inversion and interiorization, aided by the loss of myth, which permits knowledge of that which formerly one was embedded in. The inverted natural direction allows one to know for oneself what was unthinkingly attributed to nature (recall that, in myth, one believed that the act of creation fell to the gods). The developing artistry of Venetian mirrors, the successive self-portraits painted by old masters like Rembrandt, the Christian emphasis on the individual soul and destiny—all these historical phenomena reflect the gaze now purposely turned inward (32–33). Surely the individual is taken unawares by the expulsion from blindness and dependency when he or she realizes the presence of this unfathomable subject, this self that has apparently existed all along. Yet soon to be mesmerized by hints of depth and potential and heartened by the thrill of securing privately for oneself what previously was shared by the group, one can leisurely linger before oneself—even if now risking blindness to everything else but oneself.

Self-writing mirrors the historical background it emerges from even as it functions as a consciously shaped accounting for one's existence. So that, for example, Augustine's *Confessions* celebrates the beginning of Christianity and the glory of the individual relationship to God, while over 1500 years later, the death of God is acutely felt in a work like Elie Wiesel's memoir, *Night*, in which God is experienced as a child hanging on the gallows at Buchenwald. And a postmodern style of thought can be seen in Nathalie Sarraute's *Childhood*, where, as James Olney points out, the splitting of the narrator's ego into an "I" and a "you" indicates the attempt to seek "the unified *I* that seems to have become—to put it in the most optimistic terms—so elusive in our time" (248). To the extent that self-writing follows the culture's historical process and the individual's psychological development, it would appear to serve as a trustworthy means of bestowing meaning not only to one's life, but also to counter any subsequent experience of meaninglessness. As Shabad notes, the act of witnessing (which does characterize self-writing, even if one has no other witness besides oneself) gives meaning to what is felt to be meaninglessness and nonexistent.

But how is this small sample of a life, presented in narrative form and offered to an audience, supposed to define and affirm the self when recent philosophical thought debates the legitimacy of said subject, and, as Olney says, a unified "I" has become ever more elusive? Through narrative, a continuity between antiquity and modernity is established. Even as rupture and discontinuity threaten memory, hope, and unity, the power and presence of storytelling remain undisputed, for narrative can spaciously bring any rupture into itself, reporting an endurance that speaks no less to the individual than to the venture at self-preservation. But when a psychology that would look for the subject behind all texts gives way to a philosophy that sees through and deconstructs the very notion of the subject itself, the individual is once again stuck, philosophically deemed empty but psychologically longing to understand itself or if nothing else, to *exist*. This is especially visible in the work of Samuel Beckett, whose ending of the novel *The Unnamable* captures this dilemma: "I don't know, I'll never know, in the silence you don't know, you must go on, I can't go on, I'll go on" (476).

Jungian theorist Paul Kugler addresses the psychological ramifications of a subject no longer located at the center of human thought, the death once attributed to God having now caught up to the subject. "No longer is the speaking subject unquestionably assumed to be the source of language and speech, existence and truth, autonomy and freedom, unity and wholeness, identity and individuality. The transcendence of Descartes' 'cogito' is no longer certain. The speaking subject appears not to be a referent beyond the first person pronoun, but, rather, a fragmented entity produced by the act of speaking" ("'Subject'"). Trapped in language, unable to escape its concern for the "I" or "subject" that is now prone to shifts in identity, depth psychology finds itself unable completely to

settle on a determinate meaning of any text, including the individual not only as another text to be read, but as reading the world
through its own text. Nothing exists outside the text, says Derrida—
and that includes us (*Of Grammatology* 158). To the extent that any
sign refuses or resists a stable identification with any meaning, any
meaning becomes unbearably elusive, if not impossible. The ontological gap between event and meaning, once believed to be psychologically bridged through symbolic interpretation, is left with a
gaping hole. The "epistemological crisis" of postmodernism is such
that any theory of interpretation has "no location outside of language [. . .] and can never be a ground but only a mediation"
("The Unconscious" 315). Although such mediation is necessary,
given the need for language, consciousness can no longer be predicated on the awareness of a subject-object dichotomy. The notions
of objectivity and subjectivity themselves are easily interchangeable,
developed through and wielded by what is ultimately another text
with questionable authority. In that all interpretations are essentially fictitious, the only authority, the only ground remaining, is
that which has not been and cannot be interpreted—that which is
unknowable.

With the "death" of the self comes the end of self-writing as it
is known. If postmodernity questions the author and authority of a
text, any positing of one's self or story will ultimately dissipate
under critical examination, rendering the inclination to affirm oneself futile. The subject and author of self-writing, oneself, is just
another fiction among many and thereby unable to claim for itself
the sovereignty it believes it represents as it places its story in the
center. From a philosophical perspective, the author can no longer
be as convinced as Jean-Jacques Rousseau was of his importance as
a subject and of his originality in sharing himself with the world.
Rousseau's *Confessions*, generally considered to have inaugurated
the modern form of autobiography, opens with, "I am resolved on
an undertaking that has no model and will have no imitator. I want
to show my fellow-men a man in all the truth of nature; and this
man is to be myself. Myself alone. I feel my heart and I know men. I
am not made like any that I have seen; I venture to believe that I
was not made like any that exist" (5). And yet despite the fact that
such a declaration today would be seen as egotistical and grandiose,
and in spite of debates of the assuredness and truthfulness of sub-

jectivity, vestiges of Rousseau's sentiments remain to sustain the credibility of personal myth and inspire self-writing. Even as postmodernism proclaims the death of the subject, the inclination to assert oneself and say, "This is my story, my perspective, my truth" has not completely died. Even amid the recognition that "no autobiography can take place except within the boundaries of a writing where concepts of subject, self, and author collapse into the act of producing a text," the writing goes on (Sprinker 342).

I have already mentioned Samuel Beckett, whose corpus notably reflects the absence or impossibility of the "I," the "Not I" that is meant to be a stand-in for the removal and subsequent disappearance of the subject.[11] Beckett's goal is explicitly to "find a form that accommodates the mess" endemic in modernity, to find a way to go on when there is no way to go on, to speak even as there is no "I" to do the talking or the acting and no actions to be done (see Olney 12). And yet the "I" *is* attained through the "not I," for Beckett as author is unmistakably present throughout his entire work. The absent "I" is merely the inversion of the present "I," the other side of the same coin. Convictions of selfhood are still expressed, only negatively instead of positively. For Beckett, the impossible "I" can only be made possible through not saying "I," and even that does not guarantee the success of realizing some concept of self. The impossibility can best be expressed through a failure; were it to be transformed into success, a concrete "I," it would no longer adequately (or inadequately) do justice to the "not I." The purpose is precisely to keep failing, to fail at constructing a self or a coherent plot. Although a story of nothingness can conceivably become a story of something and the meaninglessness enveloped into a greater meaning, failure ensures that the chaos and mess Beckett sought to accommodate not succumb to an order that would invalidate or lessen it. Any urge to write and affirm one's self is countered by words that repeatedly deny themselves to the author and subject. In Beckett's *Not I*, each time Mouth gets closer to the "I," she (or he; Beckett notes that the sex is undeterminable) cries, "what? . . . who? . . . no! . . . she! . . ."

Beckett recounts a lecture he attended by C. G. Jung, in which Jung spoke about one of his patients, a young girl.[12] After the lecture, Beckett heard Jung comment, "In the most fundamental way, she had never been really born. I, too, have always had the sense of never having been born." Regarding himself, Beckett found a resonance. "I have always sensed that there was within me an assassinated being. Assassinated before my birth. I needed to find this assassinated person again. And try to give him new life" (Olney 325; Juliet 10). Without the most elemental beginning, one's actual life becomes as questionable as a search for meaning and self-affirmation. The historical and imagined details are rendered irrelevant in the face of the simple but stark question of one's unconfirmed existence. The passing over the incomplete birth, even as this passing is an attempt to *be* born, precludes any resuscitation, for who is there to be brought back to life? The issue of selfhood dissolves in the life that neither pins its hopes on the highly prized self nor on the inverted negative self, but on a life that ultimately cannot account for itself. Neither the testimony of the heroic nor the despairing self can redeem, for each side lauds itself at the expense of the other, isolating itself in the attempt to remember a self that can never be sufficiently remembered. Sidestepping the burden of personal meaning and the trouble of declaring a self, one finds refuge in between the "I" and "not I," caught in the "perhaps" that resides between "yes" and "no." "[P]erhaps they have said me already, perhaps they have carried me to the threshold of my story," Beckett wrote (*The Unnamable* 476). In the "perhaps" between self-affirmation and self-abnegation, we find something to hold on to, a story that still tries to be told—even if it fails. Here, one hopes life is endured even when it has become unendurable. We go on even when we can't.

However, if one has never been properly born, then one cannot properly die, the necessary "no" or ending is thwarted from holding its end.[13] Waiting in limbo, one is rather like a ghost or the undead, neither able to suffer the loss of meaning nor to be filled with any manufactured meaning. It is as if the moment of loss is frozen, and freezing along with it the individual who cannot abide by a life without meaning but who nonetheless clings to life—so much so that life and oneself must be preserved. Preservation, of which self-writing is one means, serves as a visible reminder that I am here, that I exist even if I cannot trust or fathom it, and that I intend to stay. Marina Benjamin observes that the fight against aging and imperfect bodies strives for everlastingness, whereas the development of cryonics, an intentional freezing in liquid nitrogen of one's corpse or just one's head if desired, takes self-preservation to its literal extreme (244, 247). In the collective, the expanding heritage industry, replete with "stately homes, theme parks, museums of industry, Tudor villages, folk festivals, medieval banquet weekends and historical walks" seeks to preserve history as it passes, not minding that the past it "is busy recreating is an ersatz one" (228). Mistaking the substitution for the real thing ensures that the theme park or museum mentality extends into everyday consciousness. Fantasies of preservation and attempts to solidify one's origins suspend the individual from the natural course of history. The individual may be thrown back onto himself, but it is a simulated self. Mourning for what is lost is eclipsed by a memory that cannot be depended on to remember, it in turn supplanted by archives, relics, and icons. One remains caught between nonbirth and nondeath, swimming in a gap littered with memorabilia, unable to experience the life desperately longed for because reality does not match the idea of what that life should be.

Benjamin contends that inasmuch as anything exists as potential heritage, a posthumous existence is guaranteed. This disposes the need for present-time while simultaneously seeks to extend the present infinitely. The world as museum serves as an immunity against endings, "a place in which recycling ensures continuity and where durability stands in for eternity" (232). Preservation functions as a sort of transcendence, moving beyond the temporal restrictions of birth and death. But to the degree that the promise of transcendence is predicated on the capturing and recreating of an ersatz history, along with the preservation of material things, what is effected is "merely technical; immortality without the gift of salvation. It is the same order of achievement as getting beyond history without having passed through the end: there is no transformation" (232). In skipping or preempting the ending as a means of preservation, by default one must also be displaced from the beginning. Thus excused from life, one is stuck in an emptiness that betrays any profession of mourning as shallow and any attempts at memorializing as insubstantial. To the extent that self-preservation functions as a contingency plan for averting future, imagined losses, it is a mourning in advance (240). Conversely, to permit or await an ending in the hope of transformation is bound to fail insofar as one places oneself in the position of choice and expectation, as if one could dictate the conditions of both ending and transformation. Either way, the individual insists on holding the reins to his or her desired transformation, not noticing or minding that that which is verifiably preserved is empty and artificial.

If the means of affirming oneself cannot withstand or overcome absence, cannot postpone the ending indefinitely, and in fact further compound the absence through efforts to find meaning, then is the task to say and do nothing? Or to try, as Samuel Beckett did, to put the impossibility of the situation into words, to get it out of himself in the attempt to give life to his assassinated being? Even as silence descends, one talks. The "not I's" still try to tell their stories of nothingness. Even as the demands for personal meaning are unable to be fully met, one is nonetheless compelled to look for that meaning. This is the nature of being human and the promise of myth, or so contend the personal mythologists, and it is one simple reason why (they say) as long as one lives, one cannot be devoid of myth. To be sure, individual stories continue to inspire, entertain, and provoke despite the skepticism surrounding the subject of the story. As Wendy Doniger says, these basic stories (what she calls myths), "the bare bones of human experience," are all that sustains (*Other* 166). But I think the collective tide cannot be ignored, no matter how much power modern heroes and mythmakers think they reclaim. And in the ensuing struggle between personal and collective notions of selfhood and meaning, the individual is beleaguered with conflicting messages, such that any response is bound to tighten rather than release the ropes keeping him suspended in midair, in between the "I" and "not I."

Whatever the individual is able to preserve (of one's self, one's story) stands on a precariously thin edge, enclosed by negativity on all sides. On one side, the perceived negativity driving the individual journey toward the self is that of existential loss—of meaning, myth, faith, soul. The response to this absence is to fill it with revised versions of that which is lost or imagined to be lost, holding up personal myth and fabricated meaning as replacements. But no matter how much the absence of myth may be denied or defended against, an intentional negativity remains. This logical (not existential) negativity is necessary for the much sought-after self-knowledge, to whatever degree the self can be known. For on the other side of loss is the negativity that comes with psychological awareness. "Seeing through" the phenomena to hidden motivations, listening for that which has not been said, cutting through appearances and discerning one's conscious or unconscious involvement in shaping one's reality—all these require an internalized negative process. It is an incisiveness that demands a relinquishment of that which was once held to be the undisputed truth. For personal myth, it requires a dissolution of the personified archetype into the psychological insight.

This logical negativity is apt to meet frustration against the individual inclination to confuse it with the existential negativity indicative of the absence of a mythic mode of being-in-the-world and then seek to render it back into a positive (like the restoration of myth). To refer back to Giegerich's critique of Jung: Jung understood that psychological insight presupposes the dissolution of myth. The soul is logically negative, Giegerich argues. But Jung's desire to find the myth in which he lived undermined his own insight about the reality of the soul. He could not allow that the existential loss of myth and meaning allows for knowledge of the soul *as* logical negativity. This existential absence, the loss of myth, is taken so personally and deemed so undesirable, that the instinct is to turn it back into a positive presence, to restore a mythic consciousness. However, the reality of these mythless times is real (and generally uncontested, regardless of how one then redefines modern myth)—so what "negativity" is actually available to convert into something "positive"? What we do have now, regardless if one contextualizes this in myth, *is* the psychological insight, irrespective if one follows through on the insight. We understand the archetypes and, through them, begin to understand ourselves and the depths of humanity. But it is the muddling and conflating of two different levels of thinking and being-in-the-world that allows the temptation to try and use the psychological insight to restore a mythic mode of being-in-the-world. This is precisely the intention behind personal myth: if enough individuals identify their personal myths, myth as a living, collective phenomenon will be restored. But philosophically it makes no sense, and this restoration act can only fortify the barrier between oneself and the rest of the world.

Even so, both the (existential) negativity taken personally by the individual and the (logical) negativity required for psychological awareness run the risk of being hindered but not necessarily negated by a larger philosophical negativity, so that whatever psychological progress is made disintegrates and personal negativity invalidated, leaving the individual no less confounded—and certainly no closer to meaning. For on yet another side of the loss and the attempts to amend the loss now lays the negativity of deconstruction, that infinite chain of abstractions and signifiers that never finds closure or containment. Although the concept of the subject is what is negated, as opposed to the empirical individual, the individual is affected, once again caught in a situation that finds no resolution.

Psychology aims to look at the ego, but now the ego can barely get behind itself to examine what it beholds before something else is revealed as doing the beholding. Without the opportunity to see through itself, the ego will continue to be reinforced as it is deconstructed. Amid the endless chain of signs, signifiers, and signified, as far as the individual is concerned, the process of self-actualization stagnates as the one authority that can validate one's existence—one's own—is unseated in favor of the unknowable. The current age may be marked by a dissolution of forms, but if the ego has no containment to dissolve or see through itself, it has no recourse but to be set loose on the world. But under the influence of postmodernism, the ego now faces a world that both needs and refutes its authority, leaving it with few options. One option is to stand still while growing in its place; such is the temptation for a personal psychology. And as the way is widened for an ego psychology to take the lead, personal mythology finds plenty of room to present its wares, even as it, no less than the individual, is perilously enveloped by negativity.

The idea of personal myth is faulty today because it depends on a modern appropriation and inflated usage of myth. But personal myth becomes completely untenable (and somewhat absurd) when considered in light of postmodern thought. Personal myth depends on both the split and correspondence between subject and object in order to maintain myth and have it be personal. But if the subject is psychologically seen through or pronounced dead, the object is accordingly rendered useless, and is far less likely to fulfill its half of the equation required to establish a mythic meaning. Personal myth is thus swallowed into the void left by the departure of its progenitor, collective myth. The individual can either follow willingly, thinking it is following something else, or wait for the absence to come to the individual. Either way, the absence is inevitable.

However, this inevitability of absence permits another view of myth to take precedence, one that incorporates and even appears to thrive on absence and in this space between the departure of subject and object. So although personal myth may be little more than an ego-driven fantasy doomed to fail in a modern and post-modern world, a different *perspective* on myth facilitates the persistent belief in myth's existence and functionality. It is this shift to perspective, particularly as seen in the mythopoetic emphasis on mythmaking, archetypal psychology's deliteralization of myth, and a Jungian-based attempt to marry depth psychology and postmodernism that constitutes the subject of the next chapter.

CHAPTER 3

The Lingering of Myth

An assumption of the absence of myth has fueled this discussion thus far. First, a sampling of contemporary myth theory was reviewed according to the different manner in which each theorist prejudges the question of the presence or obsolescence of myth. This was followed by an analysis of the "personal myth" movement, a phenomenon that receives its inspiration from the absence of collective myth and the resultant increasingly individualistic society. In both of these initial chapters, the absence of myth has been treated as an incontrovertible reality, as I have been adamant about making myth's lack of presence known amid theories and individuals that presumably cannot abide by any loss of myth and meaning for very long. Such an approach is determined to regard alleged reports of myth's healthy condition as regressive and one-sided, inadvertently perpetuating the very cultural ills that the longing for myth intends to mediate and transcend. Sightings of myth, as announced by some of the theorists previously cited, have subsequently been considered little more than modern productions bearing only the shallow imprint of its author instead of the authority of the larger, impersonal whole, that of the collective and the gods. Arguing for the absence of myth insists that contemporary theories of myth repeatedly—almost reverently, ironically—bow to myth's intrinsic absence and betray their faulty foundation. Such an ardent emphasis on the absence of myth accuses those who would still seek shelter and solace in myth of being blinded by their own hands, seduced by their own desires for meaning, and all too quick to forget that a fundamental rupture ever occurred.

However, perhaps it is appropriate to examine further this assumption of absence itself, to place it under the same scrutiny as the testimonies of myth's vitality—to see if the absence of myth can survive its own reversal. Rather than look at myth through the lens of its absence, one can look at the absence of myth through myth; more specifically, through the awareness that despite the general acknowledgment of an absence of myth, belief in myth has not been deterred or thwarted. Clearly, notions of "presence" and "absence" are neither straightforward nor isolated from each other's influence. Poststructural thought has exploded the certainties and singularities in language, and to the extent that myths are known, expressed, and recorded through language, the certainties of myth are similarly undone.[1] It may be accurate, as Eric Gould suggests, that the ancient and "original" manner of living myth is so far removed from contemporary experience that any possibility of recovery, or for knowledge of myth unfettered by imagination and language, is a pessimistic fantasy (10–11). Yet if one wants to argue for myth as an undying force; if one believes that as long as humankind needs to make sense of its world, myth will mold itself to the means and content at hand, then simply because myth looks different now does not imply that there is *not* some kind of active link to the myth of antiquity—which is precisely what I have been arguing against.

Postmodern thought, particularly its association with depth psychology,[2] is especially suited to address the evolving question of meaning and myth, precisely because its simultaneous concern for meaning and criticality toward such a notion breeds a certain indifference and therefore is able to engage the paradoxical question, "what are the myths of a mythless time?" with apparently little attachment to the answer. Such a phrase as "the myth of mythlessness," used to characterize an era that is only temporarily demythologized, is a condensed expression of the equivocation of myth. The first "myth" speaks to contemporary thought about myth, whereas the second refers back to a time of lived myth, to a divinely animated world, that few assume to still be true. Yet by combining two logically different traditions of myth in one phrase, it becomes quite easy to sustain the paradox and the belief that there is an all-encompassing notion of myth that manages to be negated while simultaneously expected to meet a modern presumption of meaning, supposedly rooted in and licensed by antiquity. But, as I hope to show throughout this chapter, rather than functioning as a problem to be sorted out, this purposeful equivocation is not only needed to keep myth alive, it is an equivocation desired for its own sake. Whether myth and its concomitant (non)belief in itself and the gods are objectively "real" or not is secondary to a deliberate ambiguity that would rather play in the space that gives rise to such a question in the first place. What is important is to recognize the limits and influence of human interpretation on theories and experience—though this need not preclude a larger, unknowable reality, or prescribe the end of myth.

Jungian analyst Polly Young-Eisendrath endorses "affirmative postmodernism," an American branch of postmodernism that while acknowledging humankind's subjective role in constructing the world, maintains a belief in human universals, "the ways in which we are all constrained by our emotions, our relational dependence, and our embodiment" (*Gender* 89). One can still live and be lived by a myth, a story that in the moment of its inception is the "truth." With a postmodern depth psychology, however, one can peer into the edges of the myth (if not its origin) and see for oneself how it serves, where it can be changed or broken down, and where it is a story no longer needing to be told. A postmodern myth may hold itself to be a true story about one's reality at a moment in time, but it carries the capacity to falsify itself within the recognition that "no myth [. . .] is a perfectly accurate account of reality" (78).

Young-Eisendrath's presupposition that myth is intended to give an account of reality is another indication that the notion of myth used in this context is modern and does not necessarily lend its support to the argument for the continued existence of a living rather than manufactured myth. Living myth is a self-display of its truth, an expression rather than an account. Lawrence Hatab writes, "A myth is not *meant* to be an explanation but rather a presentation of something which can *not* be explained (in the sense of an objective account)" (8). But again, this difference in the logical status of myth must be minimized, or treated as mere semantics, so that a mythic *perspective* can fill the vacancy left by the obsolescence of ontological myth—while daring to consider itself the same.

When Young-Eisendrath says, "Psychotherapy, when it works, changes myth into metaphor and allows us to play with a number of realities," she is treating myth as a de-objectified style of imagination, a therapeutic tool ("Myth" 2). But in the same lecture she also states, "we all need living myths. [. . .] [T]he ancient myths are still relevant in the post-modern world because they connect to the archetypal meanings of our emotions" (11, 4). Young-Eisendrath's ambiguous reasoning displays just one example of the shift to a mythic perspective that while presupposing a dissolution of living myth into abstract reflection, nonetheless equates myth with all reflection, thus making it nearly impossible to believe that an absence of myth means the end of myth.

No doubt, the permissiveness implied by a style of thought that, in another contemporary Jungian's words, "favo[rs] a plurality of positions and understandings" (Hauke 25) might find much to protest against in my discussion of myth. I am likely to be accused of being too rigid, too narrow, too literal-minded. *Mythos* (the story) has been sacrificed in favor of *logos* (rationality) and the attempt to follow myth's logical movement leans too heavily on truth and reason even as "truth" and "reason" have come to resemble suspicious words better left behind. Using archaic myth to gauge whether myth is current and authentic or not adheres to a literal definition of myth that remains stuck in antiquity and makes no allowances for a historical variation in the understanding of myth. However, the tendency to stick too closely to a linear, historical development of myth and mythology means that the mythic sense of cyclicality and timelessness is relegated to a lower status, if not disregarded. Maintaining a modern and monolithic attitude toward myth—is it present or is it absent—is outmoded and restrictive; the awareness of other religions and philosophies need not be a temptation to resist (because it is not one's inherited tradition) but an opportunity to broaden one's perspective. Sticking to outer, positive phenomena for the "truth" of the current age is itself a one-sided and sterile method, revealing little patience for imagination and little respect for the area where myth may linger, perhaps even hinting of a nihilistic preference for *no* meaning that overshadows any latent one. And yet any personal experience of myth may be granted but is essentially slighted by way of the charge that "personal myth" is an oxymoron.

But is not "postmodern myth" an oxymoron as well? Given a postmodernist reluctance to embrace positivity, coherence, center, and its unwillingness to settle on a particular meaning, demonstrated in its search "for new presentations, not in order to enjoy them but in order to impart a stronger sense of the unpresentable" (Lyotard 81), how can any myth have room to surface? For myth is all about meaning—even as, for example, Joseph Campbell's "The Symbol without Meaning," which has been read in a postmodernist vein,[3] aims to reveal this meaning negatively through a conscious *dis*engagement from symbols. Postmodernism's participation in critiquing the absence of myth thus stems less from an anti-absence stance, and even less from the insistence on a new myth, than from an attitude that seeks to see through and unglue fixations. "Postmodern is an attitude that inclines toward the interval—between I and not-I, body and world, forming and being formed," says Ronald Schenk (xi). A postmodern myth arms itself with a view of myth that teases its own definition, cracking open that which would otherwise confine. So even while postmodern theory may favor notions of absence in general over a metaphysics of presence (see Derrida, *Of Grammatology*), to argue for a staunch absence of myth (as I have done) to the exclusion of any other possibility is no longer faithful to a philosophy that requires a fluidity among perspectives. When the absence of myth is lorded over differing theories of myth, the absence itself is turned into a concept, a reified abstraction dependent on a particular meaning. To land repeatedly and aggressively on the side of an absence of myth is to commit what in the minds of some postmodern thinkers would be a sin: acting as if this perspective is the right one. No one can "master the work," says Susan Rowland. "There is no author in the sense of a point of authority or absolute control over meaning" (5).

Thus, one does not turn to a postmodern perspective to get a straight or definitive answer to the question, "what are the myths of a mythless time?" because in principle there is none to give. But it is precisely in this non-answer that any possible answer to the question can reveal itself. For it is in the subtleties and shades, in the space between, in metaphor and movement, that one can begin to track a myth of mythlessness. By no means does this imply that the gap has closed and that the cries lamenting the absence or death of the gods are to be appeased through a simple recanting. Rather the loss and suffering enables a sensitivity to that which may have always required softer, shielded eyes to see; a purposeful darkening of one's sight that leads to *in*sight, depth, and complexity. Absence then becomes the *reason for* myth as opposed to a reflection of the loss of myth. Myth requires mythlessness to allow itself to breathe unhindered by self-serving ideologies, formed by traces far more indelible than memory and no less invisible.

What if myth were actually more alive in its so-called absence than in any (imagined) antiquated time of myth? Two papers by David L. Miller illustrate this paradox, suggesting not only that absence permits a kind of knowledge not necessarily available in presence, but also that a strictly upheld absence of myth can unconsciously and dangerously mask the myths that continue to structure the world. In one lecture Miller contends that even as numerous phenomena show the mechanized, globalized, and capitalized world to be mythless and godless, other phenomena, such as ethnic cleansing in Kosovo, Chinese nationalism, Neonazism, religious warring in the Middle East, terrorist attacks at home and abroad, show that "the gods are alive and well, not to mention doing a lot of damage" ("A Myth Is as Good as a Smile" 184). Miller cites a report from a Peace Institute in Santa Barbara that estimates that "eighty percent of present ideological conflicts are motivated mythologically and religiously: it is a case of terrorism in the name of my god against your god" (184). The problem surfaces when these seemingly opposed viewpoints—myth and mythlessness—remain ensconced in their opposition, unconscious to the other's modus operandi. This can lead to a deadly "archetypal activism," where in the face of meaninglessness, attempts to experience meaning and myth compel a literal acting out of that which by nature is poetic and metaphoric (175). Miller gives the example of the shootings at Columbine High School, to date the largest school shooting in America's history, where for teenage killer Eric Harris, there was simultaneously "too little myth and too much myth" (186). Too little meaning in his suburban school life; too much myth in his escape from reality into apocalyptic Internet games and gothic imagery.

Studying myths and thinking mythically, then, even if the myths are contingent on an escape from reality (although a postmodern critique might argue, does this render them any less "real"?), provides a way to understand the soul of the world even as the world appears soulless. For Miller, myth may be "irrelevant to contemporary culture," but its absence allows one to see where myth is still extremely relevant, and more insidiously so in a culture ostensibly dripping with meaninglessness (189). Dead myths are then supplanted by live ones, as the myths of mythlessness are unearthed from their hiding places, their gripping power exposed.

The departure or death of the gods need not be construed as detrimental to the merits of myth. In another paper, Miller argues that sometimes absence helps to break illusions and literalistic thinking. Speaking specifically to the death of the clown and humor, he writes, "disillusionment removes the illusions" ("Death of the Clown" 81). He likens the coagulation of what were once understood in Greek physiognomy as four humors into a singular and objectified sense of humor to the loss of fluidity and multiplicity in contemporary psychological life. When humor is fixed, when it is forgotten that "ennui, depression, and rage are humors, too," a loss of humor is advantageous because it frees the fixation and restores the flow into life (73). But not without a price, for the loss or absence must remain in order to prevent new literalisms from taking hold, keeping the airways clear for ambiguity, possibility, and a play that does not shun sadness for an easy, superficial relief. And yet using Fellini's 1971 film *The Clowns* to demonstrate the disillusionment of humor, Miller notes, "it takes a clown to bury a clown, [. . .] the death of the clown is itself a part of the clown show" (80). The same could be said of myth. It takes a myth to bury a myth (evinced by talk of mythlessness) but this is all still part of the myth. Except one hopes, just as with humor, that the myth keeps its own failings close and purports to be neither all-knowing nor have the last laugh. Better for the myth not to admit its mythic nature if anyone is to apprehend it, for such an apprehension comes lightly.

One could think that with a postmodern myth, the gods might not remain buried underground, but neither do they stay above ground for too long, lest they suffer at the hands of mortals who still believe that the (literal) word is God. Neither fully present nor absent, the gods are found in the in-between spaces, protected from hearsay, homage, and obliteration alike. Yet any serious concern with myth or mythlessness necessitates an active engagement with this space in order to track the gods, for the gods' condition dictates the myth, even an absent one. Differing from the intent of the personal mythologist, this kind of tracking ostensibly cares little for the joining of two worlds (inner/outer, subjective/objective) within one's own being. Compelled to follow the movement of the myth for the sake of the myth and the culture, the postmodern mythmaker or myth-seeker does not choose fabrication as a means toward self-satisfaction or blissful anesthetization. Rather, the postmodern myth-seeker has no choice but to follow where the gods may lead, even if into an abyss. Such a pursuit, as Martin Heidegger observed, is the obligation of the poet (specifically, Hölderlin). For it is the poet who withstands the in-between spaces, between "the time of the gods that have fled and of the god that is coming" (*Existence* 289).[4]

"Poets are the mortals who [. . .] sense the trace of the fugitive gods," wrote Heidegger (*Poetry* 92). God's "failure to arrive" leaves an abyss in his wake, the arrival of the world's night, but traces of the gods are still discernible—by the poets who venture more daringly into the abyss (90). In singing the songs of the fugitive gods, of the unholy, the poet's "song over the land hallows," precisely because the poets "experience the unholy as such" (138). The songs of God's departure become in their act of singing God's trace and therefore holy, even if the trace remains embedded in darkness or unrecognizable. Heidegger said, "It remains undecided whether we still experience the holy as the track leading to the godhead of the divine, or whether we now encounter no more than a trace of the holy" (95), but if any shred of divinity is to be found, it is likely to be found and disseminated by the poet. As long as there is poetry and *poiesis* (Greek for making), one need not be entirely bereft, for poetry provides a foundation in the abyss. "Poetically man dwells," said Hölderlin, which Heidegger took to mean the "primal form of building, [. . .] the original admission of dwelling" (225). Poetry sings humankind into existence, not its literal dwelling with concrete materials and quantifiable measurements, but the "house of Being" (129), home to the fundamental mystery of existence even as mystery threatens to be forgotten.

It remains to be asked, can a postmodern myth allow the traces of the gods to be identified as such, or does that defeat its own purpose? The breaking of identifications and suspiciousness toward transcendence that characterize a postmodern move may prevent the myth from hardening its poetry into dogma or settling on any definitive answers as to the nature of the gods. But when myth is at stake, it is insufficient to leave the gods in idle speculation because then the myth disappoints and its absence threatens to overwhelm, wiping out any extant traces. It is my intention for the remainder of this chapter to pursue these traces of myth further, showing in the process that not only does successfully arguing for myth's presence amid a generally acknowledged absence necessitate a postmodern perspective, but also that within a postmodern myth lies a trap that has serious psychological implications. Four distinct but related lines of inquiry will assist in this pursuit of the fragments of myth and the gods, which are briefly outlined as follows:

- **From myth to mythopoesis.** The conflict inherent in the idea of a "postmodern myth" does find a meeting ground, for if "postmodern" and "myth" contradict each other, the tension between the two creates an opening, another in-between space that manages to negotiate the relationship between the two and pave the way for poets to follow. A postmodern myth realizes its own poetry in mythopoesis, wherein myth comes to be identified primarily with the creative act of myth-making and the irreducible need for reflecting, thus rendering a formal continuity of myth less problematic. However, in the process of easing one conflict, another one ensues when myths are no longer understood to be found but *made*, which in turn confers a level of artificiality to such supposedly extant myths. And yet on the other hand, a mythopoetic view of myth tacitly accepts and keeps the "myth" in its already diluted condition, presupposing an understanding of the irrevocable loss of living myth.
- **Metaphorical and archetypal myth.** This section shifts the attention to archetypal psychology's approach toward myth, which shares the mythopoetic emphasis on imagination and metaphor but specifically aims to remember the archetypal or divine quality of the image, supposedly the psychic building blocks of myth. The implicit intent is to bring the myth back even as myth

purportedly survives as a tool for psychological reflection. The particular focus on the mythical domain of the underworld as the source of the archetypal image could be seen, in a sense, as moving deeper into the gaps left by the loss of myth, toward soul and away from myth. But the continuing recourse to inner, psychological myth reveals a split between the literal and the imaginal, which causes any lingering myth to function less as a myth and more as a protective shield against outer reality as well as the soul.

- **Simulated myth.** A postmodern myth becomes more feasible in light of a postmodern depth psychology that looks to outer surfaces and simulation for an aesthetic meaning that is deemed sufficient as it is, leaving any mythic designation as basically superfluous. While conflict ensues when psychology attributes to a simulated myth or gods that play the same depth of meaning previously experienced in ritualized cultures, the continued stress on an ambiguous, fluid perspective ensures that any assertion of myth or the gods need not be taken too seriously. Always mindful of the unavoidable unknown factor, a postmodern depth psychology appears to settle itself happily inside the gaps—and yet, as exemplified primarily in this section by a postmodern Jungian, Christopher Hauke, the unknown proves to be ultimately unacceptable in that it must be filled with the possibility of a meaning that is antithetical to the spirit of postmodernism.

- **The problem of the in-between.** Having attempted to explicate the role of absence in engendering postmodern myth, this final section aims to demonstrate that what appears to be fluid and liberating becomes confining and frozen to the extent that the unseating of perspectives becomes the next maxim to adhere to. Unrestrained equivocation and a perpetual deferral of meaning may have the semblance of openness, but it is in the individual where one sees that an open system precludes the dialectical process from progressing or the logical contradictions inherent in psychology from being thought through to a new level of consciousness. Dialectics are dynamic, contradictory, not "yes" *and* "no." But the preference for equivocation precisely as equivocation becomes one-sided and undialectical and subsequently hinders one's subjectivity from developing, leaving neurosis rather than self-identity in its place (see Giegerich, *Soul's Logical Life* 25). The death of God cannot be completely revised to cover up the birth of the individual. And as long as the individual remains in limbo, it becomes easier to mistakenly identify traces of the gods with the gods themselves, rather than as a psychic reality to be integrated by the individual.

FROM MYTH TO MYTHOPOESIS

According to William Doty, the term "mythopoesis" was established by Harry Slochower in 1970, in referring to "situations in which literal meanings could no longer be tolerated by a later society, which then re-created the ancient stories in new guises" ("What Mythopoetic Means" 255). Seen primarily in poetry and fiction, the move from myth to mythopoesis is the move from a literal to a literary or symbolic application of mythical motifs. It is a move necessitated by the basic human need for connection with the world and oneself. For Slochower, myth or, more specifically, the act of re-creating the myths in writing, is especially important in "an alienated and alienating era" for such a poesis grants both artist and audience the experience of belonging to something larger and eternal, a return to unity amidst pervasive divisiveness (12). Mythopoesis reframes and re-members the continual (modern) questions of what it means to be human, what it means to live—but with the awareness that such a remembrance is made possible *by* humankind. Mythopoesis may call one's irrevocable embeddedness in life into connection, but what must be stressed is that this does not speak to a permanent, universal myth or definition of myth that remains immune from history and ideology. Slochower writes, "There is a need to de-romanticize the myth, to rescue its living relevance from the oceanic night of the romantic conception which views it as an eternal fixed substance, unaffected by empirical forces and the clash of interests" (40). But, he also notes, "historic ideologies never completely eliminate the universal vision" (40). Thus, every age has its artists, its "rebellious heroes" who reach into reality, through the fixations and past uncritical idolatries, in order to rescue the myth from itself.

However, in attempting to deromanticize the myth, mythopoesis appears to sidestep the question of myth. Myth may provide the material for mythopoesis, and yet, in doing so, it is, to some degree, usurped of its role in spawning a movement that both requires and rewrites its existence. Mythopoesis cannot rely on a stable concept of myth because the myth is unreliable, tainted by literal historicism or unmasked as political ideology. The way to "myth," then, to that ineffable communion between humankind and life, is actually *around* myth. In his book illustrating the mythopoeic process in ancient Israel, Bernard Batto expresses his desire to avoid using the term *myth* to characterize what are nonetheless mythic phenomena because he knows that myth "is the invention of modern scholarship, which has been forged through some five centuries of laborious investigation into human religiosity and intensive searching of the human psyche" (6). Although he recognizes the equivocal problems of using a term that "bears only a slight resemblance to its original meaning," he knows of no other comparable term to use in its stead (6). This is the conundrum faced by those caught in the double bind of myth: how to reflect upon the truth of myth while simultaneously knowing the reflection to be faulty or fictitious— incomplete at best, a narcissistic self-image at worst. But mythopoesis defuses the tension of this bind by shifting the focus from the myth to the act of mythmaking, in which contradictions fire the creative process, providing ever more outlets for the truth of myth to seep through undetected.

Other writers on mythopoesis concur that the benefits of myth are not necessarily dependent on myth itself, either on its presence or absence. For Slochower, myths do not exist in their own right; they are "a pictorial hypothesis about the nature of man. [Myths] enter the realm of reality in that they enable us to explain and predict events in the empirical world" (19). Max Bilen argues that the "fundamental human sense of dissatisfaction has less to do with an actual lack of something than with a feeling of nostalgia for a state now unknown to mankind" (862). Yet lest this "unknown state" (the infinite, absolute freedom) become romanticized and erroneously lodged in an earlier time of the "have's" in contradistinction to the current time of the "have not's," Bilen asserts that "no one has seen the infinite," but people have always believed in its possibility (862). The emphasis on human belief in determining reality thus renders any argument for a concrete absence of myth either superfluous or false. By relegating the function of myth to the act of creating or reworking the myth, mythopoesis successfully removes the middle-man, that concept known as myth, and with it the problems of defining or settling on that which is and has always been a placeholder for humankind's natural inclination toward meaning. Meaning thus hinges less on being utterly immersed in and bound to something larger than oneself than in the attitude and approach toward those speculations *about* what is perceived to be larger. One could argue that this very speculativeness indicates a profound and fundamental lack and impossibility of meaning, but then that would lead the argument back to assuming an absence of myth and would disregard the notion that there has never been myth, only mythopoesis.

In this respect, the mythopoetic view on myth points less to origins and creation and more to an original act of (re)-creating that which in modernity is no longer known. But somehow in the telling, one knows enough. Bilen calls for a "mythical attitude," an artistic attitude that is more likely to enable one to transcend the ordinary human condition than some elusive and evasive myth (861). Similarly, Hank Lazer stresses "a myth of making, of the profound resonance of the act of making, of the heuristic and instructive immediacy of writing" (410). The creating of the story must not be overlooked or undermined by the story being told, for myth compels the story rather than simply reflecting a creation already complete. The myth, then, is a perpetual continuation of a grander story, one that requires retelling and revising in order to be true to those who live it. "'Lived life,'" said Thomas Mann, is "life as a succession, as a moving in others' steps, as identification." "The typical is actually the mythical [. . .] one may as well say 'lived myth' as 'lived life'" (29). Without a sense of the typical and familiar, he believes, "without any possibility of resting upon the known, [life] could only bewilder and alarm" (28).

Mann's statement could indicate a reluctance to embrace the unknown and accept radical change or loss. And yet from the mythopoetic perspective, if the thread of myth trailing through time has always been spun from the minds of humankind—a continual response to the larger whole even as the whole empties—why insist on an absence of myth? Why force a severance from that which could console, inspire, amuse, in any time, alienating or otherwise? To be sure, arguing for the absence of myth as I have been doing does not advocate exile from the human race—but it does mean to suggest that the modern sense of exile or loss cannot easily be placated through myth (which today could only be a reconstructed, man-made one). However, the mythopoetic response to this sense of loss would be simply to tell its story, a story about loss believed to have been lived many times over. In such a "new" story, what is lost may not be entirely recovered, but the act of telling the story (more accurately, publishing the story) verbalizes the experience for the collective, or at least for a percentage of it. Such is the power of myth filtered through mythopoesis; shall it be minimized or denied even if the blanks of meaning cannot be filled in entirely or permanently?

Holding to the typical as mythical is the trap that the personal mythologist can fall into, in assuming that formal likenesses in human thought and experience bestow a numinous and archetypal quality to one's personal life. But mythopoesis means to highlight these likenesses without necessarily elevating them to more than they deserve. The emotions, the fantasies, the ideologies, even the relationship to the divine—these are played out on the page rather than in life, although their relevance to life is no less diminished, however distant. In de-objectifying the myth, in evaporating the object into a subjective attitude, style, or perspective, mythopoesis presupposes a level of reflection that has already thought through any concrete representation, thus precluding the need for any outer, positive response to the "myth" (such as ritual; Lazer writes, "The poem already *is* ritual action"[406]). The fictitious nature of the mythopoetic form shows this. And while the inability to be contained by a single narrative can point to a gap ever in need of new bridges, the mythopoetic mind-set sees this as necessary to its own survival. It is necessary to a symbolic reading of the myth, which is the only myth that modern, Western civilization has ever really known. "Modern myth is not an attempted recovery of an archaic form of life so much as a sophisticated, self-conscious equivalent," writes Michael Bell (2). If modernity has never been *in* myth but has always reflected it, then the pertinence of an absence of myth lessens when the discussion shifts to this means of reflecting. Emphasizing the "inescapable activity" of mythopoesis purports to ground the myth in nothing but itself, thus alleviating the problem of meaning in a world that has lost its ultimate grounding (2).

The equivocation of "myth" that proved to be problematic in determining its presence or absence, as discussed in chapter 1, finds a comfortable home in a mythopoetic or postmodern reading of myth. For the creating of the myth is a "borderline activity," bound to an "unstable bridge" as it attempts to forge connections that can never find stasis (Slochower 29). It is on the threshold, in these in-between spaces, that the distinction between archaic and contemporary phenomena blurs in service to an imaginative view of myth that is regarded as real as a literal myth, in and of itself able to transmit truth and transform. "Metaphors have the power of metamorphosis. . . . [The images] are real, as they are in a myth" (Bilen 864). An artistic rendering of myth offers a way to have one's myth without being completely and unconsciously had by it. Myth-making allows one to lift the blinders from naïveté and innocence but still be moved by the images, still wonder at the words even if there may be little behind them.

In the in-between spaces occupied by the mythopoetic myth, the tenet of "both/and" reigns. Paradoxes are to subsist as para-doxes; consciously precluding resolution, for such a resolution would belie the conflicts inherent in human nature and in the knowledge about such nature. Given that a myth's power and pur-pose now essentially reside in the human sphere, notwithstanding any lingering claim to universality and transcendence, it is there-fore appropriate to reflect humanity honestly in the mythic images as well as in the interpretations and theorizing. Thus, myth has no qualms about standing in for both truth and fiction, force and con-cept, human construct and outer reality, question and answer, pre-cisely because each term of a binary opposition cannot easily be detached from the other without effacing itself. The equivocation of myth need not represent a stagnant opposition in search of syn-thesis because the point is to sustain a double bind that while painful if personally caught in, can enable a freedom to look at both sides of the story—to see the wholeness already there. Like the well-known optical illusion depicting either an old or young woman, one cannot see both images simultaneously, although both are evidently real and both are necessary. Visually apprehending or experiencing the whole requires jumping from one perspective to the other—constantly. This reflects the postmodern questioning of singular truths and of rationality over irrationality, knowing that "subjectivity and knowledge of reality are dependent on the other" (Rowland 2). The in-between space not only allows for this reflexivity, it is enforced and strengthened by it. Susan Rowland writes that the postmodern sublime shares its Romantic predecessor, in the "pain or pathos felt in the gap between what can be conceived and what can be imagined or represented. [. . .] The sublime is the 'gaps' left between systems of knowledge as they fail to account for the postmodern condition in its entirety" (4–5).

Truth and the divine, the essence of myth, can *only* reside in the gaps, if myth were still to exist, for any attempt at concretization fails even doubly so at trying to represent what ultimately cannot be represented. The in-between spaces, the perpetual shifting of perspective, and the conscious engagement of metaphor and imagination thus work to sustain and enliven the gaps. The postmodern myth obligates an active passivity, a free-floating vantage point from which to see both terms of the opposition. Arguing for the absence or presence of myth requires that one choose a specific perspective to make one's case. But from a perspective that cannot stand still—the result is that there is no result and the question is left open for further debate or to forsake altogether. A postmodern myth thus retains the opposites but reconciles them in the manner of the Möbius strip, a two-sided strip of paper that is also only one side. In its twistedness, it necessitates a continual movement, a tracing along the strip, in order to see the whole.[5]

With this postmodern image in mind, a distinction between archaic, authentic myth and modern, constructed myth becomes more difficult to differentiate. The equivocation of myth may not be as equivocal, leaning more toward a univocal vision that finds its formal variations more in subjective experience and imagination than in outer phenomena. In an essay on primitivism and modernity, John McGovern contends that the notion of a primitive unity of consciousness is the result of a romantic fantasy borne out of "revulsion at modernity" and a longing toward an ideal, nonfragmented state (173). The myth of the "Fall of Man" and the return to God indicates a break in consciousness and a subsequent overcoming of this break, reestablishing the unity believed to have been lived by primitive societies. But, McGovern writes, neither the Fall nor the return is an historical event, though in the romantic desire to reconcile a supposed empirical reality, the events have been historicized (170). Citing the work of Mircea Eliade, McGovern writes that this myth is "universal amongst primitives and archaic peoples and that always, as with Christianity, there is a profound concern to distinguish between 'this' world and 'the other' world, time and eternity, being and history" (169). He continues:

> To the degree that romantics have conceived of divided being as a historical state, modernity, brought about by an event or events in the past, to be worked through in the present and overcome at some time in the future, they have attempted to combine together what Judaism and Christianity, ancient philosophy and primitive myth, have always seen as ontologically distinct, being and time. (169)

Any divided state to be fully overcome—that even *can* be overcome—therefore finds little authority or impetus in an earlier idea of myth. Moreover, the time of earlier myth is not without its own divisions and differentiations, which punctures any fantasy of a monistic wholeness. McGovern also cites contemporary anthropologist Daniel Miller, who refutes the idea that "individuality as we know it is solely a modern form, that in the natural condition humankind tends to be collective" (171).

When considering McGovern's argument, the distinction between differing forms of individuality as well as between two types of myth appears to be weakened. This reduces the ability to project modern concerns and desires backward onto a romanticized myth or culture, though by the same token, a formal continuity through the history of humanity does bestow a universal and perennial quality to human concerns per se, thus making it easier to believe in an unbroken myth. But from a mythopoetic standpoint, when myth is regarded as the cause or effect of such concerns, rather than as just another mode of reflecting on the world, it takes on an excess of reality, forgetting the temperance of history as well as the unknown. Holding to an absence of some entirely unified state, no less than the longing for this state, is for modernity a fantasy and an excuse to subjectively exaggerate, reduce, or deny what is now understood to be part of human nature: the separation between self and world.

Obviously, there is a profound distinction between ancient and modern notions of what the world is like, and this distinction is essential to keep in mind when addressing the living consequences of a worldview and belief system. Yet when myth is identified less with the embodied and enacted worldview than with the drive to view the world, as it is in a mythopoetic understanding of myth, then the distinction between archaic and modern reflections of the world loses its importance. Although I think such an abstraction of myth lies at the heart of confused or conflated understandings of myth, it is important to note that this shift in identification speaks less to the nature of myth and a mode of being *in*-the-world, and more to the nature of how we interpret and reflect *on* the world. In this regard, myth becomes just another reflective lens, one that, for a mythopoetic approach, is expressly chosen rather than given.

If, pursuing this line of thought, myths are now defined such that they have always been dependent on the human capacity to reflect, whether in the primary sense of a less critical expression of being alive or in the later sense of a more conscious, philosophical mode, what changes over time is *how* whatever is looked at or thought about is being reflected. The reflecting itself does not end, and each reflection is founded on another, which in turn inspires another, and so forth, "a constant *mise en abyme*" that eludes all attempts to find the beginning, end, or any assured center of meaning (J. Miller 72). Miller uses the image of the labyrinth to illustrate not only the impossibility of stabilizing words or meaning within a given text or story, but also to indicate the necessity of a complex, nonlinear, and repetitive form that is both a reflection and fulfillment of the complexity of representing the "truth" of the story or experience. Speaking specifically to the "slightly asymmetrical echoes [. . .] along the narrative lines" in myths of Ariadne and Dionysus, Miller writes, "The need for a permutation of the somewhat mysterious elements of the story is intrinsic to the story itself. It is as if no telling of it could express clearly its meaning. It has to be traced and retraced, thread over thread in the labyrinth, without ever becoming wholly perspicuous" (62, 65).

To the extent that the impetus to reflect on one's experience is intimately linked with myth, then as long as there is reflection, there is, in a sense, myth. One just enters and entertains the bigger question wherever one is in the story. And yet the problem associated with myth's equivocation surfaces again when myth is abstracted to the formal process of reflection. To strip myth down to what is a modern concern, the need to interpret the world and explain human existence, can induce the belief previously stated, namely, that reflecting on human experience somehow recalls myth. However, this is a fallacy because it conflates the formal with the substantial. It is like saying that the presence of antique artifacts in culture means that we are living in antiquity. That is absurd.

To be fair, I do not think that the mythopoetic move equates all reflection with myth. Mythopoesis is concerned particularly with the type of reflection that most resembles myth: the logic of human existence expressed in narrative form. But when a modern style of reflecting is subsumed under a generic notion of myth whose purpose of helping humanity understand its place in life is held to be constant and consistent, it becomes all too tempting to grant myth a permanent existence. Actually, to be more precise, it is not myth that is upheld, since, as Slochower contends, myths are not ontologically real but hypotheses about human nature. Rather, what the mythopoetic equivocation of myth means to uphold is *mythic meaning.* Yet whether the emphasis is on myth as an entity or an existential benefit derived from mythmaking, there is still that imagined unbroken thread traveling through time, connected to myth even as myth is deconstructed in favor of mythmaking. This only continues to feed the fantasy that myth can still fulfill humankind to the degree it once did.

When myth is abstracted such that its absence or presence becomes nearly impossible to distinguish, what myth once really was—a known reality and not a hypothesis—gets lost in the process. Myth as lost, however, seems to be the point of a postmodern approach. Reflections (texts) can be infinitely multiplied, or regressed, as Derrida says, and to the extent that myths are characterized by the continual process of reflecting on human nature, any attempt to isolate and define myth, let alone extract any truth from it, is rendered futile and absurd. Marcel Detienne believes myth to be "an untraceable form" and calls for a "myth-less mythology" (*Creation* 132), which brings the circle back to mythopoesis and its intention to free the myth. Myth is negated just enough so that it can roam with the invisibles in the in-between spaces, where it hopes to catch the interplay of reflections before it too becomes just one more rung into the abyss. Mythopoesis frees the myth from itself *because of* the abyss, because truth and meaning are no longer trusted with mere concrete representation or explication—but this act of freeing carries with it the hope that by paying allegiance to the absence, meaning is not forgotten.

"Each telling [of the myth] both displays the labyrinthine pattern of relations again and at the same time leaves its 'true' meaning veiled," writes J. Hillis Miller (65). But what is the merit of Miller's view? Are truth and meaning veiled out of necessity, or does the veiling hide the fact that without collective consensus, there is no truth? Why else would suspicions arise around something claiming to be the truth, unless the feasibility of "truth" was already long gone? To rewrite this reality along with the old myths, as mythopoesis does, is somehow to acknowledge that the lack of collective truth or meaning is acceptable because such a truth is far too complex and can never be completely revealed anyway. This circular thinking goes nowhere, except back into and around itself, but, under the rubric of postmodern thought, it is right on track.

Although a mythopoetic or postmodern attitude toward myth enables the persistence of myth, as I have attempted to show, the loss or fusion of critical and formal distinctions required for such a stance cannot completely deny the artificiality of any current myth defined by these standards. The focus on myth*making* reveals this. True myths are found and foundational; they precede rather than follow, are self-revealing rather than explanatory or critical. Or, if myths are an explanation, they are a *literal* one, which is more like a presentation of that which already is. "Myths are anonymous," wrote Lévi-Strauss. "[F]rom the moment they are seen as myths, and whatever their real origins, they exist only as elements embodied in a tradition" (*Raw* 18). Myths are not created in the sense of how poets and artists create them; myths are the living presentation of the truth of a given people. Whereas mythopoesis clearly is the result of myth (and "never wholly loosens itself from the genetic base," according to Slochower [34]), it bypasses myth out of the politicized awareness that the literal stories, the myths themselves, are no longer credible or functional on their own terms and must be converted into another symbolic meaning. The myths must be created because they are no longer being lived, which if nothing else, presupposes an absence of at least one kind of "original" myth. Given the mythopoetic emphasis on creativity, perhaps this man-made myth is sufficient because little else seems to be expected of myth. But this move provokes a split between literal and imaginal myth, which becomes problematic insofar as the imaginal, created myth is now assigned the role of returning human values to the collective. Yet this was a role previously upheld by a notion of myth that was dependent on and intimately connected to the literal, to self-evident, natural phenomena (earth as Mother Earth, sky as Father Sky). Any myth engendered by mythopoesis can only speak to the *split off* imaginal (as opposed to the *concrete* imaginal, where, as in the phenomena of myth, the imaginal and the literal are the same). Thus, any "restoration" of mythic values will be purely imaginal as well, and subsequently split off from the collective.

Mythopoesis subsists on the kind of double bind that squeezes myth just enough to make it suffer, but without carrying any process to completion. If a myth is dead or dying, any attempt that breathes new life into it, such as telling the story of the so-called absence of myth, reverses the dying process because this is then held to be another myth, now the "myth of mythlessness." As long as it takes a myth to show its own death, as in Fellini's film *The Clowns* where it took a clown to bury a clown, it becomes impossible to discern the line between a myth that has truly died and a new, constructed one that is, in a sense, faking the death of myth so that it (the artificial myth) might be taken more (or less) seriously. Then the myth of mythlessness becomes another strategy to pretend that myth is still necessary, and mythopoesis becomes the excuse to hold onto myth, rather than a creative, critical, and iconoclastic process necessitated by its absence or nonexistence. A staged burial of myth that intentionally strives to retrieve the myth does not restore faith or the gods but only glorifies one's stories and ideologies into something that mistakes all-too-human grandiosity for transcendence.

Furthermore, the emphasis on the act of mythmaking runs the risk of mitigating the very real force of death or destruction as it elevates outer phenomena and psychological changes into art, romanticizing one thing out of deromanticizing another. Artists may be the "antennae of the race," as Ezra Pound said (see Falck vi), but when myth gives way to mythopoesis, a removal from horrifying, disappointing, bland, and all sorts of other less than ideal phenomena ensues in service to an imaginative view that makes the experience more palatable. By no means is it contentious to want to honor and validate certain states, but it cannot be forgotten that such expressions may be symptoms of a real sickness that cannot be so easily sublimated into art. If mythopoesis means to rescue the myth from itself, then it must recognize that its rescue attempt is just another iteration of its own process—a telling of the same story in a new disguise and, though potentially cathartic, it can only be a partial or temporary relief.

Mythopoesis purposely suspends the myth in the in-between spaces, which renders the myth and by extension mythopoesis ultimately ineffective at fulfilling what it ostensibly intends, for the problems often attributed to mythlessness are no less resolved. One motivation for rescuing the myth from itself is expressed by Slochower: "[T]he myth unfolds the living chain which connects the recurrent recognition scenes of the human drama. They assure us that we are not strangers and alone in the world" (14). But efforts to remember that we belong to something universal and eternal, already ineffectual insofar as this needs to be proved, do not appear to be working (except perhaps for those who have a personal myth). This begs the question: is it more important and ultimately transformative to teach and not resist the reality that now we *are* "strangers and alone in the world" rather than foster illusions and salvational fantasies around myth?

Irrespective of any resolution to myth, or perhaps because of a purposeful lack of resolution, there is that continually resurfacing issue that is unique to this time, now expressed by a writer on mythopoesis. "The very term 'myth,' by combining, in its modern usage, the rival meanings of a grounding narrative and a falsehood, encapsulates this central problem of modernity: how to live, given what we know" (Bell 2). The caveat "given what we know" is only an addendum to a question that has motivated mythological studies from the beginning, even extending into the question "what are the myths of a mythless time," which still betrays some need for orientation. Even if it is a negative or intentionally ambiguous orientation, it aims to orient just the same. But modernity sets itself up for a decided lack of orientation, seen in the impossible expectations characteristic of Bell's statement. If his statement were true, myth— the *same* myth in antiquity as in modernity—would have to mean both truth and falsehood, an impossible predicament and diversionary tactic against the truth of truth and falsehood (and myth) in and of themselves. As I have tried to show throughout this study, the modern myth depends on the sacrifice of what one could call true myth. Moreover, the assertion that a modern myth can answer the question of how to live is dubious. How can any work of literature (the site of modern myths, from a mythopoetic perspective) really tell one how to live? This does not suggest that there is not some truth of human experience to be gleaned, but it seems as if the only books that presume to answer the question of how to live are those (usually nonfiction) especially written toward that end— not modern myths.

The following sections ask whether archetypal and post-Jungian psychology is better suited than mythopoesis to address individual needs, though the use of myth as a tool is no less applicable. For it is as if a postmodern psychology, by situating itself in the middle of this hall of mirrors, aims to supplant the myth by seeing through and analyzing it and assuming responsibility for the question of "how to live, given what we know." Mythopoesis may strive to recapture (or release) the heart of myth; similarly, post-Jungian psychology intends to use myth to reach the heart of the world and human nature. Whether the human and cultural heart is actually reached through layers of myth remains questionable.

METAPHORICAL AND ARCHETYPAL MYTH

Reflecting from in-betweenness is the prerequisite for maintaining an imaginal view over a literal one, and in the field occupied by archetypal psychology, this reflecting means to address the question "how to live" without needing to be asked or explicating the answer. The "aim of therapy," writes James Hillman, "is the development of a sense of soul, the middle ground of psychic realities, and the method of therapy is the cultivation of the imagination" (*Archetypal* 12). Based on C. G. Jung's assertion, "image is psyche" ("Commentary," *CW* 13, sec. 75), archetypal psychology's cultivation of the imagination primes the shifting meeting ground for psyche to know itself and, by extension, for humanity to recognize itself—in all its suffering as well as in all its glory. If the separation between self and world induces the need to reflect (or make myths, to the extent that one equates the two), archetypal psychology means to remember that these reflections are not always malleable or subject to one's choosing. The images, such as in dreams and fantasies, are autonomous and real in their own right, the primary data of psychic reality created ever anew.[6] No mere by-products of an irrevocable separation between self and world, nor bound to either an impersonal, objective world or an overpersonalized individual, the images bring to light the *anima mundi*, the soul of the world, in remembrance of the "inseparable conjunction of individual and world" (Sardello 15). Given that this psychic reality is always co-created and in flux, it cannot be confined to any solid or single realm, whether conceptual or concrete, and subsists instead in the shadows penetrating both fantasy and reality.

Archetypal psychology shares with Slochower's perspective the mythopoetic view that myths are metaphors, but is loathe to rush into interpretation or an unadorned thinking that would render the existence of myth negotiable and the need for myth obsolete. As long as mythical motifs are identified with underlying structures patterning all of life, the archetypes, it is seemingly impossible to be divested of myth. Even archetypal psychology's oft-posed question, "Who's there," an attempt to see through fixated collective and individual myths (meaning ideologies), tends to uncover a particular god or goddess—direct from the official annals of ancient mythology. However, archetypal psychology makes the progression "from archetype as a noun, to archetyp*al* as adjective" (Hillman, "An Inquiry into Image" 70). Similar to the mythopoetic process, the movement is away from a literal, authoritative myth whose symbolic meaning remains fixed to the archetypes. Rather, the move is toward an imaginative attitude that looks neither toward universals nor an established meaning, but only to the living peculiarities and likenesses of the image, in this moment, in this context.

And yet if archetypal psychology were committed to an adjectival stance, it would not be able to ask its revered question, "Who's there?" Personifying is essentially noun-making, and contrary to the psychological move initiated by Hillman. Although the move away from symbols and universals is, in theory, a move away from myth, or at least what would be considered traditional myth, how far is archetypal psychology willing to leave myth behind? Hillman says myths are *not* to be understood as "transcendental metaphysics whose categories are divine figures" (*Archetypal* 29). Nonetheless, one characteristic that perhaps distinguishes archetypal psychology from mythopoesis is that archetypal psychology explicitly seeks to remember the divine *quality*, to know that the traces the poets are following lead to the gods. It is not enough to know the myth is a metaphor. The metaphor must be aligned with the immutable psychic reality once stood for by the immortal gods. Myth may be a tool for discerning this psychic reality, but archetypal psychology reminds one that this tool works on the one wielding it all the same.

Hillman stresses that the gods of archetypal psychology are to be imagined rather than taken literally, to be psychologized rather than theologized. Yet imagining these particular metaphors, these "cosmic perspectives," constellates a religious mode or function that belongs to psyche and psychology (45). Archetypal psychology strives to restore "the fullness of the Gods in all things and [revert] psychology itself to the recognition that it too is a religious activity" (46). Hillman, following Jung, makes the distinction between a religious instinct and religion itself. The emphasis is on the god-*image* rather than a verifiable account of the existence of God; but although the image may be a psychological fact, it is no less religious or numinous. Religion, Jung wrote, is an "attitude of mind which could be formulated in accordance with the original use of the word *religio*, which means a careful consideration and observation of certain dynamic factors that are conceived as 'powers': spirits, daemons, gods, laws, ideas, ideals" ("Psychology and Religion," *CW* 11, sec. 8).

A psychological approach toward religion says that regardless of whether God can be proved to exist or not, the fact that there are these forces that animate, inspire, seize, and grace us, as well as compel belief in and devotion to such forces, indicates a reality that is psychological as it is religious. The same logic could be applied to modern or postmodern myth. Insofar as the need to hypothesize about reality finds myth to be a useful form in which to contain and express these hypotheses, the question of myth's absence or presence becomes as much a psychological one as it is mythological. One's beliefs and motivations are examined and questioned as much as any "outer" reality of myth. From this perspective, the "death of God," one so-called piece of evidence against religion and the possibility of myth today, would indicate a change in psychology, a change in the logic of the world rather than a loss of something concrete and outside of humankind.

It is the intent of archetypal psychology to restore a mythic/ religious *attitude*, not by forging a new myth but by rekindling belief in what is already there and always available as long as humans are psychological beings. Perhaps this is what Hillman means when he says the death of God is a "monotheistic fantasy" (45).[7] For the move toward a polytheistic psychology, which shares with postmodernism the predilection for multiple points of view, "freed from ego domination" (44), means to show that not only are there many, equally valid perspectives, but that each of these perspectives carries its own divine logic. The gods may have become diseases, as Jung said, but the gods are *in* the diseases as much as in anything else, Hillman says (see *Re-Visioning* 104). Even when presumed dead, the gods are still alive; the diseased nature of the gods merely preserved in a poetic imagining. Humanity is immersed in soul. For archetypal psychology, the immersion is founded on and verified in the aesthetics and sensuousness of the psychic image. And myth, with its pantheon of god-images, is the metaphorical road toward this recognition and a soulful mode of understanding and being-in-the-world.

Again the trap succumbed to by the personal mythologist is laid bare. If one's everyday reactions are endowed with more power than they warrant, the individual's sense of self turns grandiose, and even the gods, now anthropomorphized and stuffed inside the individual, become an inflated concept, as if the psychic reality they stood for could *only* be apprehended in this personified form. One way to curb this inflation is to attend to the dream, though the dream, even more so than myth, tends to be overly personalized and runs the risk of being forced to answer ego concerns (how instinctively one says, *my* dream, or, *I* had a dream, equating this 'my' and 'I' with the ego). Yet because the dream is a less filtered psychic phenomenon, it perhaps speaks the truth or intent of myth more clearly than a manufactured myth can, which in its narrative formulation has already passed through a greater degree of reflection.[8] To be sure, reading the dream on its own terms does not usually lend itself to the kind of satisfaction received from traditional narrative structure, nor does it necessarily provide an unambiguous meaning readily applicable to waking life. But it is precisely because of this, of not pandering to the ego's notions of comprehension and meaning, that archetypal psychology stresses the dream's ability in authentically revealing the imaginal. The dream *is* the image; "it contains its own configurations of meaning independent of systems of interpretation" (Schenk 52). The dream-image is complete unto itself, "an irreducible and complete union of form and content" (Berry 64). "Stick to the image" is archetypal psychology's motto. Follow its texture and weave (59), play with the syntax, say what it is *like* and not what it *is*—all this intends to protect the image from hasty interpretations and ego-inspired translations that speak about the dream rather than listening to what the dream has to say. Through the listening, the dream's meaning, or what it implies, as Patricia Berry says (64), becomes clear—though indirectly and freed from a suffocating subjectivity.

Attending to soul by way of the dream is to travel deep into the mythical domain of the underworld, where ever since Freud, the images have been believed to originate (see Hillman, *Dream* 10). "To arrive at the basic structure of things we must go into their darkness," Hillman says, following Heraclitus's fragment, "Nature loves to hide"[9] (26). But Heraclitus is positing a metaphysical, not a postmodern idea. And for archetypal psychology, no less than postmodernism, there is no "basic structure"—only fictions. Moreover, simple darkness is not enough for archetypal psychology. It must be matched with its metaphorical, mythological equivalent in order to defend the dream-image from restrictive theories, such as Freud's theory of repression and Jung's theory of compensation, and enable its fullness and richness to be known—on its own terms. And for this Hillman calls on Greek mythology and its vivid imagery of Hades, Pluto, Tartarus, the river Styx, and so forth, to serve as analogies for unconscious processes and the darkest, deepest depths of soul, the "unknown which is the source of all depth

psychology" ("Image" 68). *Underworld* and *depths* imply spatial local-
ities, but they are meant to serve as *perspectives,* as the movement
into the gaps and in-between spaces that shades one's sight, adding
a deathly or ghostly overtone to that which in waking, ego consciousness is often held certain and invulnerable.

However, does the correlation of dream and myth inadvertently seek to elevate the dream's significance? Joseph Campbell
said, "The myth is the public dream and the dream is the private
myth" (Campbell and Moyers 40). To call a dream a myth is to
imbue it with public status, bringing to mind the shaman who
dreams for the collective. To call the dream a *private* myth not only
reduces what it means to be a myth, but also bestows the dream
with more power and numinousity than it rightfully possesses.
There are no private shamans. Certainly one dreams for oneself,
but either the images are not very numinous, precluding the
mythic appellation. Or, an overalignment with a personal numinous experience obscures concrete, phenomenal changes wrought
by a waking consciousness that proves to be the downfall of the
dream. Wolfgang Giegerich refers to Jung's encounter with an
African chief, who, when asked about his dreams, replied that since
the coming of the white man, there was no reason to dream anymore. "The medicine man who had formerly negotiated with the
gods or the fates and advised his people had lost his raison d'être.
The authority of the medicine man had been replaced by that of
the District Commissioner" ("Opposition" 15).[10] Insofar as the
dream is displaced and stripped of its "metaphysical raison d'être"
(ibid.), the status of soul, by extension, is also displaced—but the
soul is misread in its apparent displacement as perceptions of soullessness and mythlessness come to dominate. What was a change in
condition or a change in the soul's opus comes to be solely identified with loss. No doubt, a kind of irrevocable loss occurs when the
need for dreaming is obviated, but it is, paradoxically, the insistence on and persistent belief in myth as a form and a means for
reflection that refuses to cave in entirely to the loss and render contemporary experience as entirely meaningless. And yet, it must be
noted, this equivocation of myth is no less culpable in its subsequent misrepresentation of soul.

Again, Hillman does not literalize the underworld. He is reading it archetypally, imaginally, in a manner that, though emphasiz-

ing a deathly perspective from down under, breathes blood into the image so that it is not some heady abstraction. But does the need to add value belie the fact that there is little value to be had? Does the dependence on metaphor for insight clothe and cloak it rather than release it? As a tool for reading the dream or for illuminating psyche, myth becomes other than a mere reflection. It is not only the means by which the reflection comes about, but suffuses the reflection with images and language that are specified by a particular way of thinking and seeing. The reflection is cushioned by the very tool meant to illuminate it—myth. Even if myth is eternal, it cannot be immune from the specific culture whose mode and object of reflection change with time. Mythopoesis itself tracks and is an embodiment of these changes in myth, arising, as Slochower says, "in periods of crisis, of cultural transition" (15). The cultivation of an archetypal or mythic consciousness does not insist on restraining the gods in some archaic myth because the intent is to discern the imaginal meaning from the literal event. The point is to notice where the gods are still alive *psychologically*. "What the Greeks said their Gods asked for above all else, [. . .] was not to be forgotten, that is, to be kept in mind, recollected as *psychological facts*" (Hillman, "Once More into the Fray" 5). Yet the idea of a "mythic consciousness" connotes its own confinement when it shuns the literal and concrete in favor of the imaginal or psychological, forgetting that, in myth, the literal and the imaginal are as one. The physical act of paying homage to the gods through ritual and sacrifice *was* the imaginal remembrance and tribute to psyche. Nothing else was required. For the Pueblo culture visited by Jung, it is the literal event of the sun rising that provides what only we would term imaginal meaning. The idea of "psychological facts" and "seeing through" the literal to the imaginal belongs to *this* time. Thus, it could only be in a time when myth is no longer present, or necessary at least, that the literal comes in opposition to the imaginal. Any current myth that requires a splitting off of the literal in order to psychologically "remember" it, which is what a mythology as psychology approach does, can never completely satiate insofar as the literal is denied. In this respect, mythic consciousness becomes the opposite of what it purports to be.

When psychology is treated as mythology, it loses, to some degree, the negativity required by its own in-between spaces, the gaps in which the separation between self and world dissolves. Myth may be a metaphor for looking at something else, but when that something else is granted more power and symbolism than it is worth, such as the dream-image, *because* of how myth as a tool is used, then myth has no choice but to follow suit and become something more than *it* is. The insistence on going under to reclaim blighted, underworldly perspectives in service of soul becomes the desire for unconsciousness rather than consciousness, preferring instead to be taught by images that may be snapshots from another time or storybook than living images of psychic reality created anew. Freeing the myth from itself thus necessitates its negation, similar to the downward move made by Hillman—though this time freed from the underworld. The emancipation of myth, however, demands that the severing from an animated, ensouled world (already visible in technology and science) cannot simply be transposed to a metaphorical or soul-like reading of the world and expect not to have an irreversible impact on the status of soul as well as on any "new myth." A "remythologizing" that wanted to reflect truthfully the time in which it was rooted could not come about through rewriting the old stories or seeing the gods in the diseases because when the gods and soul were displaced, such as when the coming of the white man to Africa replaced the reason for dreams, the need for the gods and myth as the carrier for soul was obviated. And as the gods and myth become de-hypostatized, swallowed by the gaps required for the imaginal perspective that replaces the literal one, the psychic reality formerly connected to the gods becomes more comprehensible—on its own, naked terms.

Yet literal, positive phenomena cannot be so easily dismissed, for the present form of the soul's mystery, of the numinous is on the outside, or so Giegerich argues ("Opposition" 20). He writes that in antiquity, the soul's major work was realized through dreams, shamanic journeys, visions—inner experiences that formerly spoke for the whole but have since lost their collective relevance and meaning. But today, the work that speaks to the whole is not myth and dream but rather phenomena like globalization and profit maximization that render the individual and individual inner experience *psychologically* irrelevant, if not obsolete (15). This psychological obsolescence might be difficult and painful for the individual to accept, but its significance to the individual is entirely personal. Taking this obsolescence personally can only defend from the larger, objective force—what the soul wants—by cocooning itself in an egocentric psychology that is no less sheltered even as it professes to lower itself before the soul. It is tempting to balk at the notion that psyche's logic has discarded the individual, not only because on the surface one tends to identify psychology with personal problems that need therapeutic attention, but also out of the reaction to a seemingly harsh, anti-individual, pro-economy collective. Greg Mogenson writes, "The individuation process, far from being an anachronism as Giegerich claims, continues to be the psyche's logical responses to the forces in the world that would disenfranchise the individual" ("Response"). Resonating with the philosophy of personal myth, this statement reflects an aversion to the psychological repercussions that come with the loss of myth and a no longer ensouled natural world. The fallacy lies in the belief that individual determination and passion can override or reverse a collective process by refusing to cater to it, rather than accept the decentering of the individual. Once again this betrays the need for some personal meaning in a world that is obviously not fulfilling it—at least in the manner expected. One can stick to one's dreams, whether waking or sleeping, for reassurance of meaning, but when the status of dreams themselves loses its psychic foothold, how effective or lasting can such a reassurance be?

By placing (or returning) the emphasis on soul over individual concerns and behavior, archetypal psychology, continuing the venture begun with the inception of depth psychology, aims to restore a psychological or religious attitude—but there is nothing to restore if one maintains the inescapability of soul. The world may no longer be ensouled as it once was, but this does not mean that the soul of the world requires any restorative or search-and-rescue efforts on the part of the individual or on the part of a school of psychology (as if such a thing were even possible). It requires only the willingness to remove the veils and be penetrated by *its*—the soul's—meaning, which may or may not reflect one's preferred ideas or feelings about meaning. The problem is not that the individual has become psychologically irrelevant. Rather, it is the persistent expectation of a kind of meaning and fullness that can no longer be equated with or accessed by myth. If, as Giegerich contends, the soul's locus is in public phenomena (even individual "inner" work is becoming increasingly disclosed, as seen in the confessional psychospeak, hyper self-awareness and reality TV permeating popular culture), then the former purpose of myth and dreams is no more. Not merely shorn of their collective and archetypal power, myth and dream have become superfluous. The incapacity to satiate the deep, bottomless desire for meaning need not be regarded as a failure but rather as an indication that these forms are no longer necessary for containing the soul's work or supplying said meaning—which may also be unnecessary.

SIMULATED MYTH

Given the redundancy of myth, perhaps a postmodern myth is not so contradictory after all, and a postmodern psychology can address the question, "how to live, given what we know" without relying on myth. To some extent "myth" is dropped. Its expendable status is revealed in the looking to outer, surface, depthless images for value and a meaning that need no further travel beyond their own aesthetic play. One postmodern Jungian theorist, Christopher Hauke, writes that even as the simulacrum has replaced the real, one can nonetheless experience value in that. He uses Princess Diana as an example, a woman whose life and even more, her death, generated tremendous public response. "No original [of Diana] had ever existed" for the millions who mourned her, "but the postmodern subject 'discovers' affect through the image, imagining that they are feeling for a person 'behind' the image" (69). Although it may appear as if the infiltration and influence of Hollywood and Disneyland in redefining culture shows no shortage of affect, for the postmodern, such massive displays of feeling indicate that these feelings are not "readily available to the fragmented, decentred subject" (68). The simulated Princess Diana provides a blank screen on which humanity can project certain qualities otherwise felt to be lost. But the affect is phony. It needs the simulation to be experienced because there is nothing substantial to contain it. Instead affect is the empty adoration of a personage whose realness held little interest or value to the collective. The collective worship of Diana was predicated on a romantic fantasy, a fairy tale, but in a postmodern world, the fantasy is enough. "Fantasy is more real than reality. [. . .] We hardly dare face our bewilderment, because the solace of belief in contrived reality is so thoroughly real" (Daniel Boorstin; see Kearney 252).

In postmodernity, the point is to stick with the simulation because the original does not exist (although only really "sticking" with it until another image entices). But in needing to point expressly to the original's nonexistence, one clings to the *idea* of the original nonetheless. The simulation is itself deceptive and deceived (more like a bad relation to the original than something wholly other). Although the subject has died, leaving behind an empty shell of an image that must suffice, rather than sloughing off the shell like a dead skin, the simulated image is made virtuous, infused with the hope that the simulation can be more than a contrivance or strong feeling. But the good news for postmodernists is that the death of the subject and the ego as constructs signals the end of an "individual subjectivity as a self-sufficient field and a closed realm in its own right, [. . .] condemn[ed] to the windless solitude of the monad, buried alive and condemned to a prison-cell without egress" (Fredric Jameson, qtd. in Hauke: 67). A purely unique individuality may be an impossible fantasy, but the demise of subjectivity ushers in a liberation from ego constraints and a connection with the world at large. The world connection may currently be held predominantly by emotionalism, sentimentalism, tourism, and escapism—industrialized affect—rather than the unemotionality and sobriety characteristic of a formerly ritualized culture. Yet inasmuch as postmodern consciousness deems *play* as the dynamic force behind the shifting of perspectives, the simulated substitute can easily and without reproach stand in for the function of the real (see Schenk 9; Derrida, *Writing* 289).

This is a time of "hyper-reflexivity," Hauke says, where the fish are "aware, for the first time, of the water they inhabit" (74). Consciousness is no longer predicated on the connection or mediation between pairs of binary oppositions, nor is it defined by making something concretely unknown concretely known. "Perhaps there is no 'something else,' something lost or unconscious, that is 'freed' or 'recovered' or 'discovered' by the process of fostering greater consciousness. Perhaps this process of greater consciousness [. . .] is the 'freed' thing itself. [. . .] The process is *it*: conscious awareness's 'aim' is the 'achievement' of itself: consciousness expressing itself" (78–79). Thus, whatever pathologies are wrought by mythlessness need not be fixed or seen through to some other deeper, psychological meaning; they are necessary as they are. Hauke suggests that difficult postmodern phenomena, such as "mass homogenization, superficiality, loss of [personal] affect, distance and selfhood," are evidently what it is required by consciousness to manifest itself (79). And it is this act of noticing that is the fulfillment of consciousness; the act is complete unto itself and requires no curative therapies. Moving toward the fictitious and simulated nature of things thus does not have to be regarded as a shallow dependence on a contrived meaning. Rather it is an accurate reflection of the unknown and inevitable alienation of human experience. This approach does not ask that unbridgeable distances between text and experience, event and meaning, be bridged by myth or even mythopoesis. The task is to leave the gaps as they are, to recognize the limits of representation and the impossibility of original knowledge without pessimistically and passively yielding to it or trying to amend it.

For Hauke, problems raised by the postmodern condition are not the issue, but the "psychological activity in response to it, is" (79). A postmodern depth psychology, necessitated by the gaps between experience and representation, precludes complacency or a nihilistic attitude in the face of fictions and interpretations that can never fully grasp reality precisely because it moves toward and stays with the unknown. It is this willingness to "work within a paradigm of not knowing," with the unconscious and unconscious processes, that creates a connection between depth psychology and postmodernism (201). Hauke makes a distinction between the erroneous representation of the unconscious as a concrete entity (which implies a something and is therefore not entirely unknown) and an absolute not-knowing—which "requires the concept of the unconscious" but is not to be identified with the concept (205). The realization that there is no "ultimate explanatory principle" dissolves the presumed authority and transcendence of that which proves to be little more than ideology (Kugler, "The Unconscious" 316). But it leaves in its wake a simulated meaning that, having sacrificed certainty, nonetheless permits a play of images to display a meaning that means nothing more beyond its display (and is still allowed to be called "meaning"). But as it is with mythopoesis, where the creating of the story supersedes the story told, the replacement of the real by the display need not interfere with living experience. One need not be unduly threatened by the abyss; texts and images may mask the unknown, but if everything is essentially a mask, with each one only able to reveal another mask behind it, then use the mask, postmodernism says. No matter if the image as mask "has no relation to reality whatsoever," as Jean Baudrillard states, for reality itself has become entirely questionable, thus precluding the need for a truthful representation (6).

On the surface, Hauke's view of consciousness rings true: he seems to accept that "this is it." There is little to alter or suppress or resist because whatever is happening is "a necessity and essential to the manifestation of consciousness" (79). But Hauke's notion of consciousness is empty. Awareness is not specified or deepened; it is content to reside in the hall of mirrors erected by postmodern thought. This would not be so troublesome were it not for the lingering concern for an original, concealed in talk of its impossibility and in the concerted efforts *not* to resist the gaps in knowledge. It is as if he offers a postmodern depth psychology as reassurance, something to hold onto amid the unknown. But having something to hold onto is not only counter to postmodernism, it is also a grasping for something that is simultaneously denied (or at least deconstructed) within postmodern thought—meaning. The reassurance of a postmodern depth psychology is itself founded on an illusory idea of truth that is content to remain as little more than a play of fictions or rejected truth. A postmodern depth psychology has already relinquished the psychological task of seeing all the way through to what lies *behind* rejected truth, beyond the no longer tenable dichotomy of "true" and "false."

According to Hauke, in order to ensure that the postmodern condition not be viewed as a shallow or empty consequence of humankind's evolution, and to assert value and credibility to a constant fluctuating of perspectives, history has to be dislocated (25ff). What was previously held to be incontrovertibly real is rewritten, or more precisely, *un*written, in the attempt to unearth what in a concrete, historical manifestation remained hidden. The deconstructive move toward shifting hierarchical structures, such as the former privileging of masculine over feminine, rationality over irrationality, literal over metaphorical, and so forth, demands that history itself be regarded as just another perspective. Adhering to a strictly historical view is prone to an "over-rigid imposition of an historical grid on human life as if there were not many other ways of thinking about what is going on in contemporary society" (Hauke 25). The displacement of history is an attempt to experience "difference in equality—rather than superiority and inferiority in opposition" (Adams 235). It intends to affirm the validity of the "other," but it is an other that does not neatly fit into a static, a priori category. What is other, such as the unspoken voices of those who have been dominated and subjugated or one's disowned psychological material, is also always in flux, necessitating its own unraveling as it is comprehended.

However, in my view, the loss of history leaves a cocoon in its place, a bubble floating through space, just like the free-floating signifiers spoken of in deconstructive philosophy. To lose history is to lose the soul's history, the cultural realization of consciousness, and the cadences of myth—even if myth is timeless. Depth and authenticity are forsaken, and one grounding still available is renounced in favor of a view that tries to be as aware, all encompassing, and politically fair as possible. But in the process, the firmness, necessity, and inescapability that come not only with affirming one's place in history, but also through the mere fact of living through it, are relinquished so that if it is not quite anything goes, then at least almost anything can be rewritten, and as long as the unknown is held supreme, anything is possible. The postmodern gaps do not *want* to become embodied and cannot be embodied as long as emphasis repeatedly returns to the unseeable, unknowable layer behind, underneath, above, infusing and coloring any permanent attempt at representation. Though postmodern Jungians do not render inessential or impossible an active engagement with the concrete (and historical) world, consciousness depends on unconsciousness. Consciousness is founded on an "embodied, intentional ambiguousness," an absent-presence that does not shun knowing or direct, visceral experience, but retains the limitations inherent in the endeavor (Schenk 45).

Whereas postmodern philosophy leans toward the deconstructive moves of deliteralizing and dislocating, a postmodern depth psychology maintains the possibility of meaning, even as the meaning is momentarily deferred. "[P]ostmodern culture—for all the accusations of its addiction to the image, its losses of history, the subject and a critical distance—is also expressing passionate concern for the refinding of human values, for *rebirth*: not in terms of modernity and 'what went before' [. . .] but in terms as yet unknown, in language as yet unspoken" (Hauke 49–50). Despite the ostensible willingness to be with current phenomena as they are, with little need to endow them with a deeper layer of meaning, talk of "rebirth" not only denies the death of the subject, it also betrays the restorative effort. It reveals the hope that something else can and will come to impart a new beginning for humanity, a new life emerging from the ashes. Except the new, as of yet unknown life is not entirely new; it is the hope for reclaiming, however disguised, something not irretrievably lost. Hauke does not use the word *myth* in this context, but his words speak directly to the sentiment expressed by those who acutely feel the loss of myth in current times. He writes, "Postmodern views offer depth psychology the chance to restore its Otherness, its spiritual and religious element which was always the ground from which it sprang but which became lost through depth psychology clinging to, rather than continuing to challenge, the modernist values within which it emerged" (209). He stresses that "what is at stake is a certain Otherness," which need not necessarily be attached to God or the gods, but, by virtue of being other than an egocentric consciousness, somehow possesses a religious element (209).

Here is another equivocation: Hauke wants to be postmodern but does not want to accept the loss that goes with it, preferring instead to nullify the postmodern logic in psychology's attempted "resacralization of culture" (Andrew Samuels, qtd. by Hauke: 209). This is akin to archetypal psychology's polytheistic approach, wherein the gods are mere metaphors, psychological tools for illuminating plurality that nonetheless warrant reverence and respect. Whether one thinks of the divine as a quality or an entity, a poetic image or a transcendent reality, one is still attached to the divine even as it is purportedly cancelled. The postmodern allowance for an Other that may or may not be sacred but by its sheer quality of otherness *is* sacred in and of itself, just enough, manages to mitigate both the power of the unknown *and* the gods. One can't have it both ways. For the death of God and God to exist simultaneously, both psychological realities are diffused and confused, assuredly leaving what Boorstin called a bewilderment that can barely be faced. Moreover, the focus on a simulated affect indicates that whatever gods are believed to be still roaming this world are also simulated. If the simulacrum is all there is, there is no reason for the divine. It seems as if the yearning for God is so desperately unfulfilled that everything and nothing is sacred anymore; the blurring of history's edges combined with a dissolving of realities turning contemporary culture into a no man's land. Hauke ends his book by quoting art critic Arjen Mulder, who in commenting on painter David Salle writes, "Whatever science and technology say, the immortals have never left us. [. . .] They stolidly guard the continuity of the imagination, whose product they themselves are. The gods are with us. And they want to play." And then Hauke's closing sentence reads, "Let's make sure we are in when they call" (286).

A conspicuous fallacy seals Hauke's book. If the gods are a product of the imagination, one need not worry about being in when they call; one has only to dip into the imagination and conjure them up. Hauke's final statement undermines, in part, the core of his entire argument. An absence of myth, a lack of transcendence is crucial to the postmodern philosophy. This renders its coupling with Jungian psychology problematic. Yes, postmodernism is permissive, the no-space of the "both/and," where the paradox, puns, and plays of language indirectly reveal the truth in a truthless time. But the meaning that issues from such linguistic play is only a semblance of meaning, an aesthetic one in which there is nothing to believe, nothing to hold to as a metaphysical given and commit oneself to, such as it was when meaning inhabited the earth. "Appearance itself is all that is necessary when perceived through the aesthetic eye unmediated by concept" (Schenk 58). Sticking to the image may elucidate and elaborate the image and offer some sort of meaning on its own terms, but there is little at stake and little to fear. It is said, "It is a terrible thing to fall into the hands of the living God" (*New Testament*, Hebrews 10:31).[11] Gods that play are like god-lite, a watered-down version of what was once worshipped and feared in deep conviction but now are supposed to laugh along with (or at) the rest of us at the impossibility of such a conviction today. When a postmodernism psychology attempts to claim for itself a transcendent meaning out of a simulated one, its psychology can only be an inflated one, its gaps sanctified not by God's grace but by hot air. Expectation or hope of rebirth sounds as if a postmodern depth psychology is the secret way to a new myth, a contradiction even postmodernism cannot swallow without choking on its own backbone.

Both postmodern depth psychologists and proponents of mythopoesis seem to say that it is naïve and perhaps even dangerous to assume that one can still be completely and unthinkingly immersed in myth—but it is equally naïve and dangerous to think that one can completely escape myth. Whether its fragments hover in the gaps, waiting to be remembered or reborn or mourned; whether it subsists as a pale reflection of what it once was or lingers only in an individual's imagination, myth, from a postmodern perspective, demands rather than precludes a sophisticated level of reflection and interpretation. Not simply composed of metaphorical images, myth has become the metaphor. A postmodern myth knows that even if the question of meaning is not meant to be and cannot ever be resolved, it can at least creatively and authentically as possible display the loss of meaning in such a way so that it becomes much more. Postmodern myth may be a placeholder for nothing substantial, only unanswerable questions (about origins, identity, etc.) that become further adrift in an infinite labyrinth where the resounding echoes of these questions become the only thing tenable. But if such a myth is a placeholder barely covering a direct passageway into the abyss, postmodernism seems to show that it is no more or less a placeholder than anything else. Perhaps it is a more appealing substitute, and one more inclined to be mistaken for an embodied rather than a vacuous depth, as depth psychologists are apt to believe. Yet whether absence paves the way to myth or myth is a denial of the absence, "absence" and "myth" are now inextricably linked, thus making it difficult outwardly to refute *any* absence (or presence) of myth. And the only way to sustain the paradox of both having and not having myth is to enter the gaps—but not a gap devoid of myth. It is the gap as threshold, as a permanent transitional or in-between space where the transparency of myth is not seen as an overlay blocking experience, but rather a gateway into a metaphorical, poetic dwelling.

THE PROBLEM OF THE IN-BETWEEN

The three schools of thought I have introduced in this chapter (mythopoesis, archetypal psychology, postmodern depth psychology) each contribute toward the argument for myth's sustained presence in a demythologized world. One area in which the theories could be said to intersect is the in-between spaces or gaps, which serve as the "foundation" for current myth, when all other foundations have disintegrated. Accordingly, to give myth the benefit of the doubt, the vitality, necessity, and inescapability of the gaps have been repeatedly underscored throughout this chapter. And yet on closer examination, the fluidity of the in-between spaces may not be as fluid as it appears. In deference to an unbridled tolerance and ambiguity, the play actually freezes in the no-space it means dartingly to navigate, ultimately unable to follow its own parameters. The depth psychological recourse to myth and the postmodern reworking of history and fantasizing about reality, a "looking backwards in order to look forwards" (Hauke 32), creates a pivot where one is essentially standing still, only able to make half circular motions. Perhaps that is its purpose. Patricia Berry contends that even stopping is "a mode of animation"; in the "awe-full image of stopping [stony Medusa] there is a rush of wings [Pegasus]," movement within stasis, insubstantial air within matter (161).

So to say the both/and stance is fixated in its easy allowances under the guise of maintaining a flow—is this not an ego standpoint demanding a kind of linear movement? Such a straightforward position is exactly what practitioners of archetypal and postmodern psychology seek to dislocate and place in a much deeper, infinite context. However, to remain purposively ambiguous to keep the flow eventually becomes a stopping that cannot be redeemed by its inner animation. It is like a withdrawal in which one sticks rather to a clear, gelatinous mass at the expense of making a decision, aiming for an answer, and making a point that isn't defined by its lack of being a point. Ambiguity and infinite open-mindedness blunt the piercing, generative vitality of any assertion while securing it from reactivity and opposition when it hedges behind the both/and. Myth itself has receded and become immune from criticism in that it can successfully stand in and argue for whatever is desired of it. Although a kaleidoscopic, virtual reality may be the predominant or favored reality in this wired culture, it nonetheless cannot delete the specificity and pointedness of the human being, or undermine the capacity and necessity for human thought and reflection. Even as the psyche is objective and autonomous, "a life that is its own end," it still "lives through us and needs us to give expression to it" (Giegerich, "Opposition" 24). The individual may be psychologically obsolete, but at the positive, empirical level, one still needs to live his or her life.

By no means does archetypal or postmodern psychology evade reflective processes or discount subjectivity. But the dilemma ensues when a polytheistic perspective tries to have it both (or all) ways—and subsequently ends up having it no way. Credibility knows no bounds or definition as every assertion has multiple addendums and contradictions, other layers that differ from but also enhance their precursor. Resistance is futile because resistance itself loses its edges when it dissolves into whatever it was resisting, precipitating a dynamic play and merging between the two that supposedly reveals a fuller, more complex meaning. But the contents of the psychological process meant to convey this are diluted. If, for example, one reads possibility and meaning into expressions of meaninglessness, such as Hauke's vision of rebirth, then the predicament is no longer so dire. The force of the meaninglessness is subdued as its own contents leak out of a back door that may instinctively recoil from such stark negativity but nevertheless traps the individual in a false sense of security, insidiously and mistakenly led to believe meaning is on its way. This circularity of postmodern thought is misleading. Although it may seem as if its openness repeatedly guides thought and experience back into itself for further interpretation or extrication, it is a circularity that remains open. Its logic rests on a partial negativity that serially seeks to undo unity, endlessly moving from one meaning to the next as it embraces a purposeful fragmentation. Even an "affirmative postmodernism" that does not discard universals cannot abide by any center for too long because the center keeps moving. The task is precisely to "discover and rediscover the boundaries between the unchangeable and the changeable in our lives" (Young-Eisendrath, *Gender* 90).

At the end of the previous chapter, the individual was left barely suspended on a tightrope, helplessly surrounded by negativity in the form of a loss of meaning and myth, the negative, discerning process required for psychological self-awareness, and the hard-not-to-feel personally negativity underlying deconstruction's "death of the subject." And in the impossibility, double binding of it all, the paralysis and impotence that accompanies the realization of 'not-I,' as Samuel Beckett expressed, the individual is empirically alive but psychologically, subjectively still yet to be born. "Assassinated before my birth," Beckett felt (Juliet 10). Postmodernism may indeed accurately show the fallacies inherent in trying to settle on any answers and assert one's authority, but the psychological consequences are such that the individual process of being born is thwarted. One's necessary subjectivity is subsumed under a philosophy that can never allow containment and thus never permit any psychological process to complete itself. As Thomas Ogden writes, "The dialectical process is centrally involved in the creation of subjectivity. [. . .] [T]he capacity for degrees of self-awareness ranging from intentional self-reflection [. . .] to the most subtle, unobtrusive sense of 'I-ness' by which experience is subtly endowed with the quality that one is thinking one's thoughts and feeling one's feelings" (208–09). But when the dialectical process gives way to incessant difference, deferral, and disunity, it precludes any sustained and contained connection of opposites. Subjectivity is obstructed such that there cannot be an "I," no here I stand, no fully being born unto oneself. Resting on an absent center, the "I" that would otherwise recognize itself in opposition to what is "not-I" then identifies with the not-I. And when confronted with an unavoidable absence that threatens to overwhelm, that "not-I," it becomes much safer and easier to turn to the in-between spaces, where the feelings of an invisible, meaningful depth lend purpose to one's nebulous existence. But the price for this meaning is such that by lingering in the gaps, the individual has little chance or reason to become an individual, to form that "I."

Another contemporary Jungian theorist, Donald Kalsched, writes, "We prefer not to think about genuine pathology in some branches of Jungian psychology. We would rather talk about the importance of 'pathologizing'—its potential 'meaning'" ("Hermes-Mercurius" 115). The pathology he is specifically referring to is attributed to those individuals who are stuck in in-betweenness, lost in a dissociated fantasy state, "which is neither imagination, nor living in external reality, but a kind of melancholic self-soothing compromise which goes on forever—a defensive use of the imagination" (106). Kalsched's patients use fantasy to deny and rewrite their painful histories (similar to the postmodern move), but their prolonged retreat into an inner world, which once provided a numbing but protective care, proves to be self-sabotaging and immobilizing when they attempt to engage with the real world. These individuals cannot hope for healing by sticking to the image because their capacity for imagination has no grounding, not even the grounding of their own life history. Choosing to live in limbo, Kalsched writes, such individuals fear and avoid an inner *coniunctio oppositorium*, a joining of the opposites that helps the individual individuate and come into one's self. The split-off fragments must not be allowed to return to consciousness so that the individual can come into his own because there is no strong enough ego-self that can contain the return of the repressed (104). And the paradox these individuals suffer is that while they carry out the basics of living, they also carry with them their unlived lives—a paradox or tension of the opposites that never achieves reconciliation, never finds transcendence, and experiences the gaps as permanently unbridgeable.[12]

This "genuine pathology" discussed by Kalsched, the self-annihilating and dismembering powers he finds operative in individuals, carries a certain applicability to the postmodern fascination with and near idolatry of the in-between spaces. It speaks to the reluctance to leave the realm of potentiality and enter reality, to *exist*. It speaks to the mythopoetic rewriting of the real, a lingering in an imaginative state of being or mind that is split off from the literal and, moreover, cannot abide by the literal because that would depotentiate the imaginative. Thus, the creative potential turns inward, heedless of the ordinary and the concrete. One remains unaware of the stopping and withdrawal from reality caused by this splitting between the imaginal and the literal, which leaves the individual (or the theory) lost in the ethers or perhaps the underworld where some may say it is tracking the pulse of the soul. Even so, in moving away from a stifling literalizing and an overbearing ego toward the shades and subtleties of the invisible realm, another literalization edges its way to the forefront. For the dissoluteness and deconstructive tendencies of the gaps become literalized to the extent that one cannot or does not want to get out.

Yet why concern oneself with subjectivity and being born if the prevailing philosophy has declared the death of the subject and psychology has unseated the ego from center stage? Because from both a psychological and philosophical perspective, that is, objectively and logically, being born is already happening; it is just taking time before it is noticed. In the same passage proclaiming the death of God, Nietzsche wrote, "This tremendous event is still on its way, still wandering—it has not yet reached the ears of man. Lightning and thunder require time, the light of the stars requires time, deeds require time even after they are done, before they can be seen and heard" (96). Just because it will take a long time for humankind to realize the psychological and philosophical consequences of the death of the God does not mean it did not logically happen. It does not mean that the individual is not without its own obligation to come into one's self. Part of the process of realizing the death of God *is* to be psychologically born. The events are inextricably linked. One can no longer remain an innocent bystander, dependent on the gods. And ever since the late eighteenth and the nineteenth century marked the beginning of the extrication from a dependence on nature and the move toward the controlling and production of nature, humankind has indicated that it does not even want, let alone need, the gods. Although to be less subjective, it would be more precise to say that the soul or world, objective reality, has already shown that the gods are no longer necessary for living.

Even so, it is probably safe to assume that few in Western civilizations would in fact want anything outside of oneself to dictate what to do, notwithstanding any New Age resurgences in surrendering to a higher power. The American Dream, which can tailor itself to incorporate any spiritual rebirth, still operates on the belief that one can determine one's life however one chooses; given the opportunity and resources, once can easily rewrite the old life into something new. But the discrepancy, especially apparent in spiritual revivalist tendencies, is revealed when humanity lives like there are no gods—but nonetheless finds ways to cling to them, or to the idea of them. Living as if there are no gods but otherwise wanting them creates another double bind that is unnecessary but sets up a default whereby one has little recourse but to fall into the gaps. Here it becomes impossible to accept both unconditional presence

(I am here, I must make my own decisions) and absolute absence, exemplified in the inclination to piece fragments together in order to mitigate the effects of a fundamental rupture, the death of God.

The inability truly to be with absence, contrary to the postmodern repeated return to the unknown, can also be evidenced in the popular death culture, which has seen a proliferation of "how to die" books, lessons that would not be needed unless absence was generally avoided or feared.[13] The main intent of such books, though, is how to live. The hope is that if one can act as if every day were the last one, one's life would be richer and more meaningful. It is like trying to learn how to live with an absence of myth through absence—but again with the back door that such a route will lead back to myth. There is an artificiality or pretense to books whose authors try to instill the message that one should act as if one has one year to live, as one author (Levine) recently undertook because, once again, it sends a different kind of message, namely, that an average, ordinary life is not enough. Life itself is withdrawn from reality in order to infuse the life of such books. (Would one truly want to spend one's final days reading books on how to spend those days?) Furthermore, for some it is not so easy suddenly to snap out of a stupor and turn one's unlived life into a fully lived one, which is what authors who make it a point to remind one of one's mortality mean to incite.

Perhaps the how to live and die movement does perceive the stuckness of the both/and, and in recognizing the ghostly subsistence of many tries to push them in a solid direction. Yet this overlooks the fact that many choose to remain in the gaps, choose to leave every option open, preferring not to be born, only partially to exist. To the extent that one stays heartened by potential and defers entering reality, then one will naturally find comfort and perhaps an imaginary salvation in myth, but it is a salvation with little substance to save. On the surface, the individual wants meaning, wants to feel alive, but becomes enwrapped and trapped by a yearning so infatuated with itself that it does not recognize its emptiness. It is a yearning that cannot see there is nothing answering it.

Postmodern or mythopoetic myth is no less of a ghost, its traces no more than whispery tendrils trying to wrap itself around an absent past while groping for a present it cannot completely grasp. When myth is the both/and, it, too, is not quite alive and not quite dead. An absent presence or present absence is just another way to talk about ghosts—which is precisely the point. Cultivating a mythic consciousness today encourages a deathly living and embraces the living dead, joining the extreme opposites of life and death into a "poetic basis of mind" that straddles the opposites without overstretching (Hillman, *Archetypal* 14). The "sickness," says Berry, "is not knowing the ghost, not hearing its echoing insubstantiality in language [. . .]. Reality *is* equivocal" (137, 139). Using Shakespeare's *Hamlet* as her template, Berry expounds the archetypal psychological need for the spaces, for the ghosts, created by the poisoning, plays and double meanings of language. Psychological work is "secured by a half-visible presence, a deeper ground with darker demands" and if the psychological is any "thing" at all, she writes, it is a mythopoetic re-making that "is at once a remembering in service of the ghost" (145). Similarly, David Miller uses ghosts as a means of talking about the ineffable, the "other-worldly" that is also "this-worldly," the postmodern Other, "whether in the form of 'meaning,' 'God,' 'truth', beauty,' or 'goodness' [. . . that] defers forever in the repetitions of its account the blessed assurance of resting in a fixated end" (*Hells and Holy Ghosts* 176, 187).

Both Miller and Berry are concerned with a psychological burying of the dead, which is actually a remembering of the ghost (or myth, insofar as one holds to the equation of mythology and psychology). There can be no real, final resting for this ghost. Not only must the liminal quality of the in-between spaces be prevented from becoming either too opaque or negated, but also the work is never done; there is always more to remember, more to see. Thus, a "proper burial" is one that, for example, unearths repressed psychological content while an "improper burial" can ensue when one holds tightly to an "objectively fixated egoic reality," not knowing when something has died, or at least needs to be loosened from its fixations (Miller, *Hells and Holy Ghosts* 157–58). Then the improper burial actually becomes a forgetting, having forgotten that some remembrances are harmful when unhesitatingly believed in. The kind of burial that buries egoic fixations so that deeper layers of psychological insight can be unearthed necessitates a mythic perspective. It is the mythopoetic move that is able to break through literal barriers and descend into the depths for a deeper and more soulful understanding. In this regard, the problem previously

alluded to, that of using myth to bury a myth, might not be so problematic if, by burial, one actually means remembering, a salvaging
of the remains of myth and the gods from literalistic fallacies.
Then, of course, it is appropriate to revert to a mythic perspective,
for what better to mirror myth than a mythic frame of mind?

Yet to the degree that this kind of remembering intentionally
points to invisible presences of something still alive, an integration
or completion of a psychic process is still required to bring it into
consciousness, to fully "remember" the invisible influence. It is not
enough to perceive the mythic ghosts, the traces of the gods, and
then extol their presence. Archetypal psychology's reluctance
toward closure and clarity ensures that the ghost remains ghostly,
but if the ghost is left lingering, it remains a semispiritual, objectified existence—and nothing happens. In his *Memories*, Jung wrote,
"It has always seemed to me that I had to answer questions which
fate had posed to my forefathers, and which had not yet been
answered, or as if I had to complete, or perhaps continue, things
which previous ages had left unfinished" (233). Insofar as the cultivation of a mythic consciousness becomes the goal, the questions
the dead leave behind to be answered persist unanswered because
what has died is not allowed to remain dead. To use Miller's
metaphor, the dead have not been properly buried; we have not
remembered the deeper psychological layer of the end of myth and
death of God. And without a proper burial for what has died (such
as the gods), there is no allowing for the psychological insight to
take hold and penetrate the living. Thus, whatever questions the
dead have remain in limbo as well, neither belonging to the living
nor able to be set to rest, and subsequently unable to progress or
give way to the next generation of consciousness. "Remember me"
cries the Ghost in *Hamlet*, as Slochower reminds us (329). But when
remembering the ghost means remembering it precisely *as* a ghost,
not quite belonging to any realm, it is a betrayal of the in-between.
Neither material nor spiritual, but a little bit of both. And one kind
of final resting or literal burial gives way to a resting in the gaps that
in resisting the literal, becomes no less fixated in its imaginative
stance. It is a halting that stands at but refuses to cross the threshold into soul.

Lingering traces of the gods could indeed be identified in the
repressed psychic material once contained in the form of the gods.

For example, Kalsched amplifies individual self-sabotage by way of the darker side of Hermes-Mercurius. Hermes is usually found at the boundaries and border crossings, mediating between worlds above and below as a psychopomp or "accompanier of souls." But in his diabolical side, he does the opposite of mediating or bringing together. He "tears apart" (the Greek *dia-bollein*); he tries to dissolve the inner world "in altered states of oblivion in order to keep it away from unbearable anxiety" (95). Addictions depict one such state of oblivion. The trace of the god, in this case, would be found in uncovering an aspect of self-sabotage in one's compulsive eating or alcohol bingeing ("inner murder") and connecting it with the image of the diabolical Mercurius. By amplifying sabotage by way of the archetype, one literally gets a bigger, richer picture of sabotage.

No doubt, a conscious remembering of the ghost or trace of the god understands the danger inherent in repressing psychic material and aims for integration, even if the remembrance falls short into the gaps. We would want to "remember" the black Hermes-Mercurius so that we could understand more fully and recognize the quality of sabotage without unconsciously identifying with or repeatedly enacting it. The images of the god teach us, and, in this respect, it is necessary to unearth the trace (the quality of sabotage), lest it stay forgotten or become hardened. But there is a different sort of danger; namely, when it is the gods themselves who are imagined to be prematurely buried underground as opposed to the psychic realities formerly connected to them. Bringing back the ghost (remembering the god) then becomes another disguised move toward unconsciousness when some sort of divine, concrete entity (no matter if only partially or invisibly embodied, just a trace) is brought back into consciousness *along with* the psychological insight. Mercurius is no longer a god in his own right; Mercurius is now an image and a placeholder, more of a shorthand that helps to explain a particular psychological complexity. Kalsched's discussion of the diabolical side of Mercurius is not intended literally to revive the god. It is to amplify what self-sabotage means by way of this particular image. Though I think proponents of archetypal psychology would say they are doing the same thing, there is the tendency to act as if Mercurius as a psychological shorthand means that Mercurius as a god still lives. This is what I think muddles the whole issue. It is the way to have it both ways, to have both mythic meaning *and* the psychological insight that comes with seeing through the myth. But when we try to have it both ways, the psychological insight is blunted and whatever meaning is found is bound to disappoint because it cannot be sustained by anything outside of one's personal, usually ego-inspired proclivities.

Perhaps the problem lies in the inability or unwillingness to let the ghost die and accept the severance once and for all, to understand the death of God on its own terms without turning it into egocentric ammunition against polytheism. If the unwillingness to bury the ghost is the case, then the ghostliness of the in-between spaces becomes a necessary receptacle—the *only* receptacle—that can contain this equivocal view of reality. Only a shifty and shifting realm could hold the fragments together without irrevocably succumbing to a nonmeaningful madness.

The gaps can be no less a cocoon than an unquestioning belief in myth, and more insidious of a trap when one believes there is no need to get out. One remains cocooned in the idea, in the imagined freedom and luxury of imagination. One is seduced by the divine quality of the invisible, unfathomable mysteriousness of the gaps. In the space where paradox rules, one has one's gods and one's self, too. God may be dead, but one can find comfort in searching through the cracks in the ground for the surviving pieces and cradle them in one's arms, believing that one is still being cradled in turn. A postmodern myth may strive to free the myth from ideology and superior claims to an unrelenting truth while not forsaking a universal continuity to human existence. But even this move cannot deny that in an infinite deferral or possibility of meaning, there is nothing for the myth to refer to anymore. Whatever traces tracked by the poets then show themselves to be nothing more than traces of fossilized gods or echoes of our own humanity.

CHAPTER 4

The Negation of Myth

God may be dead, and his traces may lead to little more than a dead, mirroring end—but this doesn't mean that God has fully disappeared. What I am referring to is the idea of "God" that still manages to serve as a placeholder for the *telos* of human consciousness, even in a demythologized world. Though this God can be referred to using other terms, such as presence, wholeness, Source, Spirit, Being, the point is, to steal a phrase from Heidegger, "Something other reigns" (qtd. in Knowles: 294). This reigning "other" has propelled numerous discourses, distinct in their methodology and content, but bound by the attempt to root out some purpose to human—though non-ego centered—existence and find cause for faith. Setting myth aside momentarily, I would like briefly to cite a few examples from recent Western thought.

GOD AFTER "THE DEATH OF GOD"

Existential Theology

Paul Tillich exhorts the modern mind to think of the "God above God."[1] That is, modern humanity must think through the emptiness and anxiety attributed to the death of God as well as the concept of God that dies and leaves nothing behind in order to reach that level of being that transcends theism and the duality of I/thou or subject/object. Without transcending the God of theism, God is seen as "a being, not being-itself. As such he is bound to the subject-object structure of reality, he is an object for us as subjects.

At the same time we are objects for him as a subject" (184–85). This, Tillich argues, deprives individuals of their complete subjectivity, incites an unsuccessful revolt against the tyranny of an objectified, all-knowing God, promotes anxiety and the pervasive sense of meaninglessness, and ultimately prohibits an authentic encounter between God [being] and man. But when one summons the "courage to be" (apprehends the God above God) from *within* the meaninglessness, for as Tillich says, "Even in the state of despair one has enough being to make despair possible," then one meets God in absolute faith (177). "The decisive absence of faith is resolute faith," wrote Georges Bataille (*Absence* 48). The "God above God," the God who invokes little faith, is the God who has not been codified into definitive belief laden with undue expectations and therefore clears the way (a *via negativa* of sorts) for a state of being that can fully affirm life as it is.

Existential Philosophy

Martin Heidegger's notion of Being similarly strives to reach, or more precisely, to *think* that state of being preceding all existence, a groundless ground that exists beyond the constricting subject-object bifurcation and presents (unconceals) a mysterious whole always already present. "[W]e should [. . .] equip ourselves and make ready for one thing only: to experience in Nothing the vastness of that which gives every being the warrant to be" (*Existence* 353). This Nothing is not to be confused with the nihilistic anxiety and despair Tillich perceived to be infecting humankind's spiritual life. Rather, it is a "*fundamentum concussum,* a bottomless abyss—a Nothing that contains Everything" (Knowles 325). Though any confident foundation for truth may have been wrested from human apprehension, truth as *aletheia* (unconcealment or unhiddenness) is secured nonetheless. The relationship between Being and Nothing carves the way for other, hidden truths to present themselves: the unsaid, unseen, and unrealized—the formless that precedes every form.

Depth Psychology

C. G. Jung's psychology project, with his notions of wholeness, individuation, Self, Transcendental Function, *Mysterium Coniunctionis,*

Unus Mundus, and synchronicity, to name a few examples, is also intended to attain a level of unity or totality of self and world that engenders a being-in-the-world not limited by dualistic and ego-biased thinking and experiencing. Jung's usage of the term *psychoid* corresponds to the formless or Nothing as it "cannot be directly perceived or 'represented,' in contrast to the perceptible psychic phenomena" ("Synchronicity," *CW* 8, sec. 840). This level of the psychoid or objective psyche cannot be circumscribed by any boundary, yet it permeates all of psychic life. It "refers to a postulated level of unity prior to the differentiation of what we experience separately as matter and spirit. The psychoid contains a level of the archetype in its unknowable 'suchness'" (Corbett 113). Though Jung spoke less of God and more of the God-*image*, Jung's psychology project may be seen, as Corbett argues, as "pure theology or speculative metaphysics and not practical psychology [. . .] in spite of Jung's disclaimers" (174).

Postmodern Theology

Thomas J. J. Altizer argues that the death of God is a necessary precondition for experiencing the ever-present, ever-renewing moment of Being. "The death of God, which brings to an end the transcendence of being, the beyondness of eternity, makes Being manifest in every Now" ("Eternal" 243). The Kingdom of God is at hand, on earth, but only after belief in a sovereign, transcendent God has been abjured. Embracing with an unequivocal "yes" Nietzsche's eternal return brings humankind down to earth as well, into its own body and subjectivity. At the same time, subjectivity is surpassed in that as one experiences and accepts the world in exquisite presence, all preconceptions of meaning stemming from a dualistic perspective (e.g., subject-object split) dissolve. "[Y]es-saying delights in the resurrection of the brute reality of things" (244). But the "brute reality" need not always be experienced as brutish, for total affirmation and embodiment amid the negation of God have the power to usher in an utter love for existence as it is—precisely because it is life as such. This is assuming, however, that one possesses the will and courage to say yes to *everything*. "All things are entangled, ensnared, enamored; if you ever wanted one thing twice, if you said, 'You please me, happiness! Abide, moment!' then you wanted *all* back. All anew, all eternally, all entangled, ensnared, enamored—oh, then you *loved* the world" (Nietzsche, *Zarathustra*, "The Drunken Song," sec. 9–10; qtd. in Altizer, "Eternal" 244–45). Joy cannot be isolated from sorrow; we cannot be isolated from the world.

New Age Spirituality

The propagation of the "do-it-yourself" spiritual movement continues to inspire lay seekers with an accessibility and clarity of ideas loosened from theological doctrine and philosophical abstruseness. Neale Donald Walsch's *Conversations with God* presents an internal dialogue between author and God, who defines Himself as "All that Is *and* All that is Not" (24). God is pure energy; the formless that took multitudinous forms so that God could know Itself through humankind. God reminds Walsch that experience far outweighs the Word of God as a measure of truth and that every statement of *what is so* is a prayer already answered. Eckhart Tolle's *The Power of Now*, drawing on Christianity and Buddhism, teaches readers to know they are not their minds and to engage fully the present. Here, in the Now, one is freed from the vortex of thoughts that attracts psychological suffering as one comes closer to experiencing Being, "the eternal, ever-present One Life beyond the myriad forms of life that are subject to birth and death" (10). Tolle prefers *Being* to *God*, because Being "has the advantage that it is an open concept," unlike the word *God*, which has long been closed (11). And Byron Katie similarly endeavors to free one from suffering-inducing thoughts by prompting one to consider, "Who would you be without your story?" (thework.org; see also Katie's *Loving What Is*).[2]

୭୭

The purpose of this extremely cursory introduction is to try to highlight a consistent and persistent thread in thought and culture; namely, the realization or striving for the realization and experience of a mode of being-in-the-world that embodies a totality of body and mind, soul and spirit. What is desired is the cultivation of an awareness that strives to be free from Cartesian barriers without regressing into a "primitive" mentality. It is the call toward a purer, higher, deeper consciousness, the yearning for consciousness to come home to itself. It is to see fully through the vestiges of the deposed God and the individual ego-self that once stood in contradistinction to God such that what remains is the wonderment of existence itself. Like the Zen parable for enlightenment depicted in the ox-herding woodcuts, one's ordinary life becomes enlivened with a heightened awareness of the self-evident mystery and interconnectedness making life possible to begin with. The expansion of consciousness thus becomes the answer to the question of where meaning is to be found in a culture bereft of transcendental signifieds or signifiers. This meaning is to be found in direct experience and in a self-knowledge that eventually leaves the self behind as one embraces the world, as it is so. Meaning is in the unadulterated presence of "This is it!" and the wordless understanding of a sigh or simple "Yes."[3]

EXCURSUS ON DECONSTRUCTION AND DEPTH PSYCHOLOGY

Even the influence of postmodern thought, particularly the movement known as deconstruction, is not completely at odds with this trajectory of human consciousness, despite deconstruction's requisite deferral of meaning. What the authors cited earlier have in common is the awareness of this pervasive duality in thought and experience, for example, I/thou, subject/object, inner/outer. Through their theories they have tried to overcome this split, to reach a higher level of awareness that is capable of encompassing both sides of binary oppositions. The deconstructive move similarly tries to overcome the opposites, yet rather than remaining bound to Western metaphysics by identifying some overarching construct that can hold the opposites (Being, God, Spirit), the overcoming occurs through dissolution. This dissolution occurs through a dynamic thought process that plays the opposites against each other, rather than move upward to an ontological, all-encompassing source immune from criticism. In deconstruction, one stays committed to the text; one is, in a sense, firmly committed to the ground, even as that ground is decimated beneath one's feet.

Stanley Romaine Hopper is one author who does not see a contradiction between deconstruction and the inclination to reach a presence of Being. In his analysis of deconstruction, he considers Derrida's "text" to "function symbolically like 'Being'" (*Way of Transfiguration* 286). There is nothing outside the text; there is nothing outside of Being. For deconstructionists the dualism inherent in traditional ontotheological thinking may not be overcome in a systematic closure (such as Being), but the problem is bypassed in Derrida's (and Heidegger's) reversal of language, such that "mystery [. . .] is now no longer inscribed within 'being,' but 'Being' is inscribed within 'Language'" (282). The determinacy of the Word is displaced by the infinite openness of word(s). Yet as Hopper notes, "Deconstruction must [. . .] be inscribed within a larger context. [. . .] It cannot be *nothing* that is deferred" (294, 287). The words do not exist in a vacuum; the larger context is psyche and its imagistic or poetic way of communicating. So while a fixated meaning may be deferred, the word itself leaves a certain residual meaning that opens a gateway into what Hopper calls a "psycho-poetics of depth" (290). "[T]he text itself is nothing—a conglomerate of gutteral and labial sounds." But if the words were not already expressions of (placeholders for) a psychic image or truth, there would "be nothing *inside* the text either" (286–87). For Hopper, deconstruction itself is a metaphorical movement in that its serial openness prohibits fixations and evokes "fresh recognitions," but one must not stop there (295). Or, rather, one must stop and look downward and inward, move *through* the words where at bottom sits the abysmal opening to psyche and the presence of Being.

Although "Being" is a metaphysical construct that technically does not exist under the rubric of deconstruction (and as such would indicate that Hopper has modified deconstruction somewhat to fit it against the backdrop of psyche), nonetheless I concur that this philosophy bears some relevancy to what I have been attempting to elucidate: the striving for a deeper, higher, unitary consciousness. Deconstruction's undoing of hierarchical binary oppositions effectuates an opening that, although it may resist being confined and categorized as a "totality" or "*coincidentia oppositorum*," nonetheless contributes to an apprehension *of* the totality that presupposes a union of opposites. "Deconstructive criticism constantly errs along the / of neither/nor." It necessitates "a dialectical inversion that does not leave contrasting opposites unmarked but dissolves their original identities" (Taylor, *Erring* 11, 10). The "neither/nor" carries little of the permissiveness demanded by the "both/and," but they are related just the same.[4] Neither/nor is the other, negative side of the both/and, attached to nothing as the both/and purposively equivocates between everything. Both of these conjunctional maneuvers reside in the margins, in the in-between spaces. Whereas the both/and seeks to apprehend positively the whole of reality, the neither/nor serves as a negative entrance into something that is not a "thing," whose logic already *is* negative.

Being or God is a concept represented or experienced through the manifold, sensuous manifestations of words, images, and phenomena, but the concept itself points to that which is wordless, sense-less and image-less. God is not a "thing," and there have been many testimonies to this. Angelus Silesius said, "God is a pure no-thing, concealed in now and here: the less you reach for him, the more he will appear" (Mitchell 89). Meister Eckhart prayed to God to be free from God. A Buddhist koan says: if you meet the Buddha, kill the Buddha. Accordingly, to move through the concept of "Being" or "God" (or Buddhahood) to its underlying reality or unconcealed presence, one has to enter by way of thought or contemplation, such as what Heidegger termed *Gelassenheit,* the attitude of letting be. This is not to equate thought with one's personal thoughts; the purpose is to reach a state of knowing beyond the Cartesian cogito. The move to thought, such as indicated in the move from *mythos* to *logos* 2500 years ago, represents a move from the objective, splitting of cognition to a subjective unity of knowledge. This is not personal or private subjectivity, but subjectivity as "absolute interiority" (Giegerich). It is the interiorization and knowledge of the utter containment by God or Being; subjectivity in the Hegelian sense, as World Spirit (or as Jung's subjective universe), where "knowledge is knowledge of one subject by another—a calling of deep unto deep" (Eckman 95). It is a kinship between subjects, whether material or psychic, engendered and enlivened by a "reflective recognition and affirmation," really by love.

The deconstructive spin pushes further into this no-thingness so that what must be thought is not the idea or presence of God but the "*unthought.*" Theologian Mark C. Taylor takes Tillich to task for failing to think this unthought or "the *difference* between Being and beings."[5] Taylor contends that the notion of the God above God still remains committed to the God of the ontotheological tradition, a tradition generally understood to have foreclosed. Even when God is transposed from *a* being to the power of Being, such as in Tillich's interpretation, "God is affirmed even in our most radical denials" (*Tears* 83). But if God has died or Western metaphysics has reached its logical cessation, then what requires consideration is the "*impossibility* of presence." This does not portend total absence, but rather a presence that cannot be represented and, as Taylor suggests, cannot be thought either (84). The Parousia is deferred, but what is present and available (and necessary, for Taylor) is the traversing, plunging into, stumbling, and erring along those in-between spaces. Unlike some of the postmodern depth psychologists discussed in chapter 3, Taylor abides by the postmodern spirit and refuses to fill the gaps with *anything*. He works hard, in my opinion, to preserve (though preservation is inimical to deconstruction) the ambiguity and, more crucial, the discomfort that accompanies the failure of language and writing—even thought—to convey the possibility of presence *now*, at this point in humankind's capacity for awareness.

Like Hopper, I think it is possible to look at deconstruction from the perspective of a larger whole, psyche. If one turns to Wolfgang Giegerich's theorizing of depth psychology, one finds in operation similar negative and negating principles intrinsic to deconstruction, such as criticism, dismantling, disruption. Giegerich is unrelentingly critical of the positivism that has ensnared Jungian depth psychology, whether it is a reified unconscious, the emotional and regressive attachment to dead myths and rituals, personalized gods/goddesses/archetypes believed to be "in us," or archetypal psychology's mesmerization with the image and reluctance to "see through" all the way to soul. None of this is true to the soul and the soul's logic (purportedly the task of psychology proper), which, being negative, can only be thought after it has been imagined or pictorially represented.[6] Otherwise, psychology remains promised to inflated ego ideals and little else. Thus, in a process of "absolute-negative interiorization" Giegerich, using Hegelian language, subjects psychology to what was unthought but intuited in Jung: the notion of soul.

Absolute-negative interiorization is a process that works on a psychic image such that slowly what the image once referred to is negated from within until there is nothing concrete left, no substrate to the image; there is only its truth, its *logos*. Akin to the alchemical process of distillation, the image is held within a vessel (the soul) and worked on as the image's content dissolves into psychological awareness and understanding, which is, one could say, what describes the modern psychological method of reading mythic images. For example, in *The Soul's Logical Life*, Giegerich takes the myth of Artemis and Actaion and thinks through its images and its movement to get to its own particular logic, to understand what this myth is saying about the soul. The psychology of the myth has little to do with the *literal* tearing apart of a hunter (turned into a stag) by his own hunting dogs (and certainly less to do with one's inner Artemis and Actaion). Rather, Giegerich examines the *logic* of the hunt, the wilderness, the transformation into a stag, and so forth. Though space prohibits me from explicating his theory further (his conclusion is that this myth depicts in narrative form the notion of the Notion or Concept itself), the point I wish to emphasize is that the images in the myth are dissolved into thought, worked on until the inner logic or truth of the image becomes clear. The intent of this alchemical thought process is to "reach" the soul, to know the soul *as* soul and not mistake it for its images, which always point to an underlying psychological truth. The finger pointing to the moon is not the moon itself. Yet as the soul has no concrete, literal edge and is not an existing entity that can literally be reached, to "reach" it requires a continuing process that sees through concrete referents so that the psychological reality behind the phenomena (which "exists" as logical negativity, Giegerich says) becomes available to knowledge.

Granted, a major difference preventing depth psychology and deconstruction from becoming entirely simpatico is the issue of deferral and openness. Both discourses are concerned with decentering the ego, though deconstruction goes much further in that the ego can never catch up to itself. With an endless chain of signifiers, the ego can never examine itself and therefore cannot be completely defeated or, to be more exact, cannot truly be decentered and put into perspective against other centers or necessities

of consciousness. Both deconstruction and depth psychology seek
to undo binary oppositions, although deconstruction keeps the
opposites dissolved and *un*-united, purposely keeping the other as
wholly Other. This is unlike Jungian depth psychology's notion of
soul that already includes its own other, such as in the archetype of
the Self, which represents the wholeness and totality (integrating
all oppositions) of the individuated individual. Both discourses
move against nominalism and the stagnation of literalized, fixated
meanings, though to the degree that psychology remains committed to the individual, there persists a drive for meaning that cannot
be deferred. And whereas depth psychology tries to assist the individual in establishing his or her own center, the lack of closure and
impossibility of center endemic to deconstruction can obstruct the
development of individual subjectivity. The result, as I discussed at
the end of the previous chapter, is that the individual ends up
being psychologically stuck in the in-between spaces, neither fully
existing nor nonexisting.

Although the idea of infinite openness may be problematic for
the development of a healthy ego, for the soul it is less of a compli-
cation. Again turning to Giegerich. He takes Heraclitus's Fragment
45—"You would not find out the boundaries of the soul, even by
traveling along every path: so deep a measure does it have"—as
measure that the logic of soul has no measure, is limitless (Kirk and
Raven, qtd. in Giegerich, "Is the Soul 'Deep?'": 1). "Heraclitus's
reflection, rather than altogether depriving us of a sense of boundary, brings about a transportation of 'boundary' from the sphere of
the real into that of the mental or notional, from the 'object' (the
soul, psychological reality) into the 'subject,' from the ontological
to the logical" (Giegerich, "Is the Soul 'Deep?'" 6). The soul has
been interiorized or, more precisely, consciousness has become
aware of the interior nature of the soul. This is not an interiority to
be taken personally (*my* soul, *my* thoughts, *my* feelings, etc.). It is an
impersonal, objective interiorization, a process of reflection that
inverts a mythic mode of being-in-the-world to a psychological one.

What was once projected completely outward, in nature, is
inverted such that one becomes conscious of that which was taken
for granted and infused with divine, magical powers. One no
longer looks at the sun as the Father God who works in profound,
mysterious ways; one becomes conscious *of* the sun as a star, as a

mass of energy, heat, and light. And the meaning of the symbol (sun as God) becomes available *as* meaning, as psychological insight into what it signifies, for example, to *internalize* the sun and hold it as a guiding center within one's self. In a psychological age, the symbols are no longer innocently and unthinkingly lived or living as they were during myth; they have become interiorized or "psychologized" (Hillman). Much of Jungian-influenced writing assumes this to be true; books are filled with the psychological meaning of the symbols of myths and fairy tales. I have already referred to the Sumerian myth of Inanna-Ishtar and her descent to the underworld. A psychological reading of the myth understands it as a depiction of the feminine initiation into one's essential and powerful femininity. In a psychological age, the image has been inverted and interiorized; the projections are removed from the gods and goddesses, from natural phenomena and taken in. The sun, for most of the world, is neither Father nor God. The life is not in the images; it is "in" us, but this in-ness is the opposite of itself; it is, rather, the awareness of how much we are in life.

"We are hopelessly enclosed by the soul. There is nothing outside the psyche, no other, nothing new" (Giegerich, "Deep" 7). But what we are enclosed by cannot be literally, empirically accounted for, unlike in myth, where one could look to the sky, earth, and waters and physically see one's containment. As itself, however, the soul is logically negative, atemporal, and outside of a positive, empirical existence—as opposed to the soul's *expression* in concrete, historical phenomena. Anything can be an expression of soul (which implies that anything has its own necessity. This makes it much harder to say that something should not have happened [such as the end of myth] and instead asks that one willingly look into and listen to the phenomena that have occurred or are occurring.).

Though outer phenomena provide an opening *into* soul, they are not to be conflated *with* soul and with what remains hidden from the senses. Yet, Giegerich also says, one has to search for the boundaries of the soul to realize the impossibility of such an effort, to know the soul *as* logically negative and atemporal. This, in my opinion, is not wholly unlike Taylor's demand to think the end of theology, along with "the disappearance of the self, the end of history, and the closure of the book"—all in order to know the impossibility of God's presence or rebirth. The loss is irrevocable and incurable, Taylor says, but in the liminal time emerging from the loss, a new kind of postmodern (negative) religious ("a/theological") reflection is made possible. "[D]econstruction is the 'hermeneutic' of the death of God" (*Erring* 8, 6). Can deconstruction also be considered a hermeneutic of the soul? For psychology, one must also think the end of religion and myth, piercing through layers of representation so as to know the soul in its true "form" (which is not really a form). But perhaps this is too simplistic a comparison, for the issues of subjectivity and closure remain one site of clashing between depth psychology and postmodern theory. And yet to risk another simple conjecture, it may be all in the timing. Depth psychology midwifes the (psychological) birth of the individual, whereas postmodernism appears to have skipped the birth of the subject (or the growing pains) and gone straight to its (psychological) death.

In answer to the question of whether deconstruction could be considered a hermeneutic of the soul, Giegerich would most likely say, no, because that overlooks and underestimates deconstruction's obligation to infinite deferral. In depth psychology, he argues, one must be committed to reaching the boundary of soul— even if the soul cannot be measured. For it is only when one realizes the soul's *lack* of boundary that one reaches the boundary. Heraclitus' fragment shows the dialectic of closure *and* openness. It is a contradiction that is necessary to understand the logic and inescapability of soul, but to attain this level of awareness one must first do the work, so to speak. "The road is not the goal. The goal is the actual, committed arrival at, and ever deeper penetration into or submission to the 'no' of the 'no boundary' insight" ("Is the Soul 'Deep?'" 27). One enters further into the no-thingness that is soul, but it is a negative, alchemical process that does come to an end or attains closure when one reaches (through thought, Giegerich stresses) the union of opposites, the *unus mundus.*

This is quite contrary to the deconstructive philosophy insofar as the infinite sequence of signifieds and signifiers promises that the process never ends; there will always be more to deconstruct. The process of penetration into and negation of words and images (texts) in deconstruction is open-ended and nondialectical. It is, as Taylor says, "unspeakable [. . .] not simply unknown but is unknowable" (*Tears* 68). But without some sort of logical containment, without the "boundary" part of the "'no boundary' insight," it becomes virtually impossible to penetrate further into *one* thing or idea and thus attain a higher or deeper level of awareness and fuller knowledge of what the text or idea is conveying. In deconstruction, awareness is dispersed and undone more than it is deepened.

Then why even raise comparisons between depth psychology and deconstruction if ultimately they stand in opposition to each other? Because I still maintain that both contribute something of value in the move toward a higher consciousness. And why I think deconstruction is particularly worth mentioning in a discussion of meaning after myth is because as a philosophy it, unlike the examples cited at the very beginning of this chapter, is already working from outside the system of Western metaphysics. It is, like Giegerich's approach to depth psychology, truthful to the reality of the loss of myth and meaning in a way that the other authors are not. By dissolving the ontotheological framework, the discourse is shifted downward and inward, to a negative level of consciousness that is not only more truthful to the negative nature that is soul or Being, but also refuses to allow a hidden God to rise up and assume His presence once again. This is unlike the blending of depth psychology and postmodern theory discussed in chapter 3 precisely because Giegerich is unwilling to disavow the loss of myth and slip it back into consciousness. He takes psychology as a natural consequence of the death of God, *not* as a means to introduce a hidden God. As he states, he is moving from the ontological to the logical. If there does remain a metaphysical element to the notion of soul or an objective psyche as the unity of all existence, it is a metaphysics of absence, *not* presence.

Though the process of absolute-negative interiorization differs from a serial, open-ended process of negation ("radical negativity," Taylor says), it is this process of negation and dissolution with which I am primarily concerned, and, more specifically, how it directly pertains to myth. However, before getting into what I mean by the negation of myth, I would like to return to where I began, to the noted move toward mending the split inherent in dualistic thinking and the attempt to realize a higher consciousness that encompasses the whole.

Myth and Consciousness

The persistent belief in the presence and necessity of myth in a time when the notion of consciousness itself is being made conscious raises a particular question: could this movement toward greater consciousness somehow bring humankind "back" to myth? Not literally back to antiquity but to a new kind of being-in-the-world that corresponds to the existential meaning experienced in mythic life? Could a deeper consciousness bring about the "new mythology" that Joseph Campbell saw as "a social as well as spiritual necessity?" (*Inner* 19). Or the myth that Jung felt humanity had "such urgent need of" and which could begin to tend the "long-forgotten soul of man?" (*Memories* 333). Myths are the source of meaning, and Jung's myth of meaning, wrote Aniela Jaffé, was a new myth of consciousness. "The metaphysical task of man resides in the continual expansion of consciousness at large, and his destiny as an individual in the creation of individual self-awareness" (140). Is this "myth of consciousness," then, a "new religion" with reignited capacity to fulfill and guide the collective at large?[7] Can a metaphysics of absence function the same as a metaphysics of presence and thus effect a reinstatement of religious truth—even after the gods/God have died?

Before proceeding, however, I think it is useful first to address the reasoning behind this exploration. Initially, it might seem that an intentional correspondence of myth and consciousness today is strange and anachronistic, for the whole pursuit of awareness and truth has been contingent on the departure from myth and religion and the gravitation toward science and philosophy. To some degree, the question is unnecessary because the mere ability to equate myth and consciousness suggests that we already understand what myth is and what it does. It indicates that myth has already dissolved from the phenomenal to the formal, from a substance contained within physical nature (the content of myth) to the nature (logic) of the container itself. As psychological rather than mythical beings, we are subjects who now look *at* myth. What was once projected onto nature is withdrawn into a reflecting consciousness dependent on an overcoming of myth. Like Lévi-Strauss, we can understand the logic of myth by way of analyzing its structure.

Moreover, the whole process of consciousness entails becoming aware of something that is *un*conscious, something previously unknown. Myths, on the other hand, are never hidden. They are expressed, celebrated, spelled out in detail, reenacted in ritual. Myths are the stories that are *told*, not the ones waiting to be unmasked. Equating myth and consciousness, then, wouldn't make sense. Myth would have to go underground so that it could then be unearthed and brought to light. Though this view does describe some current approaches to myth, it depends, as I have been arguing, on an equivocation and redefining of myth, a suppressing of something long gone in order to keep it alive (even if barely breathing).

Furthermore, consciousness cannot lead to myth, nor is myth a means to consciousness, for myth itself is *already* a product of consciousness. Myth is simply one very early form of reflection, present at a particular stage of consciousness and human history. Because myth has been dead for some time, other forms of reflection have come in, such as religious consciousness, philosophical consciousness. There is no reason to think that the expansion of consciousness would or even could effectuate a return to myth—unless myth is inflated and equivocated such that it supplants the larger and quite common concept—*reflection*. This view, which supports much of the modern and postmodern approaches introduced in this study, would have to be founded on the fact of myth's continual and inescapable existence, but history has shown that neither myth nor the gods are everlasting.

Undoubtedly, it would be far more suitable and accurate to engage this evolving of consciousness outside the discourse of myth. Yet I think asking whether consciousness (and by consciousness I do not mean mundane awareness but the nature of consciousness itself) could be a "new myth" merits attention for several reasons. For one thing, it speaks to those who manage to argue for both a persistence of myth and a development of consciousness. This is especially apparent among Jungian depth psychologists, who, while they may not outwardly propose the formation of a "new religion," nonetheless defend myth's formative and nonnegotiable power in realizing the goal of individual and collective consciousness. The equation of myth and consciousness is another way of saying that mythology is psychology, one of the more prevalent views among Jungian-oriented writings. For example: "Psychology is mythology" (Guggenbühl-Craig, *Old Fool* 35). "Mythology is psychology, misread as cosmology, history, and biography" (Campbell, "The Fairy Tale" 33). Recall Jung's observation about himself: "Now you possess a key to mythology and are free to unlock all the gates of the unconscious psyche" (*Memories* 171). Perhaps the more appropriate question would be: as psychology supplants myth, does it (psychological awareness) retain an existential and meaningful equivalency to real myth? This would address the Jungian perspective more directly, though I am primarily using the more neutral term *consciousness* rather than *psychology* because it encompasses similar intentions in other strains of thought not outwardly focused on psychology.

In essence I am asking, *can* there be myth today? No matter how formalized or psychologized myth becomes, does it still maintain a vital connection with archaic myth? That is the question this study has repeatedly confronted and answered in the negative. Then why continue to ask it? For one thing, to the extent that the absence of myth continues to be denied or recontextualized, it is necessary to consider the possibility and conditions for myth's sustained existence, to falsify my own argument so as to get closer to the reality of myth today. This is what I began to do in the third chapter, in engaging the question as to how myth can be perceived as present while its absence is acknowledged. What I found is that while the impression of postmodern thought on depth psychology facilitates the acknowledgment of the negative nature of consciousness, its no-thingness, consciousness from this perspective still remains contextualized within a present-absent myth. Absence is seen for its role in engendering myth rather than as a consequence of the loss of myth and rupture in consciousness. Absence is even accepted as necessary to the continuation of an idea of myth that serves to deliteralize and destabilize any proclaimed hold on truth—but the myth itself is far from absent. Relegated to the realm of the imaginal, the postmodern, present-absent myth does not flinch when its content is emptied or seen through or exchanged for a different perspective; rather, the myth is upheld as vital for providing an equally vital flexible and metaphorical mode of awareness.

Yet there is a difference between finding traces of myth lingering in the 'both/and' of the in-between spaces of imagination, and collectively standing between the time of myth and a consciousness that has yet to be fully realized. It is one thing to ask whether there is myth today and another to ask whether we are between myths. One can concede the absence of myth and purport to accept the ramifications, but it becomes entirely another matter when one believes this collective in-between space is really a waiting room for something better, more life affirming to come. Then the guiding question is no longer, how or where myth is today, but whether the realization of greater consciousness will restore meaning to life. To me, this is the final question that must be asked as one travels further into the absence of myth, for without addressing this possibility, the absence of myth has not been fully thought through.

Without thinking the absence of myth through, the equivocation of myth remains problematic, misleading, and falsely seductive, leading one to think that modern attempts to reclaim, redefine, and recontextualize myth succeed. Even if this was the case, and the equivocation of myth pointed to a truth beyond a particular theorist's desire for a kind of existential meaning and the surface similarity of using the same term, the equivocation must be brought home, so to speak. Whether ending the equivocation pronounces the absolute end of or a new beginning for myth, either outcome is insufficient to leave myth hanging, where it has been subject to gross misappropriation. Reality today may be equivocal, as Patricia Berry says, but myth never was. If one means seriously to engage the question of still being in myth or of a deeper consciousness leading to a kind of existential meaning equivalent to myth, then one cannot be equivocal either.

This chapter picks up where I left off from the previous one, only the difference between my approach and that of the postmodern depth psychologists is that the "myth" I am associating with consciousness is not a present-absent one, but a negated one. With regard to negation, I think one can assert a connection between myth and consciousness, but, as I will aim to explicate, it is a connection that depends on the dissolution of one (myth) so that the other (consciousness) may begin to be realized *as* consciousness. A negated myth is not the same as a mythic consciousness, whereby one places a mythic lens over a particular phenomenon or psychological complex to reveal previously unconscious elements. What I mean by negated myth is the penetration into the nature of myth itself such that its form has no choice but to dissolve, to give way to the consciousness that has endeavored to comprehend the myth. "Resolving an enigma means shifting it to a higher level, as the first drops away."[8] And when there is nothing more of myth for consciousness to pierce through, the "new" myth is not composed of fragments that substitute for the whole—the myth is finished and a new form of consciousness emerges. However, before automatically reverting to myth's obsolescence, the supposition of whether the expansion of consciousness restores mythic meaning needs to be tested.

In brief, the remainder of this chapter will focus on the following:

- **Why not myth?** This section sets aside the problematic of equating myth and consciousness and considers the possibility that achieving greater awareness does correspond to myth. Myth, in this sense, is identified with the process of making something unconscious conscious, of disclosing truths that, for as long as humankind exists, are there to be disclosed. This is an approach that does not redefine myth so much as it looks into the heart of myth itself, into its original role as expressing the truth of existence. Yet rather than erase the distinction between differing forms of expressing truth, a correspondence between myth and consciousness asks whether or not the logic of myth informs the logic of consciousness. This would suggest an abstracted yet vital connection, if not an exact equation, between myth and modern forms of consciousness. In addition, the issues of meaning and standing outside of historical time are considered as potential correlates between myth and a newer consciousness.
- **The inessentiality of myth.** In this section I address the contradiction raised in the previous section, namely, how can such an abstracted myth or new form of reflection still be a myth? I return to two theorists discussed in the first chapter, Elizabeth Baeten and Milton Scar-

borough, to show that I have done what I accused them of: conflated myth and philosophy. And yet when the discussion of myth shifts to its logic, a philosophical approach seems more relevant. Even so, I contend that Baeten and Scarborough's approach remains more faithful to their ideas about myth than to the logic of myth itself, precisely because they do not allow the logic inherent in the death of God or absence of myth to work on the notion of myth. One can stay true to myth and not disavow the reality of myth's absence, but the result is such that myth's very necessity is made redundant. Moreover, I respond to a potential conflict between my correspondence of myth and the "end of history" and my critique in chapter 3 of Christopher Hauke, a postmodern Jungian who basically argued for the same. However, I show that he too remains bound to an old form of consciousness and subsequently does not allow the nonnecessity of the gods to work on his theory.

• **After myth.** The final section takes a brief look at the logical implications of Christianity, which represented an overcoming of myth with the fall into history and the ascension of the one, true God into the spiritualized heavens. The Christian incarnation of God into man, however, indicates that religion, as well as myth, has lost its reason for existence. The onus is on humankind, which has left the sphere of myth and religion and entered a psychological age. A reflective consciousness assumes the role that myth and the gods once had, enabling human consciousness to look inward, and to understand oneself as well as the world through this subjective lens. As such, the development of consciousness does not depend on myth, whether present or absent. It depends on humankind, who, once it gives up its attachment to myth and relinquishes the ineffectual search for a meaning to replace the loss of myth, just might be able to experience the state of presence and awareness that is, at bottom, what is desired.

WHY NOT MYTH?

"And all at once she [Harmony] understood what myth is, understood that myth is the precedent behind every action, its invisible, ever-present lining. [. . .] For every step, the footprint was already there" (Calasso, qtd. in Knowles: 366).

Assuming, for the time being, that myth is inescapable, and that to demythologize is simultaneously to remythologize, reinscribing one story against the backdrop of a larger, usually hidden one (what David Miller likens to a "computer program running in the background" ["'A Myth Is as a Good as a Smile!'" 190]), then assuredly one will find any move toward greater consciousness worthy of the appellation of myth. And yet one cannot rest so easily on an automatic designation of myth if one is to consider seriously whether consciousness is really a "new myth," for this does not think through myth. It is like calling mythlessness just another myth, unaware or heedless of the equivocation between two different "myths," one an archaic reality, the other a modern ideology. But I do not think one can afford to be so equivocal if one intends to engage honestly the issue of whether this so-called new myth is, in fact, a myth. This raises a paradox. On the one hand, one needs to get inside myth to determine its relevancy for today. On the other hand, one cannot look to the nature of old myths to determine myth's continued presence today because that runs counter to the move of consciousness itself, which has already left the gods behind.

Deeming consciousness a myth is very different from, say, detecting the gods still roaming the earth, in a transmuted form, but all the while unwilling to sever completely ties with the gods' divine prehistory. For example, although Hillman ostensibly argues for the myth*ic* over myth, his contention that Zeus has evolved, that the Zeus of today could be "any damn way he might want to be, requiring all sorts of attentions today that may not have occurred to him 2500 years ago," maintains an attachment to former forms of myth ("Once More into the Fray" 4). Archetypal psychology's archetypal reading of the world lends itself to argue quite favorably for the viability of myth. Indeed its lifeline courses with the recycled blood of the Olympic pantheon. But a myth that depends on the form or image of Zeus (or any other archetype) is logically different from a myth of consciousness. This would apparently answer the question right away: no, consciousness is not a myth insofar as myth needs to be restructured to be relevant to today. And yet if one moves behind differing forms of myth into the *reason* for myth, then I think the question stays open.

To consider consciousness a new myth is different from abstracting the narrative pattern from a particular myth and finding it relevant to one's life, such as how the personal mythologist would use the hero's journey as a model. Nor is it like looking at the stories embedded in popular culture and finding, such as Wendy Doniger does, evidence of the mythic, even when classical narrative has given way to kitsch. This is no traditional story. Life has become too complex for the singularity and stability indicative of the lived stories of ritualized myth. If anything, today's myth of consciousness would be antinarrative. It is a narrative whose rules and structure have dissolved, rendering all details entirely arbitrary and, by extension, secondary. The story is almost irrelevant to the story.[9] Accordingly, one cannot apply current methods of *sustaining* myth (in contrast to studying myth) to any authentic new myth, for such methods tend to dilute or distort the nature of myth itself, usually in the name of securing a shred of meaning. This, as I said, has little to do with cultivating a mythic consciousness, which mostly entails pinning the archetype and myth on the public figure or phenomenon.[10] A mythic consciousness functions imaginally, but to the extent that it remains attached to the mythic image, consciousness gives way to unconsciousness. What I am trying to determine is if this movement toward an expanded consciousness carries within it the same purpose as real myth. This kind of inquiry suggests that rather than an absence of myth or the installation of a new myth that secretly tries to mirror the old one, there is a correspondence and not just an opposition between the logic of myth and the logic of a modern/postmodern reflecting consciousness. Or, more precisely, since I do not wish to disavow the split in consciousness that sundered one mode of being-in-the-world from another, I am inquiring as to whether the logic of myth *informs* the logic of consciousness.

A different method of discernment is required. Not just the distinction between archaic, lived myth and modern/postmodern ideas of lived myth, a necessary distinction to make, to be sure, especially when defending the vitality or absence of myth. However, even this method of differentiating seems commonplace, given the facility to see through modern so-called myth to its ideology.[11] The capacity to identify underlying patterns and motivations is not a problem. What is debatable is the matter of personal choice: how much is one willing to notice and how attached is one to his ideology? But to consider the possibility that consciousness is a myth, in a time when collective rituals are either thoroughly dissipated or commercialized, the gods are no longer reliable, and the narrative form has exploded, requires that one peer past the specifics into the heart of myth itself, into its raison d'être. One could argue that in separating myth from its concrete expression within a particular culture, I am already unfaithful to myth and am perpetuating the equivocation I have persistently found to be so troublesome, guilty of fostering expectations for a meaning that inevitably seems to fall short. One could argue that my ability to abstract myth to determine whether the mold fits or not implies that any current myth I refer to is already intellectualized and exists in an entirely different league or logical form from the myths of antiquity. And yet if one proposes that consciousness is a myth, perhaps it is not completely illogical to suggest that myth *needs* consciousness, needs the abstraction, needs us to see through its narrative details and dispense with the rituals so that we can get to its truth, a truth that is only trying to mirror the truth of human existence.

If essential to myth is the expression of the truth of existence, then new forms of expressing such a truth are conceivably not antithetical to myth. The truth of myth bears the seeds of the truth of a consciousness no longer dependent on myth. To the extent that both a mythic and psychological consciousness are concerned with expressing the truth of the age that they exist in, there is an existential, if abstracted, link between these two forms of truth. Again to reiterate, this differs from the personal myth movement, which, though it seeks to assist individuals in finding and expressing the truth of their own lives, its spirit is such that it has not really allowed the old forms of myth to stay respectfully buried. The dilemma lies in wanting it both ways: looking backward for the solution to contemporary needs. But calling on the gods and goddesses and assuming their stories to be never-ending run counter to the move toward greater consciousness, and counter to the new myth that Jungians insist we are desperately in need of.

To cite another example from this school of thought: contemporary Jungian James Hollis feels that we are "haunted by a mythological vacuum. [. . .] [T]he experience of modernism is the anguish of yearning from within our estrangement" (25). And further: "The erosion of the great myths of Earth Mother and Sky Father has left us to search privately for images to guide and support the soul and link it to the cosmic drama. Without such linkage we are doomed to a life of superficiality. To experience one's life in depth, as part of a larger context, is the central contribution of myth" (54). Hollis believes that mystery lives on, but where and how he would counsel others to remember the ineffable is still by way of the old myths, despite their "erosion." What has eroded is not the "mythic energies" but the "vessels" that once made mystery available to humankind (146). That may be true inasmuch as the energies (though not the myth) or psychic realities remain constant and consistent throughout human history (such as love, joy, rage, and so forth). Nonetheless, Hollis's basis for the *form* of consciousness remains bound to something already long gone—otherwise why would be there be a "vacuum" to haunt us or such an "anguish of yearning"? Yet while this form of consciousness is tied to "mythic energies" in the form of the gods, he is trying to apply it to that which he knows has a new logic and thereby requires a *new* form, consciousness itself. Subsequently, consciousness is cocooned. The loss of myth gets transplanted into the individual, and the individual is grandiosely granted the power to remedy the loss by finding one's personal myth. "The meeting point of outer and inner is the individual psyche. This is where the newly formed myth will be found" (148). My contention is that this is not a "new myth" of consciousness, but an attempt to jump-start an old one—despite his claim that it is not his "intent to revive old myths" (146). A myth of consciousness, however, is not about the archetypes.

Perhaps to be truly true to the *telos* of myth is neither to abandon myth, leaving it to fester and foster illusions, nor to rewrite it and create new copy that tries to supplant an original that may or may not have ever existed, but to see through myth and help myth see through itself. When myth sees through itself, it initiates the movement from a prereflected expression of truth toward an interiorized reflection and ultimately to an absolute reflection of truth.[12] Truth as prereflection belongs to the time of archaic myth, and truth as dependence on a purely objective reflection has long been rendered epistemologically problematic. Truth as interiorized reflection could be where the mythology equals psychology school currently resides, to the degree that one looks through cultural and personal phenomena to find the underlying psychic image or invisible blueprint patterning the phenomena (e.g., looking into the terrorist attacks of September 11, 2001, for a deeper understanding of how and why such an event would occur).[13]

But reflection as truth or the truth of reflection is naked reflection; it is what endures when the hegemony of a metaphysics of presence falls. With the loss of the conceptual mirror that Western consciousness previously used to look at itself, reflection is actually freed from the confusion of appearances and the duplicity of the mirror. Such a freedom makes possible the dissolution of the distinction between subject and object and the experience of a natural mode of being-in-the-world whereby one can "retrieve Being" and "let the truth be unconcealed" (Hopper, "Introduction" xiii). The "absoluteness" of an absolute reflection in a time when there are no more absolutes is more like the process of absolute-negative interiorization Giegerich writes about, a process of negation in which the contents of soul are repeatedly worked on and changed from one logical form to another, until one "gets to" soul but as the soul exists as logical negativity, there is nothing concrete to get to, only the soul *as* negativity.[14] Similarly, greater consciousness as a new myth requires a going inward, ever deeper, *into* myth, but with the awareness that, as this is enacted, the old form of myth cannot remain the same if consciousness is going to expand and myth is going to remain faithful to its purpose of reflecting truth.

Even as old forms die, to ask the question if consciousness is a new myth may not have to be such a radical departure from myth inasmuch as one reframes the question, looking instead at the ever-evolving means for apprehending truth. This is the stance Lawrence Hatab takes in his book, *Myth and Philosophy: A Contest of Truths*. Hatab defines myth from within the context of a phenomenological analysis and Heidegger's thought, such that myth is a form of unconcealment, disclosing an existential truth that defies objective explanation. Myths "disclose *that* something is, the *first* meaningful form a world takes, the background of which is hidden. Myth is therefore not explanation but *presentation* of the arrival/withdrawal of existential meaning" (23). The form of myth itself "shifts with its content—the ever-varied and often conflicting realm of existential concerns" (33). Myth is a presentation of lived reality that must be experienced. Even so, other, more conceptualized forms of presentation need not stand in opposition to myth. Hatab believes that Heidegger's notion of unconcealment allows for a pluralism of truth in which *both* myth and philosophy serve as a kind of disclosure. Philosophy did not displace myth, he contends, it is an "*added* dimension of thought" (294). Hatab strives to integrate philosophical thinking with the lived world, bringing it, in his mind, "closer to myth" (300). He does not abandon conceptual thought; rather, he aims to place conceptual thought within the lived and living world and to show that there persists something unknowable and unreachable by abstract reasoning. And it is the effort to reach the inexplicable, whether through sacred narrative, poetry, or thought, that preserves a living connection with myth. For Hatab, both myth and philosophy point to a mysterious element of life unaffected by human reasoning.

Inasmuch as consciousness seems to retain this metaphysical element, even as it no longer depends on previous forms (such as the gods) or on traditional worship, could it not be a new kind of nondenominational, a/theological (to borrow from Taylor) "religion"? The absence of myth implies not so much a loss of "myth" per se (since myth has long been absent) but rather a loss of traditional metaphysics and religious certainty. Thus, if the modern sense of a loss of myth really points to a loss of metaphysics and religion, an awareness of an absence that is perceived not as a lack of something, but an abysmal opening into a necessary and unavoidable nothing, could possess its own metaphysical element (and numinousity for some) and as such would indicate that myth, or God at least, is not absent. Clearly, the recognition of something ineffable or unknowable persists. One modification, however, is that now the ineffable is beginning to be recognized *as* ineffable and rather than being concretized into concrete gods, its negative nature is starting to be left as it is. So, in this respect, the idea of pure consciousness *could* be a myth, but a negated or sublated one.

Consciousness would be a negated myth in that the old forms of myth dissolve out of their own redundancy, no longer bound to the natural phenomena that once solely contained the truth of myth.

Have we then or are we trying to come back full circle, but instead of being contained tightly within the ritualized circle of one's god and community, it is the circle "whose circumference is nowhere and whose center is everywhere"? (Campbell, "Symbol Without Meaning" 190). Are we entering the process of truly *knowing* myth, no longer needing the gods, symbols, or the collective, which to a reflecting consciousness could now only obscure myth? Archaic myth was about being utterly contained by and obligated to the primordial gods. It could follow that awareness of the inescapability of Being and the obligations to soul could construe a myth, albeit one already being worked by progressively greater degrees of reflection.

"Already myth *is* logos, *is* reflection, *is* thought, *is* absolute interiority. But it is logos cloaked in natural imagery, it presents absolute interiority projected into its other, the 'extended matter' of the imagination, in other words in a mode opposite to what it is about" (Giegerich, "Is the Soul 'Deep?'" 21). Giegerich cites the Greek myth of Okeanos, the Germanic uroboric Midgard Serpent, and the Egyptian primal Ocean Nun—all images that encircle and encompass the entire world—as myths that are specifically about the nature of myth and reflection itself (19). The mythic images of absolute containment and interiority prefigure the form of consciousness that is to come—not just through reflecting individuals becoming more aware but also by the myth itself. Thus, for consciousness to come into its own, the myth *also* comes home to itself. But its coming home is a death. It requires a dissolution of itself into the reflection and interiority it could only previously communicate with natural images. Now we no longer need the image of Okeanos to separate Being from Non-Being and to know (be conscious of) our containment in Being, in soul.

Joseph Campbell could also be seen as trying to bring the myth back home to itself when he argues that religious meaning can no longer be attached to any symbols. The symbol must be purposely disengaged from the meaning attached to it, flung out like a wild gander into the unknown. "Beyond both the image of god and the image of man, that we must venture to find the ultimate ground of all these guiding and protecting, edifying yet imprisoning, names and forms" ("Symbol without Meaning" 157). The "ultimate ground" is absolutely negative; it is the void, the formless, the space "between two thoughts," the face one has before he is born (156). It is in entering the unknown and relinquishing any assurance of meaning that the true "meaning" of the myth or symbol is experienced. "Our meaning is now the meaning that is no meaning; for no fixed term of reference can be drawn," Campbell said (190).

In the first chapter, I stated that the problem of Campbell's symbol without meaning is that, despite his intention to disengage from meaning, he nonetheless maintains an attachment *to* meaning. Talk of "no meaning" carries its opposite and betrays the desire for some kind of meaning, irrespective of its purported impossibility. One finds a reassurance of meaning in stating the opposite, and all the more insidiously comforting if one thinks one has handled all the ontological and epistemological bases, so to speak, by stating "no fixed term of reference can be drawn." However, I do think there is another way to read Campbell's argument. For one thing, the seeming equivocation of meaning or what looks like an open back door, ready to receive meaning as it is kicked out the front door, could appear as the necessary failure of language in writing about what exists beyond words. Although, one might ask, why even use the word *meaning*, given its tendency to come laden with hidden motivations and false expectations? Because it is possible, as Campbell's argument implies, that the usage of *meaning is* trying to establish a living connection with the meaning of living myth, though with the awareness that in *both* antiquity and (post)modernity, meaning comes from its absence (as in, meaning does not exist as something to be sought after or attained).

Myths provided meaning, but not in the sense that one might think of it today. The modern concept of "meaning" emerges after myth. It comes out of an intimation of something missing, an imagining of what must have been fulfilling for others, or an already reflected and interiorized recognition of something that requires analysis for clarity (i.e., this particular experience means something to me). But the meaning that is no meaning speaks to the complete immersion in the present moment, in the Now of one's life. It is meaning as unreflected presence; if in the moment, one does not reflect on meaning because the need is obviated.

One could speculate that the same was true for archaic cultures; they did not speak of meaning because they were embedded in it, absorbed into life through ritual and sustained by the cosmological center of their myth.

The modern notion of meaning, on the other hand, involves standing outside the moment (or myth) and talking about some other moment, generating a yearning for something to fill the emptiness or lack of center that comes with standing outside of one's own life. But the kind of meaning issuing from participation and embeddedness, whether within one's collective or individual life, *is* meaningful insofar as it is fulfilling—but only in retrospect. An articulation of a current myth of meaning requires a caveat. Conceivably we, unlike those of archaic cultures, are able to designate experiences as meaningful only because we have been outside of meaning long enough to dwell on it and to study those who ostensibly had it. We can therefore surmise that being immersed in the now is meaningful insofar as it quenches the need for meaning altogether. For a new myth of consciousness, the "meaning" is apprehended neither through ritual or a collective center but through absence, through disengagement and nonattachment. The nothingness or emptiness that is not an existential, personalized crisis but rather a gateway into the formless engendering all of life, the space between two breaths, or the logical negativity of soul— this negative opening understands the questions of meaning and meaninglessness to be irrelevant. Accordingly, meaning (and myth) could be dropped from the conversation, but in the meantime, it seems, on the way to this level of awareness one is compelled to use the same language while undoing the words after they are written. It is in this sense, I think, that Campbell's "meaning that is no meaning" can also be considered.[15]

The idea of total presence and the postmodern declaration of the end of history offer another potential point of correspondence between archaic myth and a myth of consciousness. Mythic time is outside of history; its sense of "time" bound to life repeatedly beginning anew. According to Mircea Eliade, "for religious man of the archaic cultures, the world is renewed annually; in other words, with each new year it recovers its original sanctity, the sanctity that it possessed when it came from the Creator's hands. [. . .] With each New Year, a time that was 'new,' 'pure,' 'holy'—because not yet worn—came into existence" (*Sacred* 75, 76). Examples cited by Eliade include the following: among the North American Indians, the Yokuts and the Yuki express "year" by saying "the world has passed"; for the Algonquins and the Sioux, their sacred lodge symbolizes both the universe and a whole year; in India the annual building of the fire altar symbolizes the remaking of the world and the regeneration of time; in Babylon the annual reciting of the *Enuma Elish* (Poem of Creation) symbolically actualizes the cosmogony or the Creation of the world (73ff). "It is not a matter of profane time, of mere temporal duration, but the sanctification of cosmic time" (74). Each year passes, but the passing is of the world and time itself. There is no accumulated knowledge and experience such that one might refer back to. Time exists not in numbered years and clocks, but always in original time.

The sense of being outside of history is also characteristic of postmodern thought. To the degree that history is theocentric and logocentric, such as Mark Taylor contends, then the ending of the ontotheological tradition and the dethroning of the once sovereign *logos* necessitate the end of the nature of history (*Erring* 53). There is no more linear, identifiable "beginning, middle, end," no coherent plot, and where once there was an origin, there are now only vague traces leading nowhere in particular. "[E]very ostensible transcendental signified is apprehended as a signifier caught in an endless labyrinth of signifiers. Translating theology into semiology, God dies and is reborn as a sign that points to *nothing* beyond itself" (*About Religion* 26). With the impossibility of ever recovering a primordial origin, the conclusion is indefinitely deferred, leaving one to wander amid the spaces lingering from the loss of both primal beginning and satisfying end (*Erring* 98). The death of God and the closure of His Book not only sets in motion the death of the self; for the self, Taylor argues, is grounded in God (initially exemplified in Augustine), but also the end of history, which is equally inextricably tied to a creator God (14). However, this all-around dissolution—of history, God, the self, logos—occasions, Thomas Altizer argues, the dawning of a "universal or total humanity [. . .] which negates and transcends every interior and historical identity" (*Total Presence* 96).[16] Altizer's observation that traditionally established identities are collapsing is not unlike Giegerich's contention that the individual is already psychologically obsolete. Altizer writes,

"[W]hether these [human identities] be those of nation and work, or sex and race, or marriage and the family, all sanctions for these and all such social identities are coming to an end, and coming to an end at just those points where these identities are most actual and real, as the grounds for every social and historical particularity are dissolving in our midst" (97).

While the notion of a total humanity that supersedes individual identity bears a formal if weak resemblance with the collective life of myth, the particular point I wish to stress in determining a myth of consciousness has to do with standing outside of history. Clearly, one cannot simplistically equate mythic, prehistorical time and postmodern, posthistorical time. For one thing, mythic time is sacred and establishes origins, whereas postmodern time pulses to the end of the sacred *and* the original. And yet whereas mythic time knows only the present, postmodern time is similarly forced to confront the present when nothing points to anything beyond itself, although it moves beyond presence into the impossibility of presence, into difference. Both mythic time and postmodern time could be seen as relying on very little outside of themselves for knowledge. In mythic time, one *literally* refers to nothing beyond the presence of the gods; in postmodern time, one *logically* refers to nothing, having already deconstructed any proffered referent. Postmodernism is still dependent on God for knowledge, but it is an entirely negative dependency, one dictated by an absolute lack of presence. When Taylor says that history has ended while time continues, he is questioning the possibility of knowledge after the death of God, the decentering of the Word, and the disappearance of the self. In essence, what he means by the "end of history" is the end of a former logic of the world. It is the ending of history at the level of consciousness itself, not at the empirical, positive level, where obviously history continues to be made and written.

Although this change in logic further seals the coffin on traditional myth, does it somehow bring consciousness closer to the *logos* of myth, to its logical negativity, to the Nothing that grounds Being? If myth already is reflection, though in its incipient form it appears as prereflection, as concretized images, to know myth requires the awareness of reflective capacities and limits. Knowing myth is the tracking of reflection itself, and not the pursuit of traces of the gods, which conflates a reflection *freed* from the gods *with* the gods.

Myth must be understood on its own terms. This is a fact of myth repeatedly expressed by myth theorists. For example, "Like music and art, myth must be understood in its own terms; it cannot be reduced to history or metaphor or any other substitute" (Puhvel; see Batto 8). "We need an orientation which can open up the way a myth discloses the world and shapes human existence *on its own terms*" (Hatab 19). "[I]t is impossible to speak of myth nonmythically" (Westbrook 3).

The confusion of myth erupts when the process of understanding the terms of myth stops mid-process, usually not at myth but at the idea of what myth should be. Defining myth in terms of its archetypal images or in terms of creating repetitive narrative patterns or as language and metaphor is the result of selecting just one element of myth that in a sense must freeze myth to study and keep it. Then one is no longer talking about myth but about imagination, story, and language. The problem is when myth as something other than or additional to myth is used as evidence of myth's persistence—for example, myth is language and as it is impossible to be divested of language, it is impossible to be devoid of myth.[17] But my contention is that if one seriously holds myth to be alive and well, one cannot look to modern reproductions or redefinitions of myth to verify this claim. One has to look at myth directly, deep into reflection itself, past the now deconstructed placeholders of the gods.

THE INESSENTIALITY OF MYTH

In light of these arguments, there persists the question that I have been treading on: am I still talking about myth? How can a myth of consciousness abstract itself from nature, the gods, the narrative, and an intact collective bearing witness to its truth, the prime components of myth—and still call itself a myth? The form of myth cannot be separated from its content, and in seeking parallels between archaic myth and a contemporary myth of consciousness, I have removed myth from the substance of archaic life *and* this life. However, considering a myth of consciousness is not the same as asserting its actuality. Even so, to focus on the form of myth as a means for reflecting truth to the exclusion of phenomena and experience contributes to a misidentifying of myth. When myth is no longer a reality at the phenomenal level—and I think the industrious search for meaning in large measure supports this statement—but is transformed to the level of form and thought, it becomes all too easy to look at current phenomena and imaginally root out the so-called hidden myth. Though such imaginings of myth may temporarily defer the question of meaning and appease the emptiness, ultimately what one uncovers is anything but myth.

The abstracting of myth's form from its content is precisely the ground on which I criticized two myth theorists in chapter 1, Elizabeth Baeten and Milton Scarborough. I said that they intentionally confounded the form and substance of myth in their efforts to meld myth with philosophy. In their redefining of myth to suit philosophical criteria and squeeze into modernity, their arguments denied that a fundamental rupture in consciousness ever took place and reinforced the dualism they were trying to overcome. Both took their philosophical task to be one of recovering myth or, more specifically, recovering the mind-set that sees and participates with myth, since they both argue for the inarguable presence of myth. To recall the examples I previously cited: Scarborough "brackets" reality such that even when a Stone Age tribe in New Guinea discards all signs of their myth (e.g., selling sacred objects, revealing their sacred mysteries, dispensing with ceremony and initiation), the myth persists: "broken, enervated, numbed" but with its essence alive just the same (6). His abstraction of myth focuses on a larger, undying cultural force (an "intentionality" that "orients human existence" [84]) against which the loss of the mere trappings of one myth (such as ritual, the gods) cannot presume to alter too much. The fact that the tribe did not cohere around a new myth demonstrates to Scarborough the indestructibility of a primordial mode of being-in-the-world that may inspire what looks like an outward expression of myth, but the expressions and enactments are not to be solely identified with the myth itself. The mirrors and photographs handed to the New Guinea tribe initiated the tribe's personal downfall, but did not destroy the myth; rather, they point to the epistemological difficulties in visually and concretely capturing the whole truth of myth.

Baeten abstracts myth such that theories of myth function *as* myth. Without any stable content to myth, the weight necessarily shifts to myth's form and its application in thought. Opposing theories of myth are connected in a similar purpose insofar as they each attempt to define and delimit what it means to be a human being. Baeten likens theories of myth to telling stories around a campfire, for the theory, no less than the myth, serves as a necessary form or boundary against which existential questions can be drawn out. The impetus for self-creation is an innate need, but creation needs resistance to manifest. Nature must be shaped to help form human existence; myths emerge to assist with this shaping process. Thus, a Native American creation myth in which the tribe symbolically lifts the sky with large poles made from fir trees has the same logical intent of modern theories of myth, each trying to "carve out a niche where we can live 'without bumping our heads'" (193). For Baeten, myth as form and structure loosened from the phenomena that substantiate it does not indicate an irrevocable change in myth's logic. It merely shows the inescapability and necessity of myth and, more important, the amenability of myth as a concept to address human concerns at an intellectual level to the same degree that myth previously addressed human concerns at an empirical level.

In the first chapter I suggested that Baeten and Scarborough's usage of myth ultimately cocooned myth *and* truth by implying that modern, contentless forms of myth were just a disguised rendition of original myth. However, if the task of knowing myth requires seeing through to its form, to its reality as thought and reflection, then perhaps the philosopher-mythologists are not so far off course, and, as Hatab says, philosophy and myth need not be mutually exclusive. If the purpose of myth is the self-display of a being-in-the-world that accurately reflects the logic of human existence, then a stripping down of myth *to* its form could be the appropriate expression of myth in a time that has realized the advent of philosophy and shifted the discourse on truth to the level of thought.

Scarborough's intent to look beneath the surface and beyond mirrors and other visual means of reflecting could be seen as the attempt to confront reflection *as* reflection, in all its purity. Like Hatab, Scarborough sees myth as a process of presentation and disclosure of what he (Scarborough) calls the life-world. "The ultimate assessment of myth must be of a kind suited to the nature of myth as giving expression to apprehensions of the life-world and as

functioning to provide an orientation for living in that world"
(110). And Baeten's view of myth as a form defining what it is to
be human speaks to the necessity of form that sets a boundary
against the formless, and what is impossible for humankind to
reach. Myth as boundary or threshold is to be crossed if
humankind is to achieve its *telos* inscribed within myth: "absolute
and unbounded creative freedom" that constitutes both subjective
and objective features of existence (19, 20). Although Baeten
knows that meeting the *telos* of humankind requires that myth be
overcome, it is an impossible endeavor. One cannot, at the existential level, reach the absolute. "If human being is in some respect
self-creative, we cannot be mythless and we cannot determine our
boundary as boundless, our limits as limitless, our creative constru-
als of human existence as unconditioned" (189).

Nevertheless, though Baeten and Scarborough's arguments
could both seemingly be applied toward determining a myth of
consciousness, I still maintain that their approach runs counter to
the move initiated by consciousness itself. The issue is less that they
discuss myth on the level of form, for I have been doing the same,
but that they remain bound to an *old* form that is intended to be
relevant to modern myth. And the precise point of contention
between their notion of myth and mine converges on negativity
and the absence of myth. In disavowing or trying to smooth over
the fundamental rupture that did take place in consciousness (and
by which their arguments serve as evidence), they do not allow the
negativity inherent in such a rupture to work on myth. Rather than
subject myth to the task required of modernity, modernity is tried,
at least for Scarborough, as the killer of myth. But when the idea of
loss, difference, gap, and so forth emerges out of the end of myth
and a *prœ*reflective mode of being-in-the-world, any subsequent concept of myth that means to reflect truthfully modern experience
must incorporate the negativity of loss and difference. A negated
myth is one that has integrated the absence of myth into itself, but
it must be stressed, this is not quite the same as mythlessness. The
usage of *mythlessness* tends to remain bound to archaic myth in that
it refers backward, to an earlier mode of being and source of meaning that is no more. Mythlessness misses myth, even when it purports to replace it (e.g., the "myth of mythlessness"). But a *negated*
myth, as opposed to an absent one, ultimately cares little for myth.

It sees through itself and *negates its own necessity.* The negation of myth is the result of allowing the reality of God's death to change myth's logic. As such, there is no loss to be mourned or rectified; there is only change and the moving further into a de-hypostatized reflection.

To some extent, Baeten allows myth's nonnecessity inasmuch as she defines myth as a boundary that must be crossed if the *telos* of human existence is to come to fruition. But this allowance is curtailed, for she proves to be unwilling to let the old myth void itself so that humankind can at least move closer to reaching its goal of freedom, even if in its totality it cannot be reached. Moreover, instead of the recognition that myth (in its primary sense) has *already* voided itself, Baeten tries to resurrect myth. But in her attempted resurrection, original myth is confounded with modern ideas of myth such that myth itself gets lost in the process. This needlessly complicates the issue of leaving myth behind, or, more to the point, accepting that myth has already been overcome. Though Baeten's philosophical myth appears to replace phenomenal myth, in doing so, her structural approach is projected backward such that phenomenal myth is more than erased, its whole logic is ignored, and myth becomes divorced from the reality it did have. Despite her designation of myth as a threshold, she does not approach the threshold and instead seems to prefer to rest comfortably on the side deemed "human." "Only by standing alone can human being be truly human" (211). Yet myth as a necessary boundary delimiting human from Other becomes unduly rigidified in that she does not permit what lies on either side of the boundary ever to meet and impress on each other. Instead, she prefers to keep myth in its place as the pole separating heaven and earth, unaware or heedless of the fact that the creation myth symbolized both separation *and* union of the opposites. By interiorizing the creation myth, she accepts the internal, negative nature of myth—but only partially so. The sky both literally and logically remains closed for her, and she cannot complete the process she is already in. For at the formal level with which she is concerned, the sky is *not* closed. Rather, it has fallen out of mystery into science and technology.

The sheer fact of needing to recover myth or an attitude toward myth implies a looking backward toward an older form of consciousness. The need to defend against mythlessness by subsuming it under another supposed unchanging, primordial myth similarly implies staying cocooned within a protective layer of consciousness that becomes unconscious when it shields against a less than ideal reality. Scarborough takes myth as form and reflection, but rather than consider what that form might look like today (though this is what he says he is doing), he, too, is attached to an old form. He purposely keeps myth in its *pre*reflective state. "Perhaps one of the major lessons of the *recovery of myth and the whole prereflective world* it embodies is the impossibility of finding neat answers to such simple questions" (125; emphasis added). The questions he is referring to have to do with the precise details of the "murder" of myth (perpetrator, weapon, motive), depicted in his example of the New Guinea tribe. Though he says there are no "neat answers," his whole argument implicates modernity in this "crime" (which is also not really a crime given myth's resiliency). "[T]here is something in the touch of modernity which destroys not simply some particular myth but also myth itself" (6). Scarborough would sooner return to a state in which the reflective split between inner experience and outer world never happened—but this regressive turn is very different from integrating the split *into* consciousness.

The content of myth already is dialectical. One can look at Baeten's example of the Native American creation myth to see this, with the separation and union of opposites symbolically represented in heaven ("Sky World" in the myth) and earth. If the myth thus already contains the opposites, any attempt to suppress its own inner negativity involves an aborting of the movement into reflection. Scarborough suppresses myth's negativity when he treats the split between opposites as inimical to myth (and to reflection in general), and furthermore when he disavows an absence of myth. But if there is a future to myth, it must follow myth's own logical and negative movement, which historically has witnessed the loss of myth's concrete, empirical expression (archaic, ritualized myth) and the negative interiorization of reflection (depth psychology). And as the outer shell that is myth is shed and we move further into reflection, we find that myth has become little more than a memory.

Another possible contradiction raised in this study involves the postmodern notion of the end of history. Earlier I considered the correspondences between standing outside of history and a new myth of consciousness. But, in the previous chapter, I criticized Christopher Hauke for basically doing the same. I suggested that his attempt to marry Jungian depth psychology and postmodern thought left a gaping, paralytic hole that rather than fertilizing the ground for a "rebirth" (the possibility Hauke sees in the convergence of these two fields), cocooned consciousness in a disembodied bubble. I said that the dislocating of history abates the necessity of living in one's own time and renounces the one grounding still available, thus disenfranchising the cultural manifestations of consciousness. And yet by its very definition, speaking of a myth of consciousness demands that the discourse be shifted to a different level, beyond the phenomenal and substantial. In this regard, I think one can enter the logic of a myth of consciousness (with its ending of history) without denying the historical implications for myth. The potential confusion emerges out of the conflation of differing logical forms, and can be seen in Hauke's argument insofar as he, like James Hollis (previously cited), tries to fit an old form of consciousness into what he ostensibly knows must already be a new one.

Hauke explicitly states that the rebirth envisioned by Jung and supported by postmodern theory is not to be defined by modernity or antiquity or any other time in between. This rebirth is "in terms as yet unknown, in language as yet unspoken. [. . .] It is only from the point of view of modernity itself that the postmodern appears solely as an empty, superficial condition and evidence of a decline in civilisation. From a different perspective, one that is only gradually emerging and is still constrained by having to express itself in the foreign language of modernity, the postmodern may be viewed as a radical break and a beginning" (49–50). However, despite Hauke's apparent readiness for something entirely unknown, he nonetheless maintains an attachment to the former gods of myth. This is evinced primarily in his desire to recover a spirituality that in modernity became overshadowed and lost, and, more blatantly, in his admitted recourse to the gods. Recall the closing lines of his book, *Jung and the Postmodern*: "'The gods are with us.' [. . .] Let's make sure we are in when they call" (286). Hauke's postmodern approach to depth psychology is akin to Scarborough's phenomenological approach to myth. Surface changes are conceded (e.g., not mistaking the outward representation for what is being presented or, for Hauke, knowing the outer representation as simulation), but, at bottom, there is presumed to be an unchanging, sacred source or consciousness.

In this context, however, such a layer of consciousness cannot be equated with Being, or the God beyond God, or the objective psyche, precisely because of the referral *backward* to the gods (and myth)—which is a very different turn from going *inward*. The move ever inward and deeper into consciousness must be contextualized in the time that compels or witnesses the move in the first place. And this is a time whose consciousness has inherited the death of God and the incarnation of the Christian God into man. Without attending to the reality or logic of one's own time, one leaves the demands of consciousness now for something perhaps more appealing or comfortable. Hauke's proclaimed postmodern embrace of the unknown notwithstanding, he desires to maintain a connection with an a priori sacred. The unknown becomes sanctified ("resacralized"), an object of faith that is meant to restore a lost connection with the divine simply by virtue of being unknown. It is an old source of meaning that is gone, and it is this old source of meaning he wants. In his dislocating of history, he seems to have forgotten the irrevocable change in logic that did occur, brought about by the loss of the gods, not by their mere hiding or their relocation from a literal manifestation to an imaginary one. Accordingly, he is not able to consider the nonessentiality of myth and the gods, because such a dispensing might leave him in a different unknown, or a new kind of known, with little recourse to anything but himself and humankind.

Attachment to myth or an older form of consciousness not only stunts consciousness, it also betrays the desire for a kind of meaning that is meant to satisfy today's existential lack. But this lack can never be fully satisfied as long as one persists in looking backward for the source of meaning. This intention to reinstate or remember an existential meaning speaks more to the personal motivation of the theorist and further indicates that he or she is not fully available to what consciousness demands now—without attachment to the kind of "meaning" today's consciousness may provide. One can fashion a sophisticated and convincing argument out of myth, and raise all sorts of philosophical and psychological issues that do carry relevancy for today. This, I think, Baeten, Scarborough, and Hauke do. But to the extent that their arguments are purposely couched within myth and protected by the gods (even when the myth is philosophized and the gods are psychologized), there will be a split or discordance between the theory and the cultural or psychological matters the theory is aimed to address. The trajectory toward a greater, far-reaching awareness stops short, obstructed by its own method, by the very notion of myth and the gods that is imagined to be essentially unchanging and interminably fulfilling. Consequently, the desire to achieving a nondualistic mode of being-in-the-world remains caught up in its own yearning rather than becoming realized. The idea or intimation of unity cannot come completely into its own as long as myth is held to circumscribe the vessel for this greater awareness. As long as myth is held to be a gateway *to* myth rather than *through* it, notwithstanding a more complex, formalized understanding of myth, the process of reflection will be undermined. Subsequently, the negation of myth required to know myth will be thwarted, and the concomitant cancellation of myth's necessity will be avoided. The goal of reaching a greater, more unifying consciousness will not be attained.

It is because of the move into and through myth, from prereflected expression to a greater degree of reflective awareness, that any consideration of a "new myth" of consciousness must ultimately drop "myth" from the equation. By definition, a myth of consciousness cannot be bound to myth at all. Both Baeten and Scarborough are accurate when they recognize the instability and, by extension, the nonessentiality of myth's *content*. This forces the discussion of current so-called myth (as opposed to the study of historical myth) to the level of form, which indicates that myth already is and has long been recognized as an instrument of thought. Baeten and Scarborough have, even if they do not express it as such, already interiorized and negated myth. The problem is they do not go far enough because they cannot leave myth behind, along with its long fossilized content. They maintain myth as necessary unto itself, unaware that the price for the formal myth they espouse comes at the loss of myth.

In actuality, if not always in theory, the nonnecessity of myth is a given. Recall Marcel Detienne's *The Creation of Mythology*, which demonstrates that the early mythologists, both in ancient Greece as well as in Enlightenment Europe, already treated myth as a specimen of sorts, whether to be used as a device to help further philosophical arguments or dismissed as immoral, scandalous fables. Robert Segal's essay entitled "Does Myth Have a Future?" similarly shows myth's dispensability in that he takes several modern myth proponents and discusses the incompatibility of their theories after the advent of science. In what Segal calls a "strategy of regrouping," alternative functions and subjects of myth outside the realm of science are sought in order to maintain myth's validity (*Theorizing* 21). For example, Mircea Eliade's approach claims a nonexplanatory function of myth that coexists with scientific ones. What myth particularly does that science cannot is justify and regenerate phenomena, as opposed to merely explaining them. Myth roots experience in primordial time, where the divine imperative is remembered and life is symbolically renewed.

> Myth makes the present less arbitrary and therefore more tolerable by locating its origin in the hoary past. [. . .] To hear, to read, and especially to reenact a myth is magically to return to the time when the myth took place, the time of the origin of whatever phenomenon it explains and justifies. [. . .] The ultimate payoff of myth is experiential: encountering divinity. (22)

For Eliade, myth is no less present or unavoidable in modernity than it is in antiquity. He finds myths "camouflaged" in plays, books, movies, all of which bring to life another "temporal universe" (Eliade, qtd. in Segal: 22–23).

The problem Segal has with Eliade's future prospects for myth is threefold. First, "the nonexplanatory functions of myth depend on the explanatory one" (23). Myth can only step in with its nonexplanatory role if science can no longer explain phenomena. But even social rather than natural phenomena, such as marriage and government, which Eliade credits myth with explaining, can be accounted for by the social sciences. Thus, Segal asks, "[W]hat is left for myth to explain?" Segal's second objection is that modern myths may provide an entertaining or inspiring escape from the present, but they do not return one to the primordial time of the gods or serve as a cosmic renewal. Third, any return to a primordial origin occurs not in reality, but in one's imagination. Once the experience of reading, hearing, or reenacting the supposed myth is over, so is the myth (23).

It is not just Eliade's theory of the indispensability of myth that Segal disputes. Other primary forms of this "regrouping strategy" include interpreting myth symbolically so that it does not interfere with scientific explanations of the physical world, exemplified by Rudolf Bultmann and Hans Jonas, and altering both function and subject of myth such that myth in no way encroaches upon science's territory, exemplified by C. G. Jung. In short, the problem Segal has with Bultmann's demythologizing is such that in providing a modern *subject* of myth (a symbolic reading of the New Testament), Bultmann neglects to offer a modern *function* of myth. "Perhaps for him the function is self-evident: myth serves to express the human condition. But why is it necessary to express that condition, and why is it necessary to express that condition through myth? [. . .] Why do humans need to know their condition? Bultmann never says" (26). Furthermore, though Bultmann provides a theory of myth that is supposed to be acceptable and applicable after the advent of science, he nonetheless remains attached to ancient myth insofar as a demythologized myth is meant to preserve the gods' reality, even if now transposed to a nonphysical God (27).

The fallacy of Jonas's existential approach to myth, whose subject is demythologized Gnosticism, is that, like Bultmann, Jonas fails to provide a modern *function* of myth and thus fails to make the Gnostic myth necessary for moderns. In focusing on the existential aspect of myth to the exclusion of the cosmogonic and eschatological aspects, the "fact of human alienation from the world, not the source of it or the solution to it, is the demythologized subject of myth" (29).[18] Yet when myth refers to the *experience* of the world rather than the world itself, the myth is diminished (thus constraining its future prospects) and its purpose entirely vague, belonging more to human nature than anything else. At the end of his essay, Segal casts his vote with Jung, stating that Jung's theory of myth, which alters the subject and function of myth to manifestations of and openings into the unconscious, "envisions the brightest future for myth" (35). However, in his reading of Jung, Segal notes that myth is not all that indispensable; it is just simply one avenue among others to the unconscious. What is necessary is the psychological function that myth serves, but not myth itself.

AFTER MYTH

Finally, if nothing else, two thousand years of Christianity have shown not that myth is hidden or suppressed, but rather that myth did indeed become thoroughly unnecessary. More than unnecessary—in succeeding myth, Christianity rendered myth impossible. Christianity represented a decisive overcoming of myth and polytheistic religion and the emergence of *historical* religion, whereby the one, true God initiated a series of events with a specific beginning, middle, and end. No longer was the world ritualistically created anew every year; with Christianity there is only one, nonrenewable origin that was planted firmly "in the beginning" instead of now. God created the world and humankind, expelled us out of Paradise, and will judge us in the end. Though this new story about God was accepted as a self-evident truth, it cannot be identified with myth precisely because of its historical nature, and, in fact, Christianity was set in direct opposition to myth. Jean Pépin notes that in the New Testament, there are only five passages that refer to myth, all with negative connotations; "'give up [. . .] studying those interminable myths [. . .] which issue in mere speculation and cannot make known God's plan for us, which works through faith'" (New Testament, 1 Tim. 1.3–4).[19]

Moreover, from a logical perspective, the shift to a monotheistic religion denotes the evaporation of myth's substance and reason for existence. In mythical cultures, the natural phenomena *are* the gods. "God (*theos*) does not signify an acting person or a supreme being; initially it was not a possible subject of a sentence but a predicate, a predicative concept. [. . .] 'God' signified a quality of real events themselves, their effect on man. The Gods of myth were natural, self-evident Gods so that it was impossible to believe in them or to doubt their existence" (Avens 38).[20] The Christian God, however, is thrust out of nature and worldly embodiment into the infinite heavens, as spirit. In his rise to the infinite, God is deprived of his earthly (mythic) substance and becomes the "absolute *behind* sensate reality" (39). But as the infinite, God is "only an infinitely diluted remainder of what he once was," having paid the price of his substantiality in order to be taken as the absolute God (Giegerich, qtd. in Avens: 39). The Christian God and the gods of myth cannot coexist. The *logos* of myth, formerly the *logos* of nature, breaks out of its natural containment and earthly embodiment to become the *Logos* itself, God's word. And there is no turning back. Once nature is deanimated and transcended, one cannot reanimate the world and revert to a posture that unquestioningly prostrates before nature. Once God's presence is transmuted from natural phenomena to the nonphenomenon of spirit, myth crumbles under the nonweight of its departed gods.

To a certain extent, Christianity has suffered the same fate as myth. The Christian God replaced the natural, self-evident gods of myth, but Christianity, too, eventually lost its convincingness in the eighteenth and nineteenth centuries, demonstrated by an intense interest in myth and the flourishing of the field of mythology. Yet looking to myth for a new or revived source of religious meaning is not only anachronistic (and possibly destined to reenact the same sequence of events or progression in consciousness from which the myth-proponent is trying to escape), but can only effectuate a band-aid solution at best. The wound, the rupture into something deeper and closer to the bone, the change in the structure of how the world is understood—all this remains beneath the surface no matter how fervently one embraces myth's cause. The task is not to look to something else to reinstate the new God or myth, but rather to accept the end of religious meaning. Not only is myth obsolete, but, at the psychological level, Western religion is, too. Christianity prescribes more than the end of myth; it carries within itself the end of its own religious authority because God becomes man; the "Word becomes flesh." And it is not until the pronouncement of God's death that the logic inherent in the image of the incarnation is carried to its psychological conclusion, thus cementing the superfluousness of religion. With the realization of the death of God, the idea of God is destroyed and the whole sphere of transcendence comes down to earth. This is not to say that God has now become immanent or been relocated inside the individual, but rather that the form of consciousness once identified with God is finished. And it is finished, metaphorically speaking, by God's own doing.

God comes down to earth, becomes incarnate in the figure of Christ "[t]o compensate, so to speak, for his lack of being" (Avens 39). Though the Christian God needs to be embodied to become real, his substance is quite unlike the substantiality of the gods of myth. The incarnation is not a reversion to a mythic conscious-ness precisely because it proceeds *from* the *Logos*, from the *already abstracted* godhead. In ritualistic and mythical cultures, however, the gods are never abstract. Mother Earth is not yet a concept or metaphor for the environment, motherhood, or birth. She simply is the Mother who requires being treated as such. Father Sun is not a mere anthropomorphized practical, astronomical event. The phenomenon of the sun *is* the manifestation of the god; it is the expression of an already given religious truth. Recall the Pueblo Indians visited by Jung: "[W]e are a people who live on the roof of the world; we are the sons of Father Sun, and with our religion we daily help our father to go across the sky. We do this not only for ourselves, but for the whole world. If we were to cease practicing our religion, in ten years the sun would no longer rise" (*Memories* 252).

The Christian incarnation, however, indicates a different logic not only of the nature of God, but of the natural phenome-non as well. When God becomes flesh, reality itself is changed. "In the saying 'the Word becomes flesh' something enormous *hap-pens*—not only to the *Logos* which descends from heaven, but also to the flesh (the terrestrial, temporal, mortal reality assumed by the *Logos*). [. . .] [T]he flesh—in its oneness with the *Logos*— acquires a radically different nature. The very idea of flesh, earth, reality is changed" (Avens 39). Giegerich sees this coming of flesh (human, earthly existence) into contact with the *Logos* (mind, reason) most prominently in the unnatural nature or "second nature" of technology.

> Technology is *Logos* because it originates in reason; it is a product of the mind, an idea. At the same time technol-ogy is flesh, because it is corporeal reality and not simply an idea. And finally, technology is that which has 'become,' because it is not something which originates out of itself (as in the case of nature) but is artificially made, the conversion of an idea into tangible reality. (40)

In a similar vein, Gabriel Vahanian sees technology as the locus of a different religiosity after the death of God (though he does not go as far as Giegerich and profess the end of religious meaning). With Christianity, nature becomes the "technique of the human," and technology becomes a means of "emancipation [. . .] from that which alienates man from himself as well as from religion" (234, 232). An unnatural nature allows for "technological utopianism," a new, nonmythical religiosity grounded on the earth, in human life, and in the present, fullness of time (242–43).

In short, the consequence of the Christian incarnation is nothing less than a revolution in Western consciousness, regardless of whether one is an official Christian. The sheer force of Christianity, not to mention the increasing influence of "technological utopianism," shows that this revolution already happened and is happening objectively, working on human consciousness at the same time as it sublimates a mythical and religious understanding of reality. One could say that Christianity is as necessary to consciousness as myth once was, for it tracks the *logos* originally seeded in myth. If myth requires its own surpassing to become known, then by necessity a new logic will have to come in to integrate and replace the old one. An unveiling of the natural images to the logic already inherent in myth will be required so that the *logos* can become known *as Logos.*

Why is this even an issue, why should myth want to be known? Christianity tells us: the *Logos* wants to be known because it becomes real. To be sure, the *logos* of myth is real, but in a different, nondifferentiated way. The realness of the mythic images never had to be discerned because they were accepted as natural facts. But they were not *known.* For myth to become known as myth, it has to negate itself, its *logos* has to be freed. The *logos* has first to *be* the *Logos* before it can come down to earth. Only now it enters a denaturalized nature, a world and humanity that is beginning to wake up and emerge from Mother Earth's womb and the protective casings of myth. Knowledge of the *logos* as *Logos,* as itself (as opposed to the logos of myth), is made possible in a world in which the inhabitants are no longer innocent, dependent children but possessors and purveyors of knowledge and awareness and the singular ability to live one's life for oneself.

Now "the question is not whether God exists, but whether man is" (Ramsey xxvii). Obviously, at the physical level, man is, for we go about the regular business of living. The question is psychological: does man know himself as a psychological rather than mythological being? "The death of the precious contents of the old mythical, religious, and metaphysical tradition was at the same time their resurrection as 'absolute knowledge' in Hegel's terms and as 'psychology' in ours" (Giegerich, "Rescue" 112).[21] The World Parents are slain so that consciousness can become self-reflective. "Now the person having the experience is both an observing subject as well as an object of the phenomena experienced" (Schwartz-Salant 116).[22] As a psychological being, one possesses the capacity to see oneself seeing, to watch oneself thinking, to reflect on one's reflections. One no longer needs myth or the gods to do the reflecting for oneself because a reflective consciousness now assumes this formerly divine role. The source of awareness is no longer held by an outer, divine being but instead becomes grounded in a human consciousness that has learned to turn its gaze inward. And the logic of a subjective consciousness unequivocally obligates one to shed permanently the protective confines of a mythic and religious consciousness that formerly looked no further than the gods and the phenomenal. Otherwise, consciousness remains suspended in its own, shrouded world: neither fully reverted to myth, since one cannot just for oneself reinstate the logic of myth, nor attuned to the reality of the already occurred negation and concomitant obsolescence of myth and the gods.

Now it is up to us. Myth's obsolescence provokes another necessity—the necessity of living one's own life, in the circumstances that one is given. Hillman connects the Greek image of Necessity (Ananke) with *amor fati,* the love of fate ("On the Necessity of Abnormal Psychology" 7). To know one's fate as necessary requires more than simply affirming it. The necessity of an age that has realized, or is in the process of realizing, psychological awareness insists on letting the relics of myth and symbol die peacefully, so that the process of reflection can continue unobstructed and permit human, not mythic, consciousness to become known and accountable to life.

All evidence points to humankind's ascendancy: the secularization of modern culture, the founding and development of psychology, the notion of subjectivity, the capacity to predict and alter nature (or at least the attempts to do so). This is not to argue for humankind's invincibility or majesty. It is to say that one's life is *psy-chologically* in one's own hands, and no longer subsumed under tribe, king, or god. Today one thinks and acts for one's self, desires for one's self, knows the world in relation to one's self. One cannot resuscitate the gods or revive myth, no matter how psychologized or intellectualized the gods and myth may be, and still profess that this restored myth propels the drive toward consciousness and speaks to the need for human responsibility. Recourse to myth and the gods only shifts the onus off of one's self to an outside, magical, mean-ing-laden source. Consciousness, then, becomes unconsciousness, and all the "power" is invested in an unknown, symbol-laden, and sacred entity (the unconscious) that then is ultimately responsible for upholding life. This undue deference of psychological aware-ness to an unknowable and therefore unmalleable Other is, in part, what frustrates Giegerich about Jungian psychology because it over-looks subjectivity and inhibits the logic inherent in psychological awareness itself.[23]

Though the end of myth and religious meaning ushers in a new form of consciousness that belongs to the human sphere, the subjectivity or self-reflexivity required for consciousness to become known as consciousness is not to be conflated with one's personal, ego-centered subjectivity. A self-reflecting consciousness is not the same as ordinary, human consciousness. It is the truth of the total-ity of lived life, which cannot be confined to the empirical person-ality's thoughts, feelings, observations, productions, and so forth. As such, total consciousness or absolute reflection cannot be attained by human beings, for the individual cannot survive the absolute-negative interiorization required to shatter all bound-aries, defenses, and forms so as to reach a pure reflection unmedi-ated by anything. This is why Giegerich specifically says that it is *psychology* that must negate or sublate itself to reach the soul, not the individual.

Even so, the individual is not without resource or obligation, because without entering the process of negative interiorization, even if one cannot complete it, human consciousness and experi-ence are unnecessarily and unconsciously one-sided. Without seeing through phenomena to the psychic image or the soul-making activity behind it, as the archetypal psychologist would say, then psychology is confined to the ego, and life is cut off from its depths and riches. And without piercing the ideologies and fantasies that everyone operates with, one's "ontological commitments" (Kugler, "Childhood" 72),[24] in order to know them *as* ideology and fantasy, then the task given to humanity is left uncompleted and it will be as if we never left myth—though with one difference: it will be a mythic consciousness that must turn its back on reality rather than celebrate it.

At the beginning of this chapter I introduced a sampling of modern philosophical and psychological theories, all with a similar element: the desire to attain a state of Being at one with the world; to achieve a unitary consciousness that is no longer sundered by the polar oppositions with which consciousness came into being, but instead incorporates difference into a greater whole. In that consciousness strives to reach a total presence of Being, one could conceivably maintain an existential connection to living myth. Both speak to humankind's containment in life, whether the container is that of the physical world or one with no solid edges, the soul. And yet I think one must not be seduced or misled by any parallels between myth and consciousness. The move from a natural containment to a spiritualized one is no small matter, for it turns the world inside out, from mythological to psychological awareness. The price for psychology, for the soulful kind of living so desired by individuals today, is such that all outmoded forms of reflection simply cannot persist. For psychology to succeed at knowing the soul, or for consciousness to *be* conscious, it has to negate the prereflective, concretistic world of myth so that the negative ground of Being is primed.

Moreover, at the personal level, one cannot expect that as myth and religion are left behind, the same existential benefits will be attainable. Earlier I said that meaning comes from being embedded in life and suggested that if one is embedded and immersed in the Now, life is meaningful, or rather, *not* meaningful because when one lives in a state of complete presence and acceptance, meaning is irrelevant; neither necessary nor unnecessary, simply a non-issue. I think this holds true, but there is a difference between being embedded in nature, held by the mythic World Parents, and being embedded in soul or consciousness, in what is implicitly if not explicitly understood to be logically negative. Even when modern movements seeking to reclaim the earth's wisdom profess to operate out of an embeddedness in nature, such as the Gaia hypothesis, it is actually the opposite of being embedded. The scientific view of the earth as a single living superorganism or even the spiritual view of the earth as a sacred web interconnecting all of life is made possible only by an awareness that looks *beyond* natural phenomena to become conscious of the extrasensory. It is a spiritualized, abstracted (negative) perspective that does not rest in the givenness of the earth but instead becomes conscious of the earth. We have to stand outside the earth to be able to see it as a single organism. In a psychological culture, the bedding is just not there—hence, the perception of a void or emptiness in the absence of God.

What if the void is necessary for consciousness? This is perhaps a rather simplistic question since discourses such as Christian mysticism, transpersonal psychology, and Eastern philosophy have long assumed this to be true. But in the individual who expressly wants meaning, or in a psychology that cannot part with mythology, this void becomes something to be filled and as such becomes the opposite of consciousness. The obstacle, then, to becoming conscious is not the absence of God or myth but what we, humankind, do with the void. Nietzsche said, "Man would sooner have the void for his purpose than be void of purpose" (qtd. in Bataille, *On Nietzsche* xiv). It may be up to us now, to know ourselves as the creators of culture and the artisans of our own lives, but the "us" becomes a hindrance when our administering and crafting are driven by the quest for meaning. The loss of God and meaning is what creates both the space for the notion of meaning to emerge *and* the temptation to want to fill that space with meaning. But what we want the space to be filled with, the space never had to begin with. It is a psychological trick or disguised detour that satisfies the ego's need for importance and protects the soul from pretentious claims made on its behalf. And yet the void is also a psychological beckoning to know it for what it is—a void that, if not taken personally, offers a glimpse of soul or Being in all its utter simplicity.

Conclusion

This study began with the absence of myth and ended with the negation of myth. In taking the absence of myth to its logical conclusion, the negation of myth is the final stop in asserting myth's obsolescence. As I have attempted to demonstrate, the absence of myth is essentially a given. This is seen in the founding and flourishing of a mythology or mythography that could only have emerged from a perspective already outside of myth; the prevailing modern and postmodern usage of myth as fictitious in contradistinction to myth's former role as the expression of truth and reality; the persistent search for something to fill an acutely felt spiritual void in life; the redefining and recontextualizing of myth to affirm or refute its collectively acknowledged absence; undue attention and demands placed on the individual as a substitute carrier for what the culture has lost; and the turn inward to a depth psychological perspective in response to the question of where meaning is to be found for the solitary individual as well as for the collective at large.

Thus, irrespective of the stand that the contemporary myth theorist, personal and cultural mythologist, or depth psychologist takes on the issue of myth's presence versus absence, these theories and theorists are all already situated within a decisive absence of myth. From this perspective quibbling over contradictory usages of *myth* almost seems trivial because no modern redefinition and ventured revival of myth can effectuate a reversal of history and return humankind to a state of being it has long been severed from. Myth today may serve as an effective and creative tool for understanding literature, politics, culture, humanity, and so forth, but myth itself?

It, for much of the world, was emptied long ago. Even the approach of a theorist like Wendy Doniger, who certainly does not treat myth as I have done, cannot be too far from this assessment. Underneath her love of a good story and the belief that we have to hang on to myths wherever and however we find them is still the recognition that myth is not a force, but a tool used in human hands. The belief in myth as a tool or lens with which to view our world and ourselves cannot be considered as just one perspective among many on a still active, divine force of myth. The absence of living myth is precisely what allows myth to become a perspective and a tool. But it is a perspective that is chosen rather than dictated; it is a tool that is picked up rather than thrust into our hands. I do not dispute the obvious, that there are recurring patterns to the human drama and that one can find solace, inspiration, joy, and much more in stories, whether from my culture or another's. But I wouldn't call this myth; I'd call it being human.

The absence of myth may indeed be so much of a given that it is not worth expounding on any further. But what perhaps warrants underscoring is the issue that has been implied throughout and pointedly addressed in the last chapter, namely, the negation or dissolution of myth as a form of reflecting. Myth simply does not apply to the current status of reflection. Collectively speaking, humankind has already progressed from a prereflective, literal, and nature-bound awareness to an imaginal, extrasensory, psychological level of awareness. Myth has been rendered unnecessary; its compact, contained unit of knowledge has exploded into human consciousness. Now we can mine the myth for its meaning. The kernels of truth once packaged in myths (and still packaged in modern narratives) have become available to us as psychological awareness into the nature of humankind, as *in*sight. The narratives are analyzed, deconstructed, dissected—metaphorically torn apart as we devour the knowledge and understanding. To be sure, many people may not take the time to analyze literature, films, plays, and so on; much of our popular cultural forms are in fact propagated to engender an escape into fantasy instead of any sort of rigorous thought process. This does not mean, however, that the analytical possibilities are not there.

The process of knowing the myth is part of the process of becoming conscious. We become aware of ourselves as autonomous individuals as well as the world in which we inhabit and whose guardian we have since become. But saying that the myth contains a psychological validity for today is not the same—cannot be the same—as being embedded in a living myth. Psychology depends on "seeing through" myth, *all the way* through to the myth's *logos*. And the myth, or anything else at the receiving end of psychological penetration, cannot survive such a gaze without being transformed into a level of knowledge now made accessible to *human* (not divine) understanding.

Because myth is concerned with the big existential questions of humankind's relationship to the world, it may appear as a still useful (and vital) vehicle with which to understand our place today in the grander, usually unknowable scheme of life. Of course any well-told story, whether contemporary or ancient, can show us another side of being human; it can seize us with evocative images and awaken deadened emotions, bringing us to a connection with life that cannot be neatly compartmentalized and analyzed. Modern mythmakers may be antithetical to living myth insofar as the myths are consciously made (as opposed to found, though perhaps artists graced by inspiration may disagree), but the stories, the poesis, still seek to tell the truth of living in a particular culture in a particular time, whatever that truth may be. Language itself may carry a mythic function because of its inherent gappiness and metaphorical nature. As Eric Gould argues, the ontological gap between an event and our attempts to make meaning out of the event points to that which remains unknown and mysterious. Here, in the gaps left over from language, the sacred is possible.

However, there is a serious logical distinction between myth as a way of being-in-the-world and myth as a way of looking at (or speaking of, writing about) the world. Equating a mythic function with living myth not only runs the risk of setting up false expectations for a kind of existential meaning that many know only by its lack, it also minimizes the fact that our thinking has become much more abstract and less dependent on the phenomenon or the mythic image (or the gods, for that matter) itself. The change in *how* we reflect on ourselves and the world has consequences, one of which is the redundancy of the myth and I would suggest the narrative as well. A life without narratives of any kind, whether deemed mythic or not, may be considerably starker and alienating, but is it entirely inconceivable? Although a complete absence of narrative of any sort may be impossible to the extent that the narrative form changes and mirrors how we reflect on the world and, if nothing else, the mere fact of one's birth and death bookends an unavoidable narrative (although if adopting a Buddhist perspective, even this is debatable). But my point is that conflating the narrative, no less than myth, with reflection itself grants an undue authority and indispensability to the narrative (or the myth). If myths depict logic of existence in narrative form, and now we see through to the *logos* itself, to the truth "behind" the narrative, then the narrative itself, like the myth, becomes secondary.

When myth is unduly identified *with* reflection or consciousness, rather than understood as something that dissolved *into* consciousness long ago, a discrepancy ensues between the means for understanding reality and the very reality we ostensibly want to understand. When consciousness is shielded by myth, it thwarts its own continuing development and undermines, if not downright denies, its historical role in already having catapulted us *out* of myth. Far from serving as a unifying force that can restore a lost connection between humankind and the divine, myth thus becomes a great detractor. Myth diverts the process of consciousness when consciousness is erroneously led back to myth, as opposed to through it and out of it toward consciousness itself, toward a greater degree of reflection. When the very process that utterly depends on the absence and negation of myth is then turned into a reason for returning to myth, perhaps in the hope of reclaiming something we didn't realize we had lost *until* we developed consciousness, then consciousness can only cave in on itself, confined to a form it has already surpassed.

To be sure, conceding the negation of myth may have little or no bearing on popular usages of the word *myth* denoting fiction or ideology. This is a shorthand that apparently works quite well in culture; one need only scan a news headline pronouncing something a myth to know that a falsehood is being revealed. But then, it must be reiterated, this depends on a completely different meaning of *myth*. In this sense, myth is concerned less with the nature of reflection itself and more with the act of exposing another perspective that intends to trump any erroneous claims to an exclusive, objective truth. In the culture at large, myth is used critically. Myth is similarly regarded suspiciously in some of the contemporary myth scholarship reviewed in this book. I have introduced the work of Bruce Lincoln, Robert Ellwood, and David Miller, who each in his own way subjects to critical analysis that which claims for itself the designation and authority of myth. Any so-called myth is not Truth handed down by the gods but is instead shaped by cultural ideologies; moreover, any theory of myth is already stained with one's personal motivations and reaction to one's time.

However, inasmuch as one views myth as part of the larger, objective process of reflection, wherein humankind has progressed from a knowledge embedded *in* nature and the gods toward an interiorized subjective (psychological) awareness *of* nature and of one's self, then I think one needs to think twice before contextualizing human experience and identity in myth. The contemporary usage of myth that intends to maintain an existential link with original, religious myth and thus function as a gateway to a more truthful living and a deeper significance to one's personal life serves, as I have been contending, as a cocoon whose sustenance is primarily imaginal and, as such, insubstantial and transitory. Whatever meaning one thus manages to procure for one's self can never be fully authentic insofar as it is contingent on a partial escape from the world as it is. But for meaning to carry the existential and spiritual depths characteristic of mythic societies, it cannot be so easily separated from the collective reality.

We cannot have it both ways. We cannot be the ones wielding myth as a tool or lens and then act as if something outside of us has all the power. We cannot in our theories presuppose an absence of myth and then use those theories to refute the absence. When God and the death of God are held to coexist in equal measure, nothing moves and consciousness stagnates. Maintaining both confuses the psychological and philosophical realities of both and diffuses the role that each of these ideas has played in the movement of human consciousness. Archetypal psychologist Patricia Berry says that reality is equivocal, but I am not sure about this. I think reality—life— just presents itself before us, and it is our fantasies (whether unconscious or conscious) about reality, our awareness, our capacity for thought and imagination, our skill with language, our ability to see many sides of the same issue that blurs the edges of certainty and makes reality appear ambiguous. It is one thing to extol the benefits of an equivocal awareness. But it is a whole other thing to apply this ambiguity to myth and then say that we are still living in myth because, as I have argued, myth was never equivocal.

There is a price to know myth, a price to have myth available as a tool, a price to become psychologically aware human beings. And the price is the complete, *un*equivocal sacrifice of living myth. I do not dispute the fervor and sometimes despair infusing the yearning to live a mythic, meaningful life. Yet I think it is a mistake to seek out a replacement for myth and to assume that some other source, whether it is a redefined myth or not, could provide a comparable existential and spiritual meaning to one's life. Part of the inheritance of the loss of myth and the subsequent obligation of affirming one's psychological birth is that one can no longer be a child (figuratively speaking) dependent on an outside source to provide the answers, whether the authoritative parent-figure is the womb of Mother Earth (myth), God, popular spiritual guidance counselors, or self-help books. The fact that humankind is literally no longer dependent on nature and that God is no longer an objective, metaphysical ground that seamlessly connects self with other is a reality that cannot be undone. In many respects, we are truly alone. Perhaps it is the fear of this aloneness that lies at the bottom of the yearning for life, people, God, even ourselves, to be so much more than everything already is. And perhaps it is this notion that life must be far more than it is that leads to the expectation that we be filled with something we do not have and cannot yet see that we might not need.

I think the operative question is not, how do I make my life meaningful, or what comes next if there is no myth to be resuscitated and no God to save me, but, rather, can this life, the one that I find myself in, be enough as it is? To live authentically, all one can really do is plant oneself as firmly as possible in the time and experiences that one encounters. Even this, however, can prove challenging. Psychiatrist Mark Epstein relates a story recounted in Sigmund Freud's 1915 paper "On Transience," where Freud was walking through the "'smiling countryside'" on a summer day with two friends. But his friends were "unable to smile back at the beauty that surrounded them. They could admire the sights, but they could not *feel*. They were locked into their own minds, unwilling or unable to surrender to the beauty surrounding them" (61–62).

Epstein, who weaves together psychotherapy and Buddhism, finds in Freud a Buddhist correlate insofar as Freud's two friends could not accept impermanence and the "decay of all that is beautiful and perfect" (Freud, qtd. in Epstein: 62); "they were unconsciously guarding themselves against engagement with something that might disappoint them" (Epstein 62). Freud realized that his friends were "trying to fend off an inevitable mourning. In their obsessional way, they were isolating themselves and refusing to be touched" (63).

The price for refusing to be touched is psychological imprisonment, trapped in a notion of reality that may defend from loss but ultimately leaves little room for any gain. If there is a loss to be mourned today, it would not be the loss of myth—for if what we have inherited is not myth's presence but myth's absence, what is the cause for grief?—but rather the loss of ideals that can never be materialized and the impossibility of being fulfilled by anything that does not already initiate from within one's self. This loss of ideals corresponds to what Peter Homans terms *symbolic loss,* "the loss of an attachment to a political ideology or religious creed, or to some aspect or fragment of one, and to the inner work of coming to terms with this kind of loss" (*Symbolic Loss* 20). This is not solely a personal loss, as in the death of a loved one or even the loss of one's private beliefs. Homans characterizes symbolic loss as sociohistorical and collective; it is the loss of the cultural symbols themselves. But symbolic losses, no less than personal ones, still need to be mourned and for the collective, Homans believes, this mourning is best facilitated through the public monument.

Homans speaks of a continuum of monument making; on one end is the more traditional, physical monument and on the other, the "countermonument," a purposeful absence of a monument, but one that is still designed to force some burden of remembrance. (Homans cites the example of a "Monument against Fascism" in Hamburg, Germany, in 1986; as an aluminum pillar became covered with graffiti [and a special stylus was made available for visitors to leave graffiti], the monument slowly vanished into the ground [22–23].) In between the traditional monument and the countermonument, however, lies the possibility for new forms of monument making. Cultural forms such as film and theater, for example, can function as monuments.[1] To that end, our so-called modern myths and mythic products, and even the study of myth, to a certain degree, could be seen as a type of monument to the symbolic loss of myth, rather than as an attempted resurrection or proof of the eternality of myth. And perhaps our churches and temples are or are on their way to becoming monuments as well (they certainly are tourist attractions for many), visible sites of memory and mourning rather than sites of restructuring from within so as to build a new house for God, as Loyal Rue suggests.

Even if the loss of myth is so much a part of our inheritance that mourning it or its ideal seems bizarre and out of place, Homans would argue that a symbolic loss could still reverberate among later generations, especially if what precipitated the loss has not been fully understood, in this case, the death of the gods/God and continuing secularization of culture. So while the despair that inspires and sustains the search for meaning, myth, or God does point to a yearning that is not being completely fulfilled, despair as a symptom in its own right suggests that we already are in the process of mourning, even if we do not identify it as such. "The inner work of coming to terms with the loss of [collective and sociohistorical] symbols is by no means always followed by generative or creative repair or recovery, but as often by disillusionment, or disappointment, or despair" (20). Part of the problem in turning to myth out of the despair over a meaningless life is that the symptoms are mistakenly diagnosed and we believe that the recovery of myth is indeed possible. Meanwhile, the mourning process, which Homans (following Freud) links directly with the psychological process of individuation, is obstructed such that there is no real "healing," or, rather, no real consciousness of the loss and no individuation.

Here is another way of saying that the end of myth makes psychology possible—and necessary. The rapid secularization of Christian culture and the loosening of collective cohesiveness following the industrial revolution birthed the psychoanalytical movement and increased interest in one's inner world. "Just as psychoanalysis belongs, in an extraordinarily sense, to the secularization of the West, so does individuation: individuation *is* secularization" (*The Ability to Mourn* 322). And individuation, Homans argues, is also part of mourning symbolic losses. "Mourning is but the first half of individuation, its backward-looking dimension; if that is successful, the forward-looking component [. . .] makes its appearance and takes the form of enjoyable curiosity about the inner, psychological world and [. . .] about its social surround" (314). The loss of religious meaning and attachment allows for psychological awareness, but, along the way, according to Homans, a period of mourning sets in. Successful mourning propels one forward; one does not look backward and inward to revive a collective loss (which is the goal of personal myth), one looks inward out of an irrevocable loss because it is here that new "meaning" will be found. Only this meaning is not the meaning that comes from being embedded in a myth, in living symbols. It is now interiorized and internalized; the meaning is psychological, whether one's insights apply to oneself or to the culture.

We have to be able to mourn, Homans says. Freud's friends were unable to "smile back" at the beautiful countryside surrounding them because they could not accept that things die. It may be true that the feverish quest for meaning is one residual effect of a larger process of mourning the end of (mythic, metaphysical) meaning. Yet I think contextualizing the search for meaning within Homans' notion of symbolic loss and mourning also begs the question: do our "mythic monuments" effectuate a real mourning or do they perpetuate a fantasy and expectation of meaning that fails to deliver? Any prolonged emphasis on mourning the loss of myth and the gods (which already *is* an ideal of myth; here there is no difference between mourning the concrete loss of myth or the symbolic loss) could easily promote a prolonged looking backward and further idealization of what is lost. Then we never turn our gaze forward; we never move on. Among the authors I've cited throughout this book, I would say that there is no real mourning of the loss of myth and meaning. The authors I've cited are either critical of myth, which implies that they are "over" myth, or they attempt to show where and how myth lives on. There is no real apprehension of a loss (and no subsequent mourning) because those who ostensibly acknowledge the loss of myth are in essence trying to prove the contrary: we still have myth; there is no loss. We just need to adjust our gaze; we have to root our current myths or find God in the abyss, in the gaps.

With regards to myth and mourning, a conundrum presents itself. The ones who would have consciously to mourn the end of myth are precisely the ones who still look for ways to prove the existence and necessity of myth. And the ones who want myth are the ones who protest against any assertions that there is any loss, symbolic or otherwise, in the first place. So then what? One cannot force the issue. But though I am ending with a brief discussion of mourning, I am not sure that this is a process that should be prescribed (and as suggested earlier, perhaps the existential despair indicates that we are already in a mourning stage, whether or not we choose it).

I wonder if the loss of myth is something that even needs to be mourned, for we have not lost our ability to respond to the world and reflect on our experience, whether those reflections take the form of sacred stories or a psychological analysis. The force that compelled myth and compels contemporary storytellers, philosophers, and artists is still active; is this not what confuses the issue of whether there is myth? Treating the end of myth or the impossibility of living mythically as a symbolic loss that has to be mourned runs the risk of granting myth a specialness that perhaps even it does not warrant. It was one way of being-in-the-world. Now there is another. Each has its consequences, its own truth. To be sure, rapid cultural changes carry particular challenges, including the loss of no longer tenable collective ideals and attachments. But I think with regard to myth, a good response would be not to mourn its loss, nor to try and unearth the gods, but rather to live one's life without the expectation that it be any different or addled with an extra layer of meaning. Would this not be the logical equivalent of living "mythically"—of living the statement, "This is it!"?

Recall that Joseph Campbell believed we desired the *experience* of living far more than life to be meaningful. But in order to experience life we have to be willing to release the attachment as to how life should be and be penetrated by life—and by things far less idyllic than bucolic summer walks. To be penetrated asks that we puncture the protective cocoon called myth, which is little more than an empty if decorative shell, such that there is something of us that can connect to this life. While the unequivocal concession to a mythless reality may be long overdue, the willingness to tend to life unhinged from blinding motivations that only cloud perception renders the affirmation of myth's obsolescence a moot point. Because in the moment of living one's life and not trying to find myth or meaning, one shows without needing to justify that reality is, in fact, enough.

Notes

1. The Absence of Myth

1. Jung, however, appears far less accepting of this fact. In his *Memories,* he bemoans the loss of a "cosmologically meaningful" life, which has left us with spiritual poverty and impoverishment. "Knowledge does not enrich us; it removes us more and more from the mythic world in which we were once at home by right of birth" (252).

2. These are perhaps three overused, clichéd citations, but by no means are expressions of mythlessness reserved for poets and philosophers. It might be worth mentioning that Joseph Campbell, more commonly remembered for stimulating a widespread interest in myth, often referred to mythlessness in his writings. For example: "We live, today, in a terminal moraine of myths and mythic symbols, fragments large and small of traditions that formerly inspired and gave rise to civilizations" (*Historical Atlas* 8). "What we have today is a demythologized world" (Campbell and Moyers 9). "Today all of these mysteries have lost their force; their symbols no longer interest our psyche" (*Hero* 390). "The scientific method has released us, intellectually, from the absolutes of the mythological ages; the divine authority of the religiously founded state has been completely dissolved" ("Symbol without Meaning" 191). "For there are no more intact monadic horizons: all are dissolving. And along with them, the psychological hold is weakening of the mythological images and related social rituals by which they were supported" (*Inner Reaches of Outer Space* 16–17).

3. See *Theorizing About Myth, The Myth and Ritual Theory,* and the six-volume *Theories of Myth* series among Segal's publications.

4. William Doty's *Mythography: The Study of Myths and Rituals* provides a most comprehensive overview of myth, covering all major approaches to myth as well as offering extensive resources for further research. Though it is interesting to observe that Doty does not really address an absence of myth as a reality in its own right, which no doubt reflects on the willingness of many myth theorists to engage with this as well. In his book, mythlessness appears primarily in quotation marks, or expressed as the "myth of mythlessness," intended to imply that an absence of myth is just another myth. "We cannot escape myth," Doty writes (454). "[M]ythic paradigms remain fully regulative of the worldview presented, even when *the form* of the materials may be expressly *antitraditional* in nature" (417). And yet in his foreword to Loyal Rue's book, Doty writes, "I suspect few of us who work regularly with public audiences can shirk any longer the necessity of acknowledging the loss of religious/mythic centers in our own audiences' experiences" (xi).

It is this kind of equivocal stance toward myth that complicates the argument for an absence of myth, as I discuss. Nonetheless, such an equivocation necessitates a discernment between differing fundamental notions of myth so as to understand not only how myth is absent, but also to try and get a glimpse into the motivations behind this kind of equivocation.

5. The Hebrew and Christian tradition "possesses what myth never possessed, a moment of exclusion, demanding a choice between the true and the false" (Clémence Ramnoux, "Philosophy and Mythology" 347).

6. Wendy Doniger, after Mircea Eliade, calls Plato the "first great demythologizer" though, as Eliade notes, Xenophanes attempted to "demythicize" myths before Plato (O'Flaherty 26; Eliade, *Myth* 1).

7. "[T]he purpose of myth is to provide a logical model capable of overcoming a contradiction (an impossible achievement if, as it happens, the contradiction is real)" (Lévi-Strauss, "The Structural Study of Myth" 229).

8. Doniger: "I am less interested in dictating what myth *is* (more precisely, what it is not, for definitions are usually exclu-

sivist) than in exploring what myth *does*" (*Implied* 1). Lincoln: "I will not attempt to identify the thing myth 'is'; rather, I hope to elucidate some of the ways this word, concept, and category have been used" (ix). This calls to mind Meike Bal's statement about mirrors: "Rather than interpreting the mirror as such, [. . .] it seems to make more sense to look not at what mirrors mean but, in a performative conception of semiotics, what they *do*" (225). Bal is drawing from Richard Rorty, who finds the accurate mirroring of nature to be epistemologically problematic and suggests an alternative approach to philosophy, namely, sustaining an open conversation (see *Philosophy and the Mirror of Nature*). Though myth today seems to function primarily as a mirror, metaphor, or lens—all designated to look through or by way of myth into something else—the focus on myth's *activity* does offset the glare, so to speak. This is part of Doniger's comparativist approach, which essentially places mythic mirrors and metaphors side by side so that they can look at and converse with each other, each one illuminating one truth or perspective out of many.

9. Sonu Shamdasani uses this phrase to demonstrate how psychological theories are "inherently shaped by and shaping the interaction that produces them." Not only is there a "mimetic dance" between the psychologist and subject, but given the multiple theories of psychology emerging out of psychology's failure to "found itself at the theoretical level as a basic unitary science," enough material is unleashed whereby any psychologist can find a correspondence in reality to his or her desired theory ("Psychology, Psychotherapy, and New Forms of Life").

10. Robert Ellwood observes a similar split in Jung's theorizing as well as in Joseph Campbell and Micea Eliade. Their theories contained a romantic, premodern longing for myth, but their methods belonged to modernity. "They were graduates of, and more often than not, professors in, that institution dedicated above all others to the fundamental worldview values [. . .], the modern university, and from its privileged, world-scanning watchtower they located and processed for their antimodernist purposes the riches of ancient myth" ("Is Mythology Obsolete?" 681).

11. For some the Earth might be "Mother," but in reality, we are no longer her children insofar as it becomes our duty to protect and save "her." Science has enabled as well as relegated the

responsibility toward that which was formally a mystery, placing the fate of the environment in our control. Numerous cultural instances support the contention that nature is to be conscientiously protected (the Environmental Protection Agency, Greenpeace, Earth Preservation Fund, Earth First) or manipulated (genetic engineering, cloning, plastic surgery, sex-change operations, biological warfare). In short, humankind and technology are changing the nature of nature.

12. Perhaps this statement is a little extreme. Lawrence Hatab argues that philosophy is an "added dimension of thought" rather than a "displacement of myth" (294). His analysis is an existential and phenomenological one, following Heidegger's notion of *aletheia* or unconcealment, so that myth is defined as a kind of disclosure, a "presentation of the arrival/withdrawal of existential meaning" (23). This is in line with Scarborough, although Hatab is not so adamant about correcting the split between subject and object, nor does he perceive any "crisis" that demands a reinstatement or recovery of myth. In his view, there is simply more than one means of disclosing truth.

13. See, for example, in Jewett and Lawrence, 17; Coupe, 9; Miller, "Comparativism" 173; Doty, *Mythography* 18, 213, 417, 442, 454. Jewett and Lawrence go so far as to include this phrase in a terse glossary of myth related terms. Their definition of the 'myth of mythlessness' is "the unexamined belief that scientific culture has transcended mythical forms of thought" (250).

14. Guggenbühl-Craig gives the example of Christmas as proof of the persistence of myth and ritual (31). There is little need to expound on the commercialization and focus on surface values of this holiday, proof, I would think, not of myth's eternality but rather that the symbols are long dead. Though to be fair to Guggenbühl-Craig, he is primarily offering a psychological analysis of culture, and when he says, "the more myths we destroy, the better" (33), I take this as an implication that not only are ideologies harmful, but myth without ideology is not possible, thus pointing to the obsolescence of true myth.

15. In another writing, Ellwood seems less caught up in the romanticism of his subjects, Jung, Campbell, and Eliade, and poses the question, "Is there such a thing as the supposed object of study of mythology, myth, at all? Ellwood agrees with Lincoln's definition

of myth as "ideology in narrative form" and goes so far as to suggest that the word *myth* be replaced to indicate a new approach to the study of myth. "We need to understand all this [myth] as modern ideological narrative and then start again with what formerly was called myth" ("Is Mythology Obsolete?" 684–86).

16. One recent example from academe: Professor of philosophy Richard Swinburne used probability theory (Bayes's theorem) to calculate whether Jesus was resurrected from the dead. Upon assigning values to factors such as "the probability that there is a God, the nature of Jesus' behavior during his lifetime and the quality of witness testimony after his death," he inserted the data into the theorem. Swinburne's results showed a 97 percent probability of the Resurrection. Emily Eakin, "So God's Really in the Details?"

17. After Lévi-Strauss, the identification of myth and language continues to support contemporary theories. See, for example, Deanne Westbrook's *Ground Rules: Baseball and Myth*. She writes, "Is there mythology today? Undoubtedly, yes. [. . .] [T]hrough language, [myth has] become internalized" (28). And Laurence Coupe in *Myth*: "[I]t is through language and it is in history that we make our myths" (98). Language *as* myth, however, is very different from the language *of* myth. Cf. Karl Jaspers who wrote, "How wretched, how lacking in expressiveness our life would be, if the language of myth were no longer valid!" (Jaspers and Bultmann 16). Jaspers is against demythologization and fears the "banal content" that would bring mythical forms down to a lower level. But this banality of everyday experience is precisely what has happened and perhaps speaks the truth of any current "myth" more than anything else.

18. From the *Yogavasishtha-Maha-Ramayana* of Valmiki. See Doniger O'Flaherty, *Other People's Myths*, 7–9.

19. The story, retold by Idries Shah and quoted by Doniger, goes like this: "Someone saw Nasrudin searching for something on the ground. "What have you lost, Mulla?" he asked. "My key," said the Mulla. So they both went down on their knees and looked for it. After a time the other man asked: "Where exactly did you drop it?" "In my own house." "Then why are you looking here?" "There is more light here than inside my own house" (146).

20. One noteworthy event: in March 2000, in Michigan, a six-year-old boy killed one of his classmates.

21. "The Rabbi from Cracow," told by Martin Buber and retold by Heinrich Zimmer. See Doniger O'Flaherty, *Other* 137–38.

22. Doniger borrows this from David Tracy, who may have been quoting Nietzsche writing about Socrates. See p. 171n36.

2. The Personalization of Myth

1. Two publications geared toward helping people find their personal myths are *The Mythic Path: Discovering the Guiding Stories of Your Past—Creating a Vision for Your Future*, by David Feinstein and Stanley Krippner, which offers a comprehensive lesson plan (complete with guided meditations and rituals) for identifying old myths and creating new ones. Understanding that "[t]he myths and rituals guiding an individual's maturation are no longer cultural strongholds that have for generations remained stable," the authors believe that "myth-making has become an intimate matter, the domain and responsibility of each person" (14). Also, *Your Mythic Journey: Finding Meaning in Your Life Through Writing and Storytelling*, by Sam Keen and Anne Valley-Fox. The authors write, "[W]e don't celebrate our myths enough. [. . .] We were all born into rich mythical lives: we need only claim the stories that are our birthright. With a little imagination each person can find within himself a replacement for the myths and stories lost when we ceased living in tribes" (1–2).

And a small sampling from a recent Internet search: A coaching program, MythoSelf ™ enables you to "[d]iscover your personal myth, your destiny from birth and learn how to be the way you were meant to be before you learned how not to be like that. We all have a myth that is unique and wonderful" <flirtzone.com/mythoterms.htm>; a coaching organization offers a course called Myths I, described as follows: "Want to influence others? Hook into the archetypes! [. . .] Myths are universal and eternal, and will increase your understanding of human nature, as well as your ability to understand and communicate with and influence others" <susandunn.cc/courses.htm>; Life Purpose Center aims to help one "find a truly meaningful career—and life vision" by exploring the depths of one's psyche <lifepurposecoaching.com>; New Millennium Consulting offers personal mythology consultations to think about one's life symbolically and help clarify one's life purpose <angelfire.com/nm/consulting/myth.html>.

As I hope will become clear throughout this chapter, I am not criticizing personal storytelling or the recognition of patterns underlying one's life. What I am critiquing is the conscious attribution of "myth" to these stories and patterns, stemming directly from this belief that the individual has a "responsibility," or that it is one's "birthright" to redeem a collective loss.

2. I thank Richard Stromer for providing me with this source. See his dissertation, "Faith in the Journey: Personal Mythology as Pathway to the Sacred," for a more in-depth look at the history of personal mythology.

3. Two Jungian-oriented authors, D. Stephenson Bond and Stephen Larsen, are discussed in this chapter, but some additional sources include James Hollis, *Tracking the Gods: The Place of Myth in Modern Life, Swamplands of the Soul: New Life in Dismal Places,* and *The Middle Passage: From Misery to Meaning in Midlife*; Robert A. Johnson, *He: Understanding Masculine Psychology, She: Understanding Feminine Psychology,* and *We: Understanding the Psychology of Romantic Love*; Clarissa Pinkola Estés, *Women Who Run with the Wolves: Myths and Stories of the Wild Woman Archetype*; Silvia Brinton Perera, *Descent to the Goddess: A Way of Initiation for Women*; Nancy Qualls-Corbett, *The Sacred Prostitute: Eternal Aspect of the Feminine*; Robert Moore and Douglas Gillette, *King, Warrior, Magician, Lover: Rediscovering the Archetypes of the Mature Masculine*; Eugene Monick, *Phallos: Sacred Image of the Masculine.*

One commonality among these books is the use of myths and fairy tales as a map for understanding a particular aspect of psychology. But the line between personal knowledge or insight and personal mythmaking grows muddled in that it becomes all too easy to identify with the archetypes and assume that a mythic overlay signals the presence and realness of the myth rather than just the insight. A psychological view of reality, supposedly necessitated by the absence of myth, becomes less psychological as well as less real when it stays behind myth.

4. Jean Shinoda Bolen does not limit her enthusiasm to feminine psychology; she is also the author of *Gods in Everyman: A New Psychology of Men's Lives and Loves.* Steven F. Walker cites Bolen as one author representative of the "incitement to archetypal inflation

[. . .] touched by currents of modern feminism and the New Age mystique of a return of a religion of the Goddess" (*Jung and the Jungians on Myth* 128). Additional works cited by Walker (and not already mentioned) include Jennifer Barker Woolger and Roger J. Woolger, *The Goddess Within: A Guide to the Eternal Myths that Shape Women's Lives*; Christine Downing, *The Goddess: Mythological Images of the Feminine*; Ginette Paris, *Pagan Meditations: Aphrodite, Hestia, Artemis*.

5. Hillman's protestations against personalizing myth notwithstanding, archetypal psychology is not completely innocent of its own pretentious tendencies vis-à-vis myth. This issue will be taken up in chapter 3, in the section "Metaphorical and Archetypal Myth."

6. There are no shortage of examples from contemporary culture to support this assertion—the personages from Greek mythology have long been designates for commercial products, such as running shoes (Nike), cars (Mercury and Phaeton), fashion (Hermes), cleanser (Ajax). And now beauty products, without needing to appropriate for their name what were once symbols, can blatantly lay claim to a higher significance. Los Angeles boasts of a store that prays over the herbs in their cosmetic line (one customer asked if this meant she could now be exempt from church) and a hair salon where the proprietor calls on a higher power to help her give nonegotistical haircuts. Laura M. Holson, "God Loves You, Especially Your Haircut."

7. According to the American Psychological Association, the United States "is in the throes of an 'epidemic' of clinical depression." New arrivals to the United States are even asked to fill out a form that asks if they have any mental disorders. Kalle Lasn and Bruce Grierson, "Malignant Sadness."

8. A 2002 study by Columbia University researchers found that the number of people treated with antidepressants increased from 1.7 million in 1987 to 6.3 million in 1997 ("More Drugs, Fewer Couches Used to Treat Therapy"). In 2001, 111 million prescriptions were written, reflecting a fourteen percent increase from 2000 (Marsa, "Battling the Blues"). And the percentage can easily increase: as of July 1, 2002, in New Mexico, the authority to write prescriptions for treating mental illness, normally held by exten-

sively trained psychiatrists, will also be granted to psychologists on completion of a short and simplified certification program (Goode, "Psychologists Get Prescription Pads").

9. Cf. a recent journal article proposing that happiness or "subjective well-being" should become the focus of public policy-making. The authors also refer to research suggesting that most people are in fact happy, or at least feel "slightly positive most of the time" (Biswas-Diener, Diener, and Tamir, "The Psychology of Subjective Well-being" 24, 21).

10. Having a strong sense of self-worth is no longer the paradigm for success, in spite of (and perhaps contributing to) the flourishing self-help industry. Three recent studies in the United States showed that contrary to previously held notions of self-esteem, "people with high self-esteem pose a greater threat to those around them than people with low self-esteem and feeling bad about yourself is not the cause of our country's biggest, most expensive social problems" (Slater, "The Trouble with Self-Esteem"). In another article, Slater examines new research on repression, which shows that "accepted interventions, like narrative catharsis, remain in use for pecuniary, political and historical reasons, reasons that have nothing to do with curing people." Not only may telling one's story (the prerequisite for finding one's myth) have no therapeutic effect, but, in some traumatic instances, was shown to make people worse ("Repress Yourself").

11. *Not I* is the title of one of Beckett's shorter plays, featuring a character called Mouth who tries to tell her story but cannot assert the "I" out of a "vehement refusal to relinquish third person" (Beckett, *Collected Shorter Plays* 215).

12. Deirdre Bair's biography, *Samuel Beckett,* reports that Beckett attended Jung's third Tavistock lecture, a series of five lectures presented from September 5 to October 4, 1935 (208).

13. The inability neither to live nor die fully has a precedent in Stoicism. Paul Tillich notes that Seneca's *libido moriendi* anticipates Freud's death drive. "He [Seneca] tells of people who feel life as meaningless and superfluous and who, as in the book of Ecclesiastes say: I cannot do anything new, I cannot see anything new! [. . .] Seneca knew (as Freud did) that the inability to affirm life does not imply the ability to affirm death. [. . .] This shows that the

Stoic recommendation of suicide is not directed to those who are conquered by life but to those who have conquered life, are able both to live and die, and can choose freely between them" (11–12).

3. The Lingering of Myth

1. Ferdinand de Saussure's *Course in General Linguistics* is generally assumed to have inaugurated modern structural linguistics through his analysis of language as a system of relations or signs, whereby meaning is the result of an entirely arbitrary relationship between a signifier and signified that is situated within its own structural system of other signifiers and signifieds. The work of structural anthropologist Claude Lévi-Strauss, in applying a similar model to his study of myth, defines myth "as consisting of all its versions" ("The Structural Study of Myth" 217). Thus, in the context of this discussion, any perceived absent myth is as necessary as a living one in constituting the structure of the whole myth.

2. In this chapter, when I use the term *postmodern*, I am referring primarily to its appropriation by contemporary Jungian-oriented psychologists and writers, such as Michael Vannoy Adams, Christopher Hauke, Paul Kugler, David L. Miller, Ronald Schenk, Polly Young-Eisendrath. Schenk writes, "The term *postmodern* ironically hearkens back to a long tradition of imagination, and while it reacts against modern rationalism, it therefore depends on it. It decenters, de-subjectivizes, or deconstructs experience so that a sense of the 'other' emerges" (8). In part, it is this relationship to the "other," usually unknown, that in the minds of its proponents ties postmodernism with Jungian psychology insofar as what is "other" finds a correlation with Jung's notions of unconscious, shadow, self, and so forth (8). Moreover, Jungian depth psychology's emphasis on image and imagination as a source and attitude of knowing, "a bridge between ideas and things" and "a mediating third position" is thought to fit neatly into the metaphysical gap between signifier and signified left by deconstructive theory (Kugler, "Imagining" 119). My focus on 'postmodern myth,' however, is meant to continue the discussion on myth, now placed within the framework of this sensibility.

However, as Kugler notes, trying to define or establish a clear referent for postmodernism belies what postmodernism, as a whole, is trying to say; namely, that there persists a semantic surplus of meaning that cannot be covered. "The lens of consciousness will always be clouded with the tropes of the text that the reader is reading or writing. The modernist-structuralist idea of a detached observer is being replaced by the idea of an intersubjectivity in which the images in the text interfuse with and alter the lens of the viewer reading the text" ("The Unconscious" 315).

Accordingly, it must be emphasized that this depth psychological appropriation of postmodernism (and, by extension, the basis of my argument) differs from postmodernism as a general, European-based philosophy. It is exactly that—an appropriation, a borrowing and filtering of certain ideas, such as otherness and in-betweenness, and inserting them into a different framework, in this case, a predominantly Jungian-based one. A truly postmodern 'other' cannot be reached by any sort of "mediating third position" precisely because its nature *is* that of otherness, and the gap between signifier and signified loses its gap-ness the moment it is covered by an imaginal bridge. The Jungian 'other' that Schenk finds indicative of a natural alliance between depth psychology and postmodernism is an internal other that is already overarched; it is one's subjective other, one's own shadow, one's self/Self. But the postmodern other cannot be represented; it is an "Other that cannot be penetrated" (Mark C. Taylor, *Tears* 84). It is "*an* other, and never *its* [the subject's] other" (Lacan, see Weber 17).

3. See David L. Miller, "Comparativism in a World of Difference," "The Fire Is in the Mind," and "The Flight of the Wild Gander: The Postmodern Meaning of 'Meaning.'"

4. The notion of in-betweenness referred to throughout this chapter takes this sense of being between gods or myths as its starting point, but quickly shifts the emphasis to the nature and contents of the in-between itself, which proves to be nowhere near as devoid of myth as it may appear. Henry Corbin's *mundus imaginalis* ("Mundus Imaginalis") and James Hillman's "poetic basis of mind" (*Archetypal* 14) are two ways to name the attitude or locale of thinking/seeing/imagining that must position itself in the gap in order to apprehend archetypal realities. It is "soul as the *tertium*, the

perspective *between* others and from which others may be viewed." (Hillman 13). "*Neti . . . neti,* 'neither this nor that': ultimate reality, or ultimately reality, is in the middle, but in a 'middle' which is not a 'thing' (Miller, *Three Faces of God* 68). (See Miller, *ibid.* 65–79, for a more thorough explication of the development of the in-between.)

5. Paul Kugler uses the image of the Möbius strip as a means of "doing away with the nominalist-realist split," the split between image and meaning. He, in turn, references Jacques Lacan as a source for this metaphor (*The Alchemy of Discourse* 94).

6. This assertion is a strong Jungian belief and tends to overlook the possibility that what may appear to be a spontaneous and autonomous image is actually a cultural and personal product and the result of a historical development. See, for example, Wolfgang Giegerich's "The Flight into the Unconscious: A Psychological Analysis of C. G. Jung's Psychology Project" and "The Smuggling Inherent in the Logic of the 'Psychology of the Unconscious.'"

7. Although the death of God may be a monotheistic fantasy, it is nonetheless a real cultural phenomenon and not a hypothesis that can be easily relativized by being contrasted with pluralistic points of view. A more honest approach might be to enter more deeply this particular pathology, the purpose of Hillman's "pathologizing," rather than offering an imaginative escape route.

8. Cf. David L. Miller, who argues that myth, in comparison with the fairy tale, indicates a more complex and differentiated reflection. "Myth and Folktale: Two Metamorphoses" 9–22, and "Fairytale or Myth?" 157–64.

9. Heraclitus's fragment has also been translated, "The true character of a thing likes to be in hiding" (Kahn 33).

10. See C. G. Jung, *Memories, Dreams, Reflections* 265.

11. This idea is similarly expressed by Jung: "To this day God is the name by which I designate all things which cross my willful path violently and recklessly, all things which upset my subjective views, plans and intentions and change the course of my life for better or worse." Interview in *Good Housekeeping* magazine, Dec. 1961, cited in Edward Edinger, *Ego and Archetype* 101.

12. See also Kalsched's *The Inner World of Trauma: Archetypal Defenses of the Personal Spirit,* for further explication on the psychological paralysis resulting from the turning of what was meant to protect the individual to self-destruction.

13. Some recent titles include Maria Housden, *Hannah's Gift: Lessons from a Life Fully Lived*; Kathleen Dowling Singh, *The Grace in Dying: How We Are Transformed Spiritually as We Die*; Sogyal Rinpoche, *The Tibetan Book of Living and Dying*.

4. THE NEGATION OF MYTH

1. Tillich's "God above God" has also been expressed as the "God beyond God."

2. It is interesting to note that this question, "who would you be without your story?" is a shift from the personal myth movement that places such value on having a story to tell.

3. The idea of a commonality transcending the borders of all spiritual traditions has long been formulated in the "perennial philosophy," which can, in its logic if not its name, be traced to Philo of Alexandria or St. Augustine (Ferrer 73). In modernity, the perennial philosophy was heralded and popularized by Aldous Huxley, who wrote in his introduction to the *Bhagavad-Gita*, "Under all this confusion of tongues and myths, of local histories and particularist doctrines, there remains a Highest Common Factor, which is the Perennial Philosophy" (12). It teaches that "man's life on earth has only one end and purpose: to identity himself with his Eternal Self and so come to unitive knowledge of the Divine Ground, [. . .] within which all partial realities have their being, and apart from which they would be nonexistent" (13). (See also Huxley's *The Perennial Philosophy*.)

Jorge Ferrer opts for a spiritual pluralism and nonhierarchical participation over the monistic metaphysical truth and essentialism of a perennial philosophy, a move that echoes James Hillman's polytheistic revisioning of depth psychology. Yet just as Hillman's allegiance to the psychic *image* does not sever all connection to a divine transcendent, Ferrer does not relinquish what he calls "Mystery" (rather than Being, God, Spirit, etc.). Now Mystery itself, it seems, has become postmodern. Mystery is now to be 'found' in the space "between the One and the Many" (191) and in "liberating defiance of all intellectual schemas that claim to theorize the whole of reality" (Tarnas, Foreword xiii).

4. Roland Barthes finds in "Neither-Norism" a similar (political) paralysis underlying the ostensible fluidity of intentional equivocation. He writes, "a final equilibrium immobilizes values, life, destiny, etc.; one no longer needs to choose, but only to endorse" (153).

5. Taylor is borrowing from Heidegger's sense of difference or *Differenz*, "which is the condition of the possibility of all presence and every present, is not a presence, and hence can never be properly present. Yet neither is it simply absent. What neither philosophy nor theology has thought (because neither can think such an "unheard-of" thought without ceasing to be itself) is that which lies *between* presence and absence, identity and difference, being and nonbeing" (*Tears* 77–78, 84).

6. Giegerich refers to the early, pre-philosophical Greek conception of *psyché* as one example indicating the soul's logical negativity. In Greek thought, the soul 'exists' either prior to existence or after it, in death. "Either way, as pre-existence or after-life, the soul is removed from life. [. . .] The term pre-existence can only have a meaning if it is the strict opposition of existence: that which precedes (and as such excludes) existence. Pre-existence is the negation of existence" (*Soul's Logical Life* 115).

7. In 1949, Max Zeller shared the following dream with Jung: "A temple of vast dimensions was in the process of being built. As far as I could see—ahead, behind, right and left—there were incredible numbers of people building on gigantic pillars. I too was building on a pillar. The whole building process was in its very first beginning, but the foundation was already there." Jung's response to Zeller's dream was to say, "that is the temple we all build on. We don't know the people because, believe me, they build in India, and China, and in Russia, and all over the world. That is the new religion." Jung told Zeller it would take six hundred years before the temple would be built. When Zeller asked him how he knew this, Jung replied, "From dreams. From other people's dreams and my own. This new religion will come together as far as we can see" (Max Zeller, qtd. in Kammen and Gold: 231).

8. "The Sphinx hints at the indecipherable nature of man, this elusive, multiform being whose definition cannot be otherwise than elusive and multiform. Oedipus was drawn to the Sphinx, and he resolved the Sphinx's enigma, but only to become an enigma

himself. Thus anthropologists were drawn to Oedipus, and are still there measuring themselves against him, wondering about him" (Calasso 344).

9. The surge of reality TV is a prime example. Though there is to some extent a plot to follow (Who will Donald Trump fire next? Which team will do a better job of redecorating their neighbor's house?), and obviously these episodes are structured by editors for dramatic effect, mostly the audience seems enthralled by these voyeuristic opportunities, content to watch regular people going about the random business of their day.

There is also the recent survey released by the National Endowment for the Arts, which indicates that the reading of fiction has declined over the last twenty years. Though, interestingly, the number of people writing fiction has increased. "We seem to be slowly turning into a nation of 'creative writers,' more interested in what we have to say ourselves than in reading or thinking about what anyone else has to say" (McGrath). This assessment fits well with the reality TV craze; television seems to be less of a medium and more of a podium available to anyone determined to seize one's fifteen minutes.

10. See, for example, Headline Muse, an "archetypal e-zine" [electronic magazine] devoted to uncovering the underlying myths and mythic patterns in current culture, politics, and cinema (<headlinemuse.com>)

11. Recall Bruce Lincoln and Robert Ellwood, two contemporary myth theorists cited in the first chapter. Lincoln traces through history, beginning with the pre-Socratics, the ideological underpinnings of self-proclaimed myths, while Ellwood examines the sociopolitical climate incubating Jung's, Campbell, and Eliade's theories of myth.

12. The word *truth*, I recognize, is potentially problematic. On the one hand, the absence of myth signals a loss of collective, objective truth, leaving in its wake private opinion and subjective interpretation. Furthermore, whatever subjective truth one claims is subject to additional scrutiny under the general rubric of postmodern thought, which seems to delight in reiterating the impossibility of truth, preferring instead to take refuge in the unknown. But myth has always been concerned with the reflection of truth. As I demonstrated in the previous chapter, the shifting logic of myth

(through mythopoesis, archetypal and postmodern myth) really illustrated a shifting logic in how we experience the world and how we reflect on that experience, each reflection trying to be truthful to its own situation. If *truth* is an iffy word, perhaps *reflection* is more acceptable. The trope of *mise en abyme*, for one thing, suggests that reflection is all there is, "a bottomless and infinite duplication" (Derrida, qtd. in Dällenbach: 170).

13. See *Jungian Reflections on September 11* for a depth psychological reading of this event.

14. "The soul does not exist, does not have an existence, is not a positive entity, nor a positive attribute of an existing entity. It is its own substance, but this substance is, or has the quality of, (logical) negativity. It is *sublated* feelings / emotions / impulses / ideas / images, and the like. It is nothing else but their *sublatedness*. This is why soul does not have an existence. It is what results from, nay, *occurs as* the logical or 'alchemical' operation of negation upon some (existing) prima materia" (*Soul's Logical Life* 134).

15. This, however, is not to suggest that Campbell is on the whole willing to part with a romantic approach toward myth and engage the possibility of myth as no longer being necessary in a demythologized world. See Robert A. Segal, *Joseph Campbell: An Introduction* 257–71, for a review of Campbell's view of myth as indispensable and entirely sufficient for human fulfillment.

16. Cf. Maurice Blanchot on Nietzsche: "Nihilism [death of God] is an event achieved in history, and yet it is like a shedding off of history, a moulting period, when history changes its direction and is indicated by a negative trait: that values no longer have value by themselves" (122). It is "the impossibility of coming to an end and finding an outcome in the end" and, as such, reverses itself to affirm life and the eternality of being (126).

17. See, for example, Laurence Coupe. "Because we and our world are constituted in language, we are always in process, in history. The best thing we can do is forgo the dream of a wordless world beyond this world, and take pleasure in the endless self-generating power of myth" (96).

18. This sense of alienation from the world is what connects, for Jonas, ancient Gnosticism and modern existentialism. "In Gnosticism one is presently separated from one's true, divine self, which itself is separated from both the true god and the true world. One

finds oneself trapped in an alien, material self that is part of an alien world under the control of an alien god" (Segal 28). Although the modern, existential self is not separated from a fixed, divine essence, the separation from one's *true* self is the place where the Gnostic myth can inform modern experience (28–29).

19. Jean Pépin, "The Survival of Myths in Early Christianity" 651. See Pépin's additional essays, "Christian Judgments on the Analogies between Christianity and Pagan Mythology" and "The Euhemerism of the Christian Authors" for further discussion on Christianity's efforts to displace and disgrace myth while claiming for itself truth and authenticity.

20. Avens is commenting on Giegerich's "The Burial of the Soul in Technological Civilization." Giegerich's original essay, "Das Begräbnis der Seele in die technische Zivilisation," is published in *Eranos Jahrbuch* 52 (1983) 211–76.

21. Giegerich is responding to Barbara Eckman's essay, "Jung, Hegel, and the Subjective Universe." Eckman contends that Jung's notion of the psychoid underlying all psychic and material reality corresponds to Hegel's view of the world as "one living system" or "one subject," both of which overcome the Cartesian and Kantian split between subject and object (91). Giegerich's rejoinder to Eckman is that the parallels between Jung and Hegel may have been drawn somewhat presumptuously insofar as Jung's conception of the psychoid is intended to overcome the bifurcation of subject and object, but, in reality, fails to do so. Jung, Giegerich maintains, remains the faithful Kantian empiricist, unable to realize fully the notion of a subjective universe as long as his primary concern with psychological results excludes *how* one comes to a result (107–08). "What is posited and claimed to exist remains 'out there,' i.e., merely objective, even if it is the idea *of* something that is also working in and through us" (108).

See also Giegerich's "Jung's Betrayal of his Truth: The Adoption of a Kant-based Empiricism and the Rejection of Hegel's Speculative Thought," for a more in-depth argument of how Jung's reluctance to move beyond (think through) an empirical psychology precluded the logical intention of his psychoid archetype of coming into its own.

22. Nathan Schwartz-Salant's 1997 Eranos lecture, "Slaying the World Parents" is a commentary on Erich Neumann's "'killing the

World Parents,' a phrase referring to an act of overcoming compulsion and unconsciousness of states as they occur in *participation mystique*" (119).

23. "The subject, you yourself, your own thinking, have to take responsibility for whatever is stated in psychology, because the only entrance to psychology is through my (each person's) own subjectivity, which in turn is only accessible speculatively by reflecting myself in some other (in a given manifestation or document of the soul) and through absolute-negative interiorization" ("Is the Soul 'Deep?'" 26).

24. Kugler writes, "Our ontological commitment is the fantasy of reality we are unconsciously moved by and which constrains our sense of reality, determined what will be experienced literally and what metaphorically" ("Childhood" 72).

CONCLUSION

1. Homans cites Jay Winter's *Sites of Memory, Sites of Mourning: The Great War in European Cultural History* and Henry Rousso's *The Vichy Syndrome: History and Memory in France since 1994* as two studies that treat film and other cultural forms as nontraditional but still effective monuments (24).

Bibliography

Adams, Michael Vannoy. "Deconstructive Philosophy and Imaginal Psychology: Comparative Perspectives on Jacques Derrida and James Hillman." *Jungian Literary Criticism.* Ed. Richard P. Sugg. Evanston: Northwestern UP, 1992. 231–48.

The Affluenza Project. <http://www.affluenza.com>

Altizer, Thomas J. J. "Eternal Recurrence and the Kingdom of God." *The New Nietzsche: Contemporary Styles of Interpretation.* Ed. David Allison. New York: Delta, 1977. 232–46.

———. *Total Presence: The Language of Jesus and the Language of Today.* New York: Seabury, 1980.

Avens, Robert. "Reflections on Wolfgang Giegerich's 'The Burial of the Soul in Technological Civilization.'" *Sulfur* (Fall 1987): 34–54.

Baeten, Elizabeth M. *The Magic Mirror: Myth's Abiding Power.* New York: State U of New York P, 1996.

Bair, Deirdre. *Samuel Beckett.* London: Jonathan Cape, 1978.

Bal, Mieke. "Mirrors of Nature." *Quoting Caravaggio: Contemporary Art, Preposterous History.* Chicago: U of Chicago P, 1999. 209–30.

Barthes, Roland. *Mythologies.* Trans. Annette Lavers. New York: Noonday, 1957.

Bataille, Georges. *The Absence of Myth: Writings on Surrealism.* Trans. Michael Richardson. New York: Verso, 1994.

———. *On Nietzsche.* Trans. Bruce Boone. New York: Paragon House, 1992.

Batto, Bernard F. *Slaying the Dragon: Mythmaking in the Biblical Tradition.* Louisville: Westminster/John Knox, 1992.

Baudrillard, Jean. *Simulacra and Simulation.* Trans. Sheila Faria Glaser. Ann Arbor: U of Michigan P, 1994.

Baumeister, Roy F. *Escaping the Self: Alcoholism, Spirituality, Masochism, and Other Flights from the Burden of Selfhood.* New York: BasicBooks, 1991.

Beckett, Samuel. *Collected Shorter Plays.* New York: Grove Press, 1984.

——. *Molloy, Malone Dies, The Unnamable.* New York: Alfred A. Knopf, 1997.

Bell, Michael. Introduction. *Myth and the Making of Modernity: The Problem of Grounding in Early Twentieth-Century Literature.* Eds. Michael Bell and Peter Poellner. Amsterdam: Rodopi, 1998. 1–8.

Benjamin, Marina. *Living at the End of the World.* London: Picador, 1998.

Berry, Patricia. *Echo's Subtle Body: Contributions to an Archetypal Psychology.* Dallas: Spring, 1992.

Bierlein, J. F. *Parallel Myths.* New York: Ballantine, 1994.

Bilen, Max. "The Mythico-Poetic Attitude." *Companion to Literary Myths, Heroes and Archetypes.* Ed. Pierre Brunel. Trans. W. Allatson, J. Hayward, T. Selous. London: Routledge, 1992. 861–66.

Biswas-Diener, Robert, Ed Diener, and Maya Tamir. "The Psychology of Subjective Well-being." *Daedalus: Journal of the American Academy of Arts & Sciences* Spring 2004: 18–25.

Blanchot, Maurice. "The Limits of Experience: Nihilism." *The New Nietzsche: Contemporary Styles of Interpretation.* Ed. David Allison. New York: Delta, 1977. 121–27.

Bolen, Jean Shinoda. *Goddesses in Everywoman: A New Psychology of Women.* New York: HarperPerennial, 1984.

Bond, D. Stephenson. *Living Myth: Personal Meaning as a Way of Life.* Boston: Shambhala, 1993.

Calasso, Roberto. *The Marriage of Cadmus and Harmony.* Trans. Tim Parks. New York: Vintage International, 1994.

Campbell, Joseph. "The Fairy Tale." *The Flight of the Wild Gander.* New York: HarperPerennial, 1990. 9–42.

——. *The Hero with a Thousand Faces.* 2nd ed. Princeton: Princeton UP. 1968.

——. *Historical Atlas of World Mythology. Vol. I: The Way of the Animal Powers. Part 1: Mythologies of the Primitive Hunters and Gatherers.* New York: Harper & Row, 1988.

————. *The Inner Reaches of Outer Space: Metaphor as Myth and Religion.* Toronto: St. James, 1986.

————. *The Masks of God: Creative Mythology.* New York: Arkana, 1968.

————. *Reflections on the Art of Living: A Joseph Campbell Companion.* Comp. and ed. Diane K. Osborn. New York: HarperCollins 1991.

————. "The Symbol Without Meaning." *The Flight of the Wild Gander.* New York: HarperPerennial, 1990. 120–92.

Campbell, Joseph, and Bill Moyers. *The Power of Myth.* Ed. Betty Sue Flowers. New York: Doubleday, 1988.

Cioran, E. M. *On the Heights of Despair.* Trans. Ilinca Zarifopol-Johnston. Chicago: U of Chicago P, 1992.

Cirlot, J. E. *A Dictionary of Symbols.* 2nd ed. Trans. Jack Sage. London: Routledge & Kegan Paul, 1971.

Cook, Albert. *Myth and Language.* Bloomington: Indiana UP, 1980.

Corbett, Lionel. *The Religious Function of the Psyche.* London: Routledge, 1996.

Corbin, Henry. "*Mundus Imaginalis* or the Imaginary and the Imaginal." *Spring* (1972): 1–19.

Coupe, Laurence. *Myth.* London: Routledge, 1997.

Dällenbach, Lucien. *The Mirror in the Text.* Trans. J. Whiteley and E. Hughes. Chicago: U of Chicago P, 1989.

Derchain, Philippe. "Egyptian Cosmogony." Trans. David White. *Mythologies.* Eds. Yves Bonnefoy and Wendy Doniger. Chicago: U of Chicago P, 1991. 91–95.

Derrida, Jacques. *Of Grammatology.* Trans. Gayatri Spivak. Baltimore: Johns Hopkins UP, 1976.

————. *Writing and Difference.* Trans. Alan Bass. London: Routledge and Kegan Paul Ltd., 1978.

Detienne, Marcel. *The Creation of Mythology.* Trans. Margaret Cook. Chicago: U of Chicago P, 1986.

————. "The Interpretation of Myths: Nineteenth and Twentieth-Century Theories." Trans. John Leavitt. *Mythologies.* Eds. Yves Bonnefoy and Wendy Doniger. Chicago: U of Chicago P, 1991. 5–10.

Doniger, Wendy. *The Bedtrick: Tales of Sex and Masquerade.* Chicago: U of Chicago P, 2000.

————. Foreword. *The Rise of Modern Mythology 1680–1860.* Burton Feldman and Robert D. Richardson. Bloomington: Indiana UP, 1972. xii.

————. *The Implied Spider: Politics and Theology in Myth.* New York: Columbia University Press, 1998.

Doty, William G. Foreword. *Amythia: Crisis in the Natural History of Western Culture.* Tuscaloosa: The U of Alabama P, 1989. ix-xii.

————. *Mythography: The Study of Myths and Rituals.* 2nd ed. Tuscaloosa: The U of Alabama P, 2000.

————. "What Mythopoetic Means." *Mythosphere: A Journal for Image, Myth, and Symbol* 2.2 (2000): 255–62.

Downing, Christine. *The Goddess: Mythological Images of the Feminine.* New York: Continuum, 1996.

————. "Incestuous Fantasies: The Myths about Myth Spawned by Freud, Jung, and Lévi-Strauss." Society for Values in Higher Education. August 1975.

Eakin, Emily. "So God's Really in the Details?" *New York Times* 11 May 2002. <http://www.nytimes.com/2002/05/11/arts/11GOD.html?>.

Eckman, Barbara. "Jung, Hegel, and the Subjective Universe." *Spring* (1986): 88–99.

Edinger, Edward F. *Ego and Archetype: Individuation and the Religious Function of the Psyche.* Boston: Shambhala, 1972.

Eliade, Mircea. *Myth and Reality.* Trans. Willard R. Trask. Prospect Heights: Waveland, 1998.

————. *The Sacred and the Profane: The Nature of Religion.* Trans. Willard R. Trask. New York: Harcourt, Inc., 1959.

————. "Toward a Definition of Myth." Trans. Teresa Fagan. *Mythologies.* Eds. Yves Bonnefoy and Wendy Doniger. Chicago: U of Chicago P, 1991. 3–5.

Ellwood, Robert. "Is Mythology Obsolete?" *Journal of the American Academy of Religion* 69.3 (September 2001): 673–86.

————. *The Politics of Myth: A Study of C.G. Jung, Mircea Eliade, and Joseph Campbell.* New York: State U of New York P, 1999.

Epstein, Mark. *Going to Pieces Without Falling Apart: A Buddhist Perspective on Wholeness.* New York: Broadway Books, 1998.

Falck, Colin. *Myth, Truth, Literature: Towards a True Post-modernism.* Cambridge: Cambridge UP, 1989.

Feinstein, David, and Stanley Krippner. *The Mythic Path: Discovering the Guiding Stories of Your Past—Creating a Vision for Your Future.* New York: Jeremy P. Tarcher/Putnam, 1997.

Feldman, Burton, and Robert D. Richardson, Jr. *The Rise of Modern Mythology 1680—1860.* Bloomington: Indiana UP, 1972.

Ferrer, Jorge N. *Revisioning Transpersonal Theory: A Participatory Vision of Human Spirituality.* New York: State U of New York P, 2002.

Giegerich, Wolfgang. "The Flight into the Unconscious: A Psychological Analysis of C. G. Jung's Psychology Project." Psychology at the Threshold. UCSB, Santa Barbara, California. September 2000. Audiotape. Soundstrue Recording, 2000.

———. "The Historicity of Myth." Reading at El Capitan Canyon, Santa Barbara, California. June 2004. *Spring Journal Books,* 2005.

———. "Is the Soul 'Deep?' Entering and Following the Logical Movement of Heraclitus' 'Fragment 45.'" *Spring* 64 (1998): 1–32.

———. "Jung's Betrayal of his Truth: The Adoption of a Kant-based Empiricism and the Rejection of Hegel's Speculative Thought." *Harvest* 44.1 (1998): 46–64.

———. "Once More the Reality/Irreality Issue: A Reply to Hillman's Reply." Online posting. <http://www.rubedo.psc.br/reply.htm>.

———. "The Opposition of 'Individual and Collective'—Psychology's Basic Fault: Reflections on Today's Magnum Opus of the Soul." *Harvest* 42.2 (1996): 7–27.

———. "The 'Patriarchal Neglect of the Feminine Principle': A Psychological Fallacy in Jungian Theory. *Harvest* 45.1 (1999): 7–30.

———. "The Rescue of the World: Jung, Hegel, and the Subjective Universe. *Spring* (1987): 107–14.

———. "The Smuggling Inherent in the Logic of the 'Psychology of the Unconscious.'" Unpublished essay, 2002.

———. *The Soul's Logical Life: Towards a Rigorous Notion of Psychology.* 2nd ed. Frankfurt am Main: Peter Lang, 1999.

Goode, Erica. "Psychologists Get Prescription Pads and Furor Erupts," *New York Times on the Web* 26 Mar. 2002 <nytimes.com/2002/03/26/health/psychology/26MENT.html?>.

Gould, Eric. *Mythical Intentions in Modern Literature.* Princeton: Princeton UP, 1981.

Guggenbühl-Craig, Adolf. *From the Wrong Side: A Paradoxical Approach to Psychology.* Trans. Gary V. Hartman. Woodstock: Spring, 1995.

———. *The Old Fool and the Corruption of Myth.* Trans. Dorothea Wilson. Dallas: Spring, 1991.

Gusdorf, George. "Conditions and Limits of Autobiography." *Autobiography: Essays Theoretical and Critical.* Ed. James Olney. Princeton: Princeton UP, 1980. 28–48.

Hatab, Lawrence J. *Myth and Philosophy: A Contest of Truths.* La Salle: Open Court, 1990.

Hauke, Christopher. *Jung and the Postmodern: The Interpretation of Realities.* London: Routledge, 2000.

Heidegger, Martin. *Existence and Being.* Chicago: Henry Regnery, 1949.

———. *Poetry, Language, Thought.* Trans. Albert Hofstadter. New York: HarperCollins, 1971.

Hillman, James. *Archetypal Psychology: A Brief Account.* Woodstock: Spring, 1997.

———. *The Dream and the Underworld.* New York: Harper & Row, 1979.

———. "An Inquiry into Image." *Spring* (1977): 62–88.

———. "Look Out: Three Occasions of Public Excitation" *Depth Psychology: Meditations in the Field.* Eds. Dennis Patrick Slattery and Lionel Corbett. Einsiedeln: Daimon Verlag, 2000. 161–74.

———. "Once More into the Fray." *Spring* 56 (Fall 1994): 1–18.

———. "On the Necessity of Abnormal Psychology: Ananke and Athene." *Facing the Gods.* Ed. James Hillman. Dallas: Spring, 1980. 1–38.

———. *Re-Visioning Psychology.* New York: HarperPerennial, 1992.

Hollis, James. *Tracking the Gods: The Place of Myth in Modern Life.* Toronto: Inner City Books, 1995.

Holson, Laura M. "God Loves You, Especially Your Haircut." *New York Times* 6 May 2001.

Homans, Peter. *The Ability to Mourn: Disillusionment and the Social Origins of Psychoanalysis.* Chicago: U of Chicago P, 1989.

———, ed. *Symbolic Loss: The Ambiguity of Mourning and Memory at Century's End.* Charlottesville: UP of Virginia, 2000.

Hopper, Stanley Romaine. Introduction. *Interpretation: The Poetry of Meaning.* Eds. Stanley R. Hopper and David L. Miller. New York: Harcourt, Brace & World, 1967. ix–xxii.

———. *The Way of Transfiguration: Religious Imagination as Theopoiesis.* Lousiville: Westminster/John Knox, 1992.

Housden, Maria. *Hannah's Gift: Lessons from a Life Fully Lived.* New York: Bantam, 2002.

Houston, Jean. *A Mythic Life: Learning to Live Our Greater Story.* New York: HarperCollins, 1996.

Huxley, Aldous. Introduction. *The Song of God: Bhagavad-Gita.* Trans. Swami Prabhavananda and Christopher Isherwood. New York: Mentor, 1954. 11–22.

———. *The Perennial Philosophy: Interpretations of the Great Mystics, East and West.* New York: HarperCollins, 1944.

Jaffé, Aniela. *The Myth of Meaning.* New York: G. P. Putnam's Sons, 1971.

Jaspers, Karl, and Rudolf Bultmann. *Myth and Christianity: An Inquiry into the Possibility of Religion without Myth.* Trans. Norbert Guterman. New York: Noonday, 1958.

Jewett, Robert, and John Shelton Lawrence. *The American Monomyth.* Garden City: Anchor Press/Doubleday, 1977.

Juliet, Charles. "Meeting Beckett." Trans. and ed. Suzanne Chamier. *TriQuarterly* 77 (Winter 1989/90): 9–30.

Jung, C. G. "Archetypes of the Collective Unconscious." *The Archetypes and the Collective Unconscious. Collected Works 9.i.* Trans. R. F. C. Hull. Princeton: Princeton UP, 1969. 3–41.

———. "Commentary on the 'The Secret of the Golden Flower.'" *Alchemical Studies. Collected Works 13.* Trans. R. F. C. Hull. Princeton: Princeton UP, 1967. 3–55.

———. *Erinnerungen, Träume, Gedanken.* Ed. Aniela Jaffé. New York: Random House, 1963.

———. "Introduction to the Religions and Psychological Problems of Alchemy." *Psychology and Alchemy. Collected Works 12.* Trans. R. F. C. Hull. Princeton: Princeton UP, 1968. 1–38.

———. *Memories, Dreams, Reflections.* Ed. Aniela Jaffé. Trans. Richard and Clara Winston. New York: Random House, 1961.

———. "Psychology and Religion." *Psychology and Religion: West and East. Collected Works 11.* Trans. R. F. C. Hull. Princeton: Princeton UP, 1958. 3–105.

———. "Synchronicity: An Acausal Connecting Principle." *The Structure and Dynamics of the Pscyhe. Collected Works 8.* 2nd ed. Trans. R. F. C. Hull. Princeton: Princeton UP, 1969. 417–531.

Jung, C. G., and C. Kerényi. *Essays on a Science of Mythology: The Myth of the Divine Child and the Mysteries of Eleusis.* Trans. R. F. C. Hull. Princeton: Princeton UP, 1978.

Kahn, Charles H. *The Art and Thought of Heraclitus: An Edition of the Fragments with Translation and Commentary.* Cambridge: Cambridge UP, 1979.

Kalsched, Donald. "Hermes-Mercurius and the Self-Care System in Cases of Early Trauma." *Fire in the Stone: The Alchemy of Desire.* Ed. Stanton Marlan. Wilmette: Chiron, 1997. 94–124.

———. *The Inner World of Trauma: Archetypal Defenses of the Personal Spirit.* London: Routledge, 1996.

Kammen, Carole, and Jodi Gold. *Call to Connection: Bringing Sacred Tribal Values into Modern Life.* Salt Lake City: Commune-A-Key Publishing, 1998.

Katie, Byron. *Loving What Is: Four Questions That Can Change Your Life.* New York: Harmony, 2002.

———. *The Work of Byron Katie.* <http://www.thework.org>

Kearney, Richard. *The Wake of Imagination: Toward a Postmodern Culture.* London: Routledge, 1988.

Keen, Sam, and Anne Valley-Fox. *Your Mythic Journey: Finding Meaning in Your Life Through Writing and Storytelling.* New York: Jeremey P. Tarcher, 1989.

Knowles, Debra Smith. "Along a Path Apart: Conflict and Concordance in C. G. Jung and Martin Heidegger." Diss. Pacifica Graduate Institute, 2002.

Krippner, Stanley. "Personal Mythology: An Introduction to the Concept." *Humanistic Psychologist.* 18.2 (1990): 137–42.

Kristeva, Julia. *Black Sun: Depression and Melancholia.* Trans. Leon S. Roudiez. New York: Columbia UP, 1989.

Kugler, Paul. *The Alchemy of Discourse: An Archetypal Approach to Language.* London: Associated UP, 1982.

———. "Childhood Seduction: Material and Immaterial Facts." *Fire in the Stone.* Ed. Stanton Marlan. Wilmette: Chiron, 1997. 54–78.

———. "Imagining: A Bridge to the Sublime." *Spring 58* (Fall 1995): 103–22.

————. "The 'Subject' of Dreams." *Dreaming.* 3/2 (1993). Online posting. <http://www.cgjungpage.org/articles/pksubj.html>.

————. "The Unconscious in a Postmodern Depth Psychology." *C. G. Jung and the Humanities: Towards a Hermeneutics of Culture.* Eds. Karen Barnaby and Pellegrino D'Acierno. Princeton: Princeton UP, 1990. 307–18.

Larsen, Stephen. *The Mythic Imagination: The Quest for Meaning Through Personal Mythology.* Rochester: Inner Traditions International, 1996.

Lasn, Kalle, and Bruce Grierson. "Malignant Sadness." *Adbusters.* June–July 2000: 28–39.

Lazer, Hank. "Poetry and Myth: The Scene of Writing, Thinking as Such." *Mythosphere: A Journal for Image, Myth, and Symbol.* 1.4 (1999): 403–16.

Levine, Stephen. *A Year to Live: How to Live This Year as If It Were Your Last.* New York: Three Rivers, 1998.

Lévi-Strauss, Claude. *Myth and Meaning: Cracking the Code of Culture.* New York: Schocken, 1979.

————. *The Raw and the Cooked: Introduction to a Science of Mythology.* Vol. 1. Trans. John and Doreen Weightman. New York: Harper & Row, 1969.

————. "The Structural Study of Myth." *Structural Anthropology.* New York: Basic Books, 1957. 206–31.

Lincoln, Bruce. *Theorizing Myth: Narrative, Ideology, and Scholarship.* Chicago: U of Chicago P, 1999.

Lyotard, Jean-François. "Answering the Question: What Is Postmodernism?" Trans. Régis Durand. *The Postmodern Condition: A Report on Knowledge.* Minneapolis: U of Minnesota P, 1984.

Mann, Thomas. "Freud and the Future." *Freud, Goethe, Wagner.* New York: Alfred A. Knopf, 1937.

Marsa, Linda. "Battling the Blues; Lighter Moods Without Drugs." *Los Angeles Times* 1 July 2002: S1

McGovern, John. "'Like Water in Water': Primitivism and Modernity." *Myth and the Making of Modernity: The Problem of Grounding in Early Twentieth-Century Literature.* Eds. Michael Bell and Peter Poellner. Amsterdam: Rodopi, 1998. 167–80.

McGrath, Charles. "What Johnny Won't Read." *New York Times* 11 July 2004.

Miller, David L. "Comparativism in a World of Difference: The Legacy of Joseph Campbell to the Postmodern History of Religions." *Common Era: Best New Writings on Religion.* Ed. S. Scholl. Ashland: White Cloud, 1995. 168–77.

———. "The Death of the Clown: A Loss of Wits in the Postmodern Movement." *Spring* 58 (Fall 1995): 69–82.

———. "Fairytale or Myth?" *Spring* 1976 (1976): 157–64.

———. "The Fire Is in the Mind." *Spring* 56 (Fall 1994): 78–91.

———. "The Flight of the Wild Gander: The Postmodern Meaning of "Meaning." *Paths to the Power of Myth: Joseph Campbell and the Study of Religion.* Ed. Daniel C. Noel. New York: Crossroad, 1990. 108–17.

———. *Hells and Holy Ghosts: A Theopoetics of Christian Belief.* Nashville: Abingdon, 1989.

———. "Myth and Folktale: Two Metamorphoses." *Mythosphere: A Journal for Image, Myth, and Symbol.* 1.1 (1998): 9–22.

———. "'A Myth Is as Good as a Smile!' The Mythology of a Consumerist Culture." *Depth Psychology: Meditations in the Field.* Eds. Dennis Patrick Slattery and Lionel Corbett. Einsiedeln: Daimon Verlag, 2000. 175–92.

———. "'Nothing Almost Sees Miracles!' Self and No-Self in Psychology and Religion." *The Journal of the Psychology of Religion,* 4–5 (1995–1996): 1–26.

———. *Three Faces of God: Traces of the Trinity in Literature and Life.* Philadelphia: Fortress Press, 1986.

Miller, J. Hillis. "Ariadne's Thread: Repetition and the Narrative Line." *Critical Inquiry* 3 (1970–71): 57–77.

Mitchell, Stephen, ed. *The Enlightened Heart: An Anthology of Sacred Poetry.* New York: HarperPerennial, 1989.

Mogenson, Greg. "Response to Wolfgang Giegerich." Online posting. <http://www.cgjung.com/mogenson1.html>.

Money, Meaning and Choices Institute. <http://www.mmcinstitute. com>.

Moore, Thomas. "Is the Personal Myth a Myth?" *Rituals of the Imagination.* Dallas: The Pegasus Foundation, 1983. 19–33.

"More Drugs, Fewer Couches Used to Treat Depression." *HealthScoutNews* 8 Jan. 2002. Online posting: <http://www.healthy place.com/communities/depression/treatment/antidepres sants/articles/013.asp>.

Murdock, Maureen. "Telling Our Stories: Making Meaning from Myth and Memoir." *Depth Psychology: Meditations in the Field.* Eds. Dennis Patrick Slattery and Lionel Corbett. Einsiedeln: Daimon Verlag, 2000. 129–39.

The New Testament. Trans. Richmond Lattimore. New York: North Point, 1996.

Nietzsche, Friedrich Wilhelm. *The Portable Nietzsche.* Trans. and ed. Walter Kaufmann. New York: Penguin, 1959.

Novak, Michael. *The Experience of Nothingness.* New York: Harper & Row, 1970.

O'Flaherty, Wendy Doniger. *Other People's Myths: The Cave of Echoes.* New York: Macmillan, 1988.

Ogden, Thomas H. *The Matrix of the Mind: Object Relations and the Psychoanalytic Dialogue.* Northvale: Jason Aronson, 1986.

Olney, James. *Memory and Narrative: The Weave of Life-Writing.* Chicago: U of Chicago P, 1998.

Otto, Walter. *The Homeric Gods: The Spiritual Significance of Greek Religion.* Trans. Moses Hadas. London: Thames and Hudson, 1954.

Paris, Ginette. *Pagan Meditations: Aphrodite, Hestia, Artemis.* Woodstock: Spring, 1986.

Patton, Laurie L., and Wendy Doniger, eds. Introduction. *Myth and Method.* Charlottesville: UP of Virginia, 1996. 1–26.

Pearson, Carol S. *Awakening the Heroes Within: Twelve Archetypes to Help Us Find Ourselves and Transform Our World.* San Francisco: Harper & Row, 1991.

———. *The Hero Within: Six Archetypes We Live By.* Rev. ed. San Francisco: Harper & Row, 1989.

Pépin, Jean. "Christian Judgments on the Analogies between Christianity and Pagan Mythology." *Mythologies.* Eds. Yves Bonnefoy and Wendy Doniger. Chicago: U of Chicago P, 1991. 655–65.

———. "The Euhemerism of the Christian Authors." *Mythologies.* Eds. Yves Bonnefoy and Wendy Doniger. Chicago: U of Chicago P, 1991. 666–71.

———. "The Survival of Myths in Early Christianity." *Mythologies.* Eds. Yves Bonnefoy and Wendy Doniger. Chicago: U of Chicago P, 1991. 649–54.

Ramnoux, Clémence. "Philosophy and Mythology, from Hesiod to Proclus." Trans. Gerald Honigsblum. *Mythologies*. Eds. Yves Bonnefoy and Wendy Doniger. Chicago: U of Chicago P, 1991. 346–52.

Ramsey, Paul. Preface. *The Death of God: The Culture of Our Post-Christian Era*. By Gabriel Vahanian. New York: George Braziller, 1961. xiii–xxix.

Rinpoche, Sogyal. *The Tibetan Book of Living and Dying*. New York: HarperCollins, 1994.

Romanyshyn, Robert. "Yes, Indeed! Do Call the World the Vale of Soul Making: Reveries Toward an Archetypal Presence." *Depth Psychology: Meditations in the Field*. Eds. Dennis Patrick Slattery and Lionel Corbett. Einsiedeln: Daimon Verlag, 2000. 193–203.

Rorty, Richard. *Philosophy and the Mirror of Nature*. Princeton: Princeton UP, 1979.

Rousseau, Jean-Jacques. *Confessions*. Trans. Angela Scholar. Oxford: Oxford UP, 2000.

Rowland, Susan. *Jung: A Feminist Revision*. Cambridge: Polity, 2002. Online posting. http://www.cgjungpage.org/jungsem.html

Rue, Loyal D. *Amythia: Crisis in the Natural History of Western Culture*. Tuscaloosa: U of Alabama P, 1989.

Sardello, Robert. *Facing the World with Soul: The Reimagination of Modern Life*. Hudson: Lindisfarne, 1992.

Sarraute, Nathalie. *Childhood*. Trans. Barbara Wright. New York: George Braziller, 1983.

Saul, John Ralston. *The Unconscious Civilization*. New York: Free Press, 1995.

Saussure, Ferdinand de. *Course in General Linguistics*. Trans. Wade Baskin. New York: McGraw-Hill, 1965.

Scarborough, Milton. *Myth and Modernity: Postcritical Reflections*. Albany: State U of New York P, 1994.

Schenk, Ronald. *The Sunken Quest, the Wasted Fisher, the Pregnant Fish: Postmodern Reflections on Depth Psychology*. Wilmette: Chiron, 2001.

Schwartz-Salant, Nathan. "Slaying the World Parents: A Paradox." Eranos Lecture Oct. 1997. *Eranos Yearbook* 67 (1998): 113–27.

Segal, Robert A. *Joseph Campbell: An Introduction*. New York: Meridian, 1987.

———, ed. *The Myth and Ritual Theory*. Oxford: Blackwell, 1998.

———, ed. *Theories of Myth*. 6 vols. New York: Garland, 1996.

———. *Theorizing about Myth*. Amherst: U of Massachusetts P, 1999.

Settegast, Mary. *Mona Lisa's Moustache: Making Sense of a Dissolving World*. Grand Rapids: Phanes, 2001.

Sexson, Michael W. "Myth: The Way We Were or the Way We Are?" *Introduction to the Study of Religion*. Ed. T. William Hall with Ronald R. Cavanagh. San Francisco: Harper & Row, 1978. 35–47.

Shabad, Peter. "The Most Intimate of Creations: Symptoms as Memorials to One's Lonely Suffering." *Symbolic Loss: The Ambiguity of Mourning and Memory at Century's End*. Ed. Peter Homans. Charlottesville: UP of Virginia, 2000. 197–212.

Shamdasani, Sonu. "Psychology, Psychotheraphy, and New Forms of Life." Psychology at the Threshold. UCSB, Santa Barbara, California. September 2000. Audiotape. Soundstrue Recording, 2000.

Singh, Kathleen Dowling. *The Grace in Dying: How We Are Transformed Spiritually as We Die*. New York: HarperCollins, 2000.

Slater, Lauren. "Repress Yourself." *New York Times on the Web*. 23 Feb. 2003. <http://nytimes.com/2003/02/23/magazine/23REPRESSION.html>.

———. "The Trouble with Self-Esteem." *New York Times Magazine*. 3 February 2002: 44–47.

Slochower, Harry. *Mythopoesis: Mythic Patterns in the Literary Classics*. Detroit: Wayne State UP, 1970.

Smallwood, Basil. "Take a Pill: The Pharmacologizing of America." *Adbusters* June–July 2000: 42.

Sprinker, Michael. "Fictions of the Self: The End of Autobiography." *Autobiography: Essays Theoretical and Critical*. Ed. James Olney. Princeton: Princeton UP, 1980. 321–42.

Stromer, Richard. "Faith in the Journey: Personal Mythology as Pathway to the Sacred." Diss. Pacifica Graduate Institute, 2003.

Tarnas, Richard. Foreword. *Revisioning Transpersonal Theory: A Participatory Vision of Human Spirituality*. By Jorge N. Ferrer. New York: State U of New York P, 2002. vii–xvi.

Taylor, Mark C. *About Religion: Economies of Faith in Virtual Culture*. Chicago: U of Chicago P, 1999.

————. *Erring: A Postmodern A/theology.* Chicago: U of Chicago P, 1984.

————. *Tears.* New York: State U of New York P, 1990.

Tillich, Paul. *The Courage to Be.* New Haven: Yale UP, 1952.

Tolle, Eckhart. *The Power of Now: A Guide to Spiritual Enlightenment.* Novato: New World Library, 1999.

Vahanian, Gabriel. "Religion and Technology." *Introduction to the Study of Religion.* Ed. T. William Hall. San Francisco: Harper & Row, 1978. 231–45.

Vernant, Jean-Pierre. *Myth and Society in Ancient Greece.* Trans. Janet Lloyd. New York: Zone Books, 1988.

Vogler, Christopher. *The Writer's Journey: Mythic Structure for Writers.* 2nd ed. Studio City: Michael Wiese, 1998.

Walker, Steven F. *Jung and the Jungians on Myth: An Introduction.* New York: Garland, 1995.

Walsch, Neale Donald. *Conversations with God: An Uncommon Dialogue.* New York: G. P. Putnam's Sons, 1996.

Weber, Samuel. *Return to Freud: Jacque Lacan's Dislocation of Psychoanalysis.* Trans. Michael Levine. Cambridge: Cambridge UP, 1991.

Westbrook, Deanne. *Ground Rules: Baseball and Myth.* Urbana: U of Illinois P, 1996.

Wiesel, Elie. *Night.* New York: Bantam, 1960.

Wolkstein, Diane, and Samuel Noah Kramer. *Inanna: Queen of Heaven and Earth: Her Stories and Hymns from Sumer.* New York: Harper & Row: 1983.

Woolger, Jennifer Barker, and Roger J. Woolger. *The Goddess Within: A Guide to the Eternal Myths That Shape Women's Lives.* New York: Fawcett/Columbine, 1990.

Young-Eisendrath, Polly. *Gender and Desire: Uncursing Pandora.* College Station: Texas A&M UP, 1997.

————. "Myth and Body: Pandora's Legacy in a Post-Modern World." Online posting. <http://cgjungpage.org/articles/pollypm.html>.

Zoja, Luigi, and Donald Williams, eds. *Jungian Reflections on September 11: A Global Nightmare.* Einsiedeln: Daimon Verlag, 2002.

Index